THE EUROPEAN OMBUDSMAN INVESTIGATED

This book is a seminal study of the European Ombudsman, focusing on current challenges and future developments by its leading expert commentators.

This open access volume traces the evolution of the European Ombudsman over its first almost three decades. Its focus however lies on the current challenges and future perspectives of this ever-innovative EU institution. It brings together leading voices from academia, EU institutions, civil society, and the European Ombudsman's office. It highlights developments and future potential in several salient fields, from data infrastructure and digital platforms over environmental protection and border protection agencies to revolving doors and industry lobbying. The collection's breadth of study and depth of expertise will mean this is required reading for scholars of EU law, from both a constitutional and consumer law perspective.

The European Ombudsman Investigated

From Old Battles to New Challenges

Edited by
Deirdre Curtin
Tanja Ehnert
Anna Morandini
and
Sarah Tas

•HART•
OXFORD • LONDON • NEW YORK • NEW DELHI • SYDNEY

HART PUBLISHING

Bloomsbury Publishing Plc

Kemp House, Chawley Park, Cumnor Hill, Oxford, OX2 9PH, UK

1385 Broadway, New York, NY 10018, USA

29 Earlsfort Terrace, Dublin 2, Ireland

First published in Great Britain 2025

A catalogue record for this book is available from the British Library.

A catalogue record for this book is available from the Library of Congress.

ISBN: HB: 978-1-50997-560-0
ePDF: 978-1-50997-562-4
ePub: 978-1-50997-561-7

Typeset by Compuscript Ltd, Shannon

To find out more about our authors and books visit www.hartpublishing.co.uk. Here you will find extracts, author information, details of forthcoming events and the option to sign up for our newsletters.

Foreword

EMILY O'REILLY*

When first elected European Ombudsman by the European Parliament in 2013, I committed to using the resources of the office to drive positive change within the EU administration on behalf of EU citizens. I would handle complaints alongside maximising the potential of the office to bring about deep and sustained change in the manner in which the powerful EU administration interacts and deals with those whom it serves.

It is tempting to make too close a comparison between the role of an Ombudsman in a Member State, and that of an Ombudsman overseeing the unique and highly complex administration of the EU. The literal geographical distance of 'Brussels' added to the complexity of its decision-making processes, and the extent of its – ever increasing – reach compels the European Ombudsman not just to deal with individual complaints as a Member State Ombudsman would, but also to bridge that gap of comprehension. One aim must be to make the EU administration as familiar to its citizens, and therefore as capable of being held accountable by its citizens, as would be the case, generally speaking, in their own Member State.

This approach explains why the office, through individual complaints and own initiative investigations and inquiries has had a significant focus on transparency, integrity and on the EU decision-making process. Citizens have a Treaty-based right to take part in the life of the Union, a right that cannot be exercised without the information necessary both to understand how decisions are made, and, if they so wish, to attempt to influence them.

In addition, the number of complaints received every year, modest when compared with the case load of a Member State Ombudsman concerned with the everyday concerns of citizens such as health, education and social protection, compels the European Ombudsman to seek out those areas of possible maladministration incapable of being captured through the standard single complaint handling process.

My approach has therefore necessarily been a hybrid one and intended to improve the citizen experience of the EU administration, and the quality of the EU administration. I place significant importance on communication for those reasons, both with the citizens and the administration. As our office is primarily public facing, we write our decisions in clear and accessible language, avoiding exclusionary and often

*Emily O'Reilly was first elected as European Ombudsman in July 2013. She was re-elected in 2014 and again in 2019.

self -reverential 'legalese' yet never avoiding the law itself, the cornerstone of our work. Under my watch, the office has retained and recruited the highest ever number of colleagues with qualifications and prior professional expertise in law.

Maladministration encompasses offences against the law but also against more general principles, such as fairness and equity. An administrative action may be legal but not 'just' or 'fair', the space in which an Ombudsman operates.

Some behaviour can be put right through individual complaints. Some such complaints have led to important change such as the European Medicines Agency proactively publishing the results of clinical trials. However, solutions to individual complaints often – naturally – address only the matter at hand and do not have a wider effect. The overwhelming majority of our inquiries each year fall into this category.

The scope and activities of the EU administration are nonetheless vastly wider than this. In recent years the EU has greatly expanded the powers of the border agency Frontex, taken on vaccine procurement and used the EU budget to help Member States pay for arms for Ukraine following Russia's brutal invasion in 2022. Behind these decisions lies a necessary but complex machinery. There are over 1000 expert groups that advise European Commission policy-makers and more than 150 committees and working parties in the Council – where Member States are represented – that do the technical negotiations on draft EU laws.

Multiple EU regulatory agencies check the safety of medicines, food, aviation and chemicals. Others monitor health and safety at the workplace, manage the EU trade mark or try to protect our financial system against future shocks. Monitoring, at times shaping, the resulting policies are thousands of lobbyists frequently better resourced than their civil society counterparts. The Ombudsman can boost the accountability and democratic scrutiny of these activities by acting proactively. It has looked into the transparency of expert groups, raised awareness about how lobbyists can unduly influence legislation, made suggestions to improve the transparency of informal negotiations (known as trilogues) on EU laws and reminded the EU institutions that work-related text messages are EU documents that need to be registered.

In 2013, I came to an office – almost at its twentieth anniversary – that had been established by my two predecessors, Jacob Söderman (1995–2003) and Nikiforos Diamandouros (2003–13) as a well-respected body that worked independently and impartially. Nevertheless, no organisation can rest on its past achievements or fail to respond to societal change or the expectations of citizens.

My aim was to ensure that the Office effected change in the EU administration to the benefit of as many citizens as possible even if they have no direct dealings with the EU institutions. The question was how to do so efficiently and with limited resources. One part of the answer was to use the considerable powers of the Ombudsman in a more strategic manner. The word 'strategic' means the identification of long-term or overall aims and interests and the means of achieving them. Just as one might be 'strategic' in the management of a family budget to ensure that everyone is as well looked after as possible, so too is my office 'strategic' in the effective husbandry of our powers and resources.

These powers include the right to start own-initiative investigations and the right to inspect all EU documents and therefore be able properly to judge whether an institution is acting appropriately. The transformation included overhauling the internal structure of the office to create teams of thematic experts in addition to a strategic inquiries team. I also established a fast-track procedure for access to document complaints.

Ombudsman inquiries can involve culture change and therefore inquiry outcomes tend to involve evolutionary rather than revolutionary change. One should not however underestimate the power of well-judged questions asking for detailed answers and explanations.

Own-initiative investigative powers highlight problematic issues without the Ombudsman necessarily having received a direct complaint. An example is the knowledge gap between how the EU legislates and how the public perceives it to legislate. The latter has tended to see EU laws as the result of an amorphous 'Brussels' over which one has little influence. The role of the Member States in shaping all EU laws has remained hidden in plain sight – allowing governments to blame 'Brussels' over policies that they actually agreed to. The Ombudsman's work in this area has led to some transparency improvements and it remains a priority for the Office.

The Office also helps the public – and even the Institutions themselves – understand why an issue is important and notably with integrity matters where the line between an action and an outcome might be a long one. One such issue is revolving doors. EU officials moving to the private sector can use their knowledge and networks to help lobby their former colleagues or to help their new place of work to lobby more effectively in an effort to shape future EU legislation in its interests. The EU institutions have rules to control this but are reluctant to use them to their full extent. Own-initiative inquiries in this area have raised awareness and improved rules implementation. Other issues concern ensuring that experts advising on EU policies or regulations do not have a conflict of interest. For the EU administration this also means checking why companies might be responding to certain EU tenders – a recent Ombudsman inquiry[1] asked the European Commission to be more vigilant after it awarded a small but potentially influential study contract to one of the world's biggest investment companies in an area of regulatory and financial interest to it.

A significant tranche of my work concerns the EU administration's fundamental rights obligations. Our strategic work has examined whether EU funds are being spent in line with those obligations and how the border agency Frontex is complying with them in its border management tasks. We have also looked into whether sufficient human right impact assessments have been carried out in the context of measures to reduce irregular migration. This work has grown significantly in recent years and this is likely to remain the case as the EU redefines its approach

[1] Decision of the European Ombudsman in joint inquiry 853/2020/KR on the European Commission's decision to award a contract to BlackRock Investment Management to carry out a study on integrating environmental, social and governance (ESG) objectives into EU banking rules www.ombudsman.europa.eu/en/decision/en/135363.

to migration and the climate crisis increasingly becomes a major driver of cross-border movement.

The EU can be very nimble when there is political will or pressure to act. The Ombudsman needs to be equally nimble in keeping abreast of new issues. This has meant timely questions to the EU administration about maintaining transparency standards during the emergency decision-making of the Covid-19 pandemic, the accountability of environmental decisions amid plans to make the EU climate-neutral by 2050 and managing potential conflicts of interests related to decisions on funding for EU defence projects. We are following developments in Artificial Intelligence and its possible implications for public administrations.

This text has focused on the work of the European Ombudsman yet the Ombudsman does not operate alone. Often it takes a series of actors such as civil society, journalists and other stakeholders to achieve change through public pressure and other means. In addition, while our ombudsprudence indicates our positive effect on the EU administration, this needs to be objectively analysed and contextualised.

We therefore decided to hold an academic conference with the European University Institute's Department of Law and School of Transnational governance in late 2022 to discuss the Ombudsman's evolving role. It brought together diverse perspectives from academia, the EU administration, civil society and the European Ombudsman Office itself. We discussed the Ombudsman's role over time, how its 'soft power' can encourage positive change, and the role of transparency in achieving accountability in the EU institutions. We also discussed new challenges and opportunities.

These excellent discussions have been further developed in this book. Many of the themes mentioned above are explored, including how the role of the European Ombudsman has evolved, how it can lend expertise and institutional authority to issues raised by public interest actors and how the Office acts as an 'influencer' for progressive change in the EU administration. I am deeply grateful to the editors, Professor Deirdre Curtin, Tanja Ehnert, Anna Morandini and Sarah Tas, for bringing this book together so quickly and professionally.

The fact that the European Ombudsman Office has grown in stature and wears its big role lightly and with assurance is thanks to the talent, commitment and enthusiasm of the people who work there. This book is both a tribute to their work and a rallying call for the European Ombudsman to continue to meet the multi-faceted challenges that lie ahead for what is commonly referred to as the 'watchdog' of the EU administration.

Contents

Contributors

EDITORS

Deirdre Curtin is Professor of European Law and the Dean of Graduate Studies at the European University Institute, Italy, where she is also the Director of the Centre for Judicial Cooperation at the Robert Schuman Centre.

Tanja Ehnert is Inquiries Coordinator at the European Ombudsman and Visiting Professor at the College of Europe, Belgium.

Anna Morandini is a PhD Researcher in European Law at the European University Institute, Italy.

Sarah Tas is Assistant Professor of European and Comparative Administrative Law at Maastricht University, the Netherlands.

AUTHORS

Onno Brouwer is Partner at Freshfields Bruckhaus Deringer LLP.

Dirk Detken is Head of Legal Affairs Services at the European Food Safety Authority (EFSA).

Mariolina Eliantonio is Professor of European and Comparative Administrative Law and Procedure at Maastricht University, the Netherlands.

Anne Friel is in-house solicitor at ClientEarth, specialising in environmental democracy and fundamental rights.

Rosita Hickey is Director of Inquiries at the European Ombudsman.

Olivier Hoedeman is coordinator at Corporate Europe Observatory (CEO).

Emilia Korkea-aho is Professor of European Law and Legislative Studies at University of Eastern Finland, Finland.

Pascal Lefèvre is Senior Expert and Coordinator for Inter-institutional Relations with the European Ombudsman in the Secretariat-General of the European Commission.

Christian Linder is Head of Unit 'Ethics, Good Administration & Relations with the European Ombudsman' in the Secretariat-General of the European Commission.

Emily O'Reilly was first elected as European Ombudsman in July 2013. She was re-elected in 2014 and again in 2019.

Aidan O'Sullivan acted as the Head of Cabinet of European Ombudsman between 2014 and 2023.

Danai Petropoulou Ionescu is a PhD Candidate at the Department of Public Law and the Department of Political Science, Maastricht University, the Netherlands.

Koen Roovers is an Inquiries Officer in the Strategic Inquiries team of the European Ombudsman.

Moritz Schramm is a researcher at the Humboldt-University of Berlin, Germany.

Harald Schumann is a journalist at Investigate Europe.

Nikos Vogiatzis is Senior Lecturer at Essex Law School at the University of Essex, Germany, and a Senior Humboldt Fellow at the Academy for European Human Rights Protection at the University of Cologne, Germany.

Laura Weemering is a member of the Public Access to Documents (PAD) team in the Legal Affairs Services Unit at the European Food Safety Authority (EFSA).

Anchrit Wille is Professor at the Institute of Public Administration, Faculty of Governance and Global Affairs at the Leiden University, Netherlands.

Introduction: The European Ombudsman Beyond Old Battles and Navigating New Challenges

DEIRDRE CURTIN, TANJA EHNERT,
ANNA MORANDINI AND SARAH TAS

For almost 30 years, the European Ombudsman (EO) has striven to ensure good administration in the European Union (EU). It has made remarkable achievements. As struggles against instances of undue influence, secrecy or incomplete accountability continue in an EU administration that assumes ever more responsibilities, its role remains absolutely pivotal. With the third EO leaving office, crucial perennial battles demand new strategies while issues related to current developments such as the digitalisation, environmental crisis and securitisation, pose distinct challenges. With innovation engrained in its DNA, the EO keeps entering new stages of its evolution in its aspiration of ensuring good administration.

This volume takes a future-facing look at the major challenges the EO faces. Drawing on experience and the successes of the past decades, it discusses approaches the EO is or should be developing. It complements the emerging doctrinal literature on the EO with stakeholder voices on its evolving and future challenges and strategies. This book thereby lends voice to those who review, rely on and produce the EO's work: academics, civil society actors, EU institutions and bodies and the EO office. We believe that this diversity of perspectives can show the many facets of the work, influence and potential of this unique EU institution. It gathers the expectations the EO encounters and the central areas and strategies it ought to consider.

In this introductory chapter, we briefly depict how the current position and strategy of the EO emerged, before highlighting the central challenges it faces. Lastly, we detail the vision of this volume and give an overview of its chapters.

I. THE ROUTE TRAVELLED: LOOKING BACK AT THE FIRST THREE DECADES

The roots of Ombudsperson (commonly referred to as Ombudsman) lie in the Swedish and Danish ideas of a citizen representative, 'guardian of the common and individual rights of people',[1] that upholds rule of law and democracy.[2] As administrative

[1] Alfred Bexelius, 'The Swedish Ombudsman' (1967) 17 *The University of Toronto Law Journal* 170, 171.

[2] Michael Gøtze, 'The Danish Ombudsman – A National Watchdog with European Reservations' (2009) 28 *Transylvanian Review of Administrative Sciences* 172, 173.

apparatuses extended, Ombudspersons should both protect individual rights and improve administration.[3] Given their task of counterbalancing ever more anonymous bureaucracies, the institution is commonly vested in an individual person.[4]

The EO was created by the Maastricht Treaty in 1992, overcoming institutional opposition after a first proposal in 1979.[5] Its mission is to strengthen the democratic character of EU governance and bring sceptical citizens closer to the often-distant Brussels.[6] This role of the EO has been shaped by both its legal basis in the Treaties and officeholders' creative interpretation thereof, as we will now recount.

Article 228 TFEU[7] established the powers for the EO to conduct inquiries based on complaints from any EU citizen and resident or upon own initiative. Their subject is maladministration of Union institutions, bodies, offices or agencies – with the exception of the judicial role of the Court of Justice. If the EO discovers maladministration, concerned EU institutions may respond to the findings within three months. The EO reports on her findings to the institution concerned, the complainant and the European Parliament (Parliament). The Parliament receives a yearly report on all EO inquiries. It elects the EO following its own election and for its term in office; it can reappoint an EO.[8] The EO is entirely independent in its work meaning that it does not take instructions from any external party. This is an essential element for EO to conduct its role of 'watchdog'.[9] Dismissal requires a decision by the Court of Justice at the request of the Parliament based on serious misconduct or lacking fulfilment of the conditions to perform the role.[10]

Maladministration, as the term determining the EO's mandate, is not further defined in the Treaty. This gives the EO the leeway to interpret it much more broadly than legality alone. For the EO, maladministration occurs if an institution or body fails to act in accordance with the law or the principles of good administration or violates fundamental rights.[11] It can include administrative irregularities, unfairness, discrimination or the abuse of power. It moreover encompasses the failure to reply, or the refusal or unnecessary delay in granting access to information in the public interest.[12]

The EO's work is further detailed in the Statute, which was revised in 2021, formalising some of its strategies and offering a 'strong and clear mandate' to

[3] Anne Peters, 'The European Ombudsman and the European Constitution' (2005) 42 *Common Market Law Review* 697, 697–99.

[4] Tom Binder, Marco Inglese and Frans van Waarden, 'The European Ombudsman: Democratic Empowerment or Democratic Deficit?' (Deliverable 8.9 Report 'Experiences with the European Ombudsman' BEUCITIZEN, 2016), 9.

[5] ibid 10.

[6] Peters (n 3) 700.

[7] ex Article 195 TEC.

[8] As has been the case for example with Emily O'Reilly, elected in 2013 and re-elected in 2014 and 2019.

[9] Anchrit Wille and Mark Bovens, 'Watching EU Watchdogs Assessing the Accountability Powers of the European Court of Auditors and the European Ombudsman' (2022) 44(2) *Journal of European Integration* 183, 187.

[10] Consolidated version of the Treaty on the Functioning of the European Union, 2008/C 115/01, Article 228.

[11] Georgiana Sandu, 'The European Ombudsman' (October 2023) Factsheets on the European Ombudsman, www.europarl.europa.eu/factsheets/en/sheet/18/the-european-ombudsman#_ftn1.

[12] European Ombudsman, 'Make a Complaint to the European Ombudsman', www.ombudsman.europa.eu/en/make-a-complaint.

the EO.[13] The revision includes notably the strengthening of the Ombudsman's access to classified EU information in the course of an investigation, and further frames the performance of own-initiative inquiries.[14] Following complaints, the EO shall attempt to solve any maladministration with the institution concerned and close the case if satisfied. It should propose solutions and cooperate with the Union and national authorities. Importantly, the EO can conduct inquiries based on complaints or on its own initiative, the latter particularly on systemic instances of maladministration. Concerned authorities must provide any requested information without delay. The EO may gather information by questioning EU officials or from whistle-blowers, who are protected when disclosing information in inquiries.[15]

The three EOs who have so far held the mandate each shaped the role with their unique perspectives.[16] The first to take the office of the EO was Finish lawyer and politician Jacob Söderman (1995–2003). He set the foundation for the EO's respected position and key strategies – pushing for transparency, collaborating with other actors and communicating proactively. Sparked by the failed Danish referendum on the Maastricht Treaty, this period saw political commitments to open and legitimise EU decision-making, promising citizens to better understand its workings. He mostly dealt with individuals' complaints, embodying thereby the 'EU-legitimizing role of the defender of citizens' rights and interests' in the good administration of the EU.[17] At the same time, the EO devised a nascent public media strategy that attempted to reach non-institutional audiences in a different and more direct way. In these pre-social media days, he *inter alia* garnered attention through an editorial in the *Wall Street Journal*.[18] He sparked irritation because in the perception of critics he dared to step outside his express powers into the public space and criticise the Commission's proposal for an Access to Documents Regulation. Even if the provisions of the Regulation[19] did not improve significantly in its final version, the response by Commission President Prodi in the journal in his own piece was an early achievement of the strategy.[20] This mandate moreover gave rise to the European Network of

[13] Ana Paula Zacarias, Secretary of State for European Affairs of Portugal, www.consilium.europa.eu/en/press/press-releases/2021/06/18/the-council-gives-its-consent-to-the-revised-statute-of-the-ombudsman-to-further-guarantee-its-independence/.

[14] European Ombudsman, 'New Statute: Ombudsman Welcomes Legal Strengthening of her Office' (10 June 2021) Press release no. 4/2021, www.ombudsman.europa.eu/en/press-release/en/142792.

[15] Regulation (EU, Euratom) 2021/1163 of the European Parliament of 24 June 2021 laying down the regulations and general conditions governing the performance of the Ombudsman's duties (Statute of the European Ombudsman) and repealing Decision 94/262/ECSC [2021] OJ L253/1.

[16] Herwig CH Hofmann, 'The Developing Role of the European Ombudsman' in Herwig CH Hofmann and Jacques Ziller (eds), *Accountability in the EU: The Role of the European Ombudsman* (Cheltenham, Edward Elgar, 2017) 3.

[17] ibid.

[18] Jacob Soederman, 'The EU's Transparent Bid for Opacity' *The Wall Street Journal Europe* (24 February 2000) www.statewatch.org/observatories/freedom-of-information-in-the-eu/1999-2007-secret-europe-reporting-on-secrecy-and-openness-in-europe/major-row-breaks-out-as-prodi-attacks-the-european-ombudsman-for-defending-the-right-of-access-to-documents-mr-soderman-replies/the-eu-s-transparent-bid-for-opacity-by-jacob-soederman/.

[19] Regulation (EC) No 1049/2001 of the European Parliament and of the Council of 30 May 2001 regarding public access to European Parliament, Council and Commission documents [2001] OJ L 145/43.

[20] Romano Prodi, 'Commission's Transparency Defended' *The Wall Street Journal Europe* (13 March 2000).

Ombudsmen as a forum of collaboration with national and regional Ombudsmen,[21] and of the addition of Article 41 on the 'Right to Good Administration' in the Charter of Fundamental Rights, an important constitutional confirmation.[22]

The second to hold the office of the EO was the Greek academic Paraskevas Nikiforos Diamandouros (2003–13). His legal approach placed much emphasis on the need for a principle of good administration.[23] As the law leaves 'maladministration' undefined, he demarcated it widely as the failure to act according to the law, human rights or principles of good administration. This definition goes beyond questions of legal compliance, albeit including them. It highlights an administrative 'culture of service' towards active citizens: acting fairly and reasonably, balancing all interests, avoiding delay and secrecy, acting courteously and with sensitivity to needs, acknowledging mistakes and improving continuously.[24] This broad and flexible vision was catalysed in the 'Public service principles for the EU civil service'.[25] It has significantly influenced the practice of the EO and EU administration.

The third EO, Emily O'Reilly from Ireland, was first elected in 2013 and re-elected in 2014 and 2019. As a former journalist and ombudsman of Ireland, raising citizens' awareness of the EO became one of her priorities. Her strategy 'Towards 2024' moreover aimed to improve the EO's lasting impact by strengthening follow-up on her work and dialogue with institutions, to ensure real-life relevance by identifying systemic trends in public administration, and to render her office more efficient and flexible.[26] Her mandate saw the start of parallel inquiries with the European Network of Ombudsmen,[27] enhanced cooperation with Parliament through committees and hearings, the set-up of a new strategic investigation unit and a fast-track procedure for access to document requests. She gave a more visible role to the function of EO, notably through her work on the issue of 'revolving doors' – the move of staff between public administration and private sector positions, giving rise to potential conflicts of interest and damages in public trust.[28]

In the first 25 years of its existence, the EO office has dealt with more than 57,000 complaints and launched over 7,300 inquiries.[29] It has demanded transparency in the

[21] The European Network of Ombudsmen (ENO), https://eno.ombudsman.europa.eu/home.html.

[22] Hofmann (n 16) 4; Jacob Söderman, 'How to be a Good Ombudsman' Issue 80 of Occasional paper (2004) International Ombudsman Institute 3.

[23] Hofmann (n 16) 4.

[24] Nikiforos P Diamandouros, 'The Principle of Good Administration in the Recommendations of the European Ombudsman' (Speech by the European Ombudsman at the EUNOMIA Project Capacity-Building Seminar on 'Ombudsman's Intervention: Between the Principles of Legality and Good Administration', Sofia, 17 September 2007) www.ombudsman.europa.eu/en/speech/en/369; European Ombudsman, 'Code of Good Administrative Behaviour'.

[25] European Ombudsman, 'Public Service Principles for the EU Civil Service' (19 June 2012) www.ombudsman.europa.eu/en/document/en/11650.

[26] European Ombudsman, 'Strategy Towards 2024' (7 December 2020) at www.ombudsman.europa.eu/en/strategy/our-strategy/en.

[27] The first parallel investigation was Case SI/1/2015/MHZ, Asylum, Migration and Integration Fund (AMIF) – role of national Ombudsman, decided on 16 September 2016; since then six more parallel inquiries were launched, see www.ombudsman.europa.eu/en/european-network-of-ombudsmen/parallel-inquiries.

[28] See Emilia Korkea-Aho, 'When the Doors of EU Administration Revolve: The European Ombudsman's Legacy and Future Action', chapter 6 in this volume.

[29] European Ombudsman, 'Annual Report 2020', 18 May 2021, 20, www.ombudsman.europa.eu/en/doc/annual-report/en/141317.

way Member States make EU law in the Council, finance ministers shape Eurozone policies in the Eurogroup and the Union negotiates trade agreements with third countries. It has guided the Commission and other institutions to communicate more accessibly and multi-lingually. It has pushed for stronger ethics rules for European Commissioners, better enforcement of rules regarding revolving doors, and guidelines on interacting with lobbyists for EU civil servants. Thereby it expanded its scrutiny beyond the core institutions to the work of bodies such as the European Border and Coast Guard Agency (Frontex), the European Medicines Agency, the European Defence Research Programme and EU-funded projects such as in educational cooperation in Latin America.[30] In this period, the EO saw growth in both its public and institutional relevance.[31]

Innovation and continuity alongside a broad interpretation of the mandate have shaped the first decades of the EO's work. All three EOs have embraced the founding treaty provision as a launchpad rather than a narrow corset. This allowed the institution to play a powerful role despite – or one may argue precisely because of – its soft power. The next section highlights major perennial battles and new challenges for coming EOs to overcome, with the fourth EO to be elected after the 2024 Parliament elections.

II. THE ROUTE MEANDERING AHEAD: ADDRESSING MULTIFACETED CHALLENGES

Which challenges lie ahead for the EO in promoting a transparent, ethical and accountable EU administration? The contributions in this book show that core battles remain unchanged since the EO's origins, while the widespread sensation of a persistent poly-crisis creates new challenges. Well-known issues, for example in institutional transparency and independence, require ever new approaches to overcome persisting hurdles. Defining developments such as the digitalisation of governance, the expansion of EU agencies in the field of security and the handling of the environmental crisis require enhanced attention. Collaborating with all its stakeholders – citizens, EU and national institutions, civil society organisations and journalists – and determining the best use of scare resources remains central. This section provides an overview of key challenges that are further developed in the chapters of this book.

As a prerequisite of accountability, transparency has always been at the heart of the EO's work. Despite achievements made, access to documents and transparency of decision-making remain high on the agenda.[32] Vigilance is also required regarding new institutional hurdles against transparency, as evidenced by the recent action of the European Commission to redact the identities of certain officials from the public

[30] See an overview by the European Ombudsman, '25 years of the European Ombudsman' at www.ombudsman.europa.eu/webpub/25years/en/index.html.

[31] European Ombudsman (n 14).

[32] Anna Morandini and Sarah Tas, 'Seminar Report: The Evolving Role of the European Ombudsman' (1 February 2023) www.ombudsman.europa.eu/en/event-document/en/165564.

register (citing data protection and security reasons).[33] This further exacerbates the opaqueness characteristics of the 'Brussels bubble'. Ongoing work on transparency is indispensable to ensure that citizens, civil society organisations and journalists can understand and review the work of the EU administration. It enables them to take an informed decision in elections with regard among others to the handling of environmental questions such as the use of pesticides, the management of EU borders in conformity with human rights and more generally the spending of EU funding. Structurally, the implementation of the Access to Documents Regulation, in place unchanged since 2001, requires adaptations to the digital age and mitigation of its dependence on applicants.[34] Yet the key concept standing out for the next decades is proactive transparency.[35] The EO, in its own work and its suggestions to EU institutions and bodies, is at the forefront of a push to publish comprehensible information on own initiative.[36] While this may seem to foretell a bright future for transparency, this core public value faces new threats of opacity: data protection and trade secrets are increasingly weaponised to avoid scrutiny.[37] At the same time, the EO has started action in the field, asking the European Commission for more transparency in its use of Artificial Intelligence in decision-making.[38]

In safeguarding the independence of EU institutions and their decision-making, lobbying remains a crucial battlefield. Its continuing importance is illustrated by reports indicating the recent Digital Services Act Package to be one of the most lobbied pieces of EU regulation of all time.[39] With some, albeit limited, achievements like the Lobbying Transparency Register made, new battles such as the Commission Regulatory Scrutiny Board – an under-observed gatekeeper for draft Union regulation – gain in contour.[40] A recent incident highlights that the European Commission still requires complaint-based EO inquiries as a prompt to drop a consultant with clear conflict of interests. This was the case of a consultancy firm which was tasked to evaluate a merger control tool despite conflicting interests due to its involvement in controversial Big Tech mergers and acquisitions.[41] Revolving doors pose similar threats to institutional legitimacy.[42]

[33] Luca Bertuzzi, 'European Commission Cracks Down on Internal Transparency over Security' (5 April 2023) *Euractiv* www.euractiv.com/section/eu-institutions/news/european-commission-cracks-down-on-internal-transparency-over-security/.

[34] See Tanja Ehnert and Koen Roovers, 'The European Ombudsman's Role in Fostering Institutional Legitimacy', chapter 10 in this volume.

[35] See Nikos Vogiatzis, 'The Evolving Proactive Role of the European Ombudsman', chapter 2 in this volume; and Dirk Detken and Laura Weemering, 'Transparency That Is Fit for Purpose: EFSA's Experience with the European Ombudsman and Proactive Transparency', chapter 13 in this volume.

[36] Morandini and Tas (n 32).

[37] See for example SK Sandeen and T Aplin, 'Trade Secrecy, Factual Secrecy and the Hype Surrounding AI Machines' in Ryan Abbott and David Geffen (eds), *Research Handbook on Intellectual Property and Artificial Intelligence* (Cheltenham, Edward Elgar Publishing, 2022) 442.

[38] See the Case SI/4/2024/MIK, Ombudsman asks European Commission about artificial intelligence use in decision making, opened 3 January 2024.

[39] Bram Vranken and Max Bank, 'Why EU Commission Dumped Google's Favourite Consultant' (2 October 2023) *EU Observer*, https://euobserver.com/opinion/157481.

[40] See Olivier Hoedeman, 'The Role of the European Ombudsman in Curtailing Undue Corporate Lobbying Influence', chapter 9 in this volume.

[41] Vranken and Bank (n 39).

[42] See Emilia Korkea-Aho, 'When the Doors of EU Administration Revolve: The European Ombudsman's Legacy and Future Action', chapter 6 in this volume.

Central focuses for future EO work arise from ongoing European and global dynamics.[43] The EU has grown significantly in the past 25 years, creating ever-more agencies that demand accountability – prominent examples in the human rights sensitive area of security are Europol and Frontex.[44] While crises have always been a catalyst for EU integration, a newly purported permanent state of multiple crises cautions to review normalised exceptional or emergency arrangements. They should never become a tool to undermine democratic oversight.[45] The digitisation and digitalisation of governance demand a watchful eye on the way administration uses large datasets, machine-learning and AI tools, particularly in collaboration with large private transnational cooperations.[46] Finally, protecting our physical environment for the next generations is a central mission of the Union that the EO should actively promote as a focus of good governance.[47]

This extensive agenda puts further emphasis on crucial decisions on how the EO should use its comparatively small resources and soft power.[48] In terms of resources, the EO cannot rely on similar staff numbers of other public accountability forums such as the European Court of Auditors. She must strike a delicate balance between helping individual complainants and pursuing more systemic inquiries, both of which are essential to its work.[49] The EO must strike the right tone, at times friendly at others stern, to convince affected institutions of implementing its non-binding recommendations and proactively moving towards better administration.[50] One piece of this strategy is following up on the EO's own work as well as communicating its impact, which is not always clearly visible.[51] Another piece is its interplay with citizens, journalists and organised civil society as well as other EU accountability institutions or forums – such as notably the Court of Auditors, the Court of Justice, the European Network of Ombudsmen and sectorial actors such as the European Data Protection Supervisor.[52]

[43] See Aidan O'Sullivan, 'The European Ombudsman's Perspective', chapter 14 in this volume.

[44] See Sarah Tas, 'The Role of the European Ombudsman in Fostering Transparency and Accountability of EU Agencies: Zooming-in on Europol and Frontex', chapter 7 in this volume.

[45] Morandini and Tas (n 32).

[46] See Moritz Schramm, 'Administrification of the Digital Single Market: A New Role for the European Ombudsman in the DSA Framework?', chapter 12 in this volume.

[47] See Onno Brouwer and Anne Friel, 'Barriers to Obtaining Information to Protect the Environment: The Role of the European Ombudsman', chapter 8 in this volume, who discuss the need for increased transparency in the field.

[48] For example, in 2023, there were 75 posts in the Ombudsman's establishment plan, see European Ombudsman, Annual Report 2023 (2024), 32.

[49] See Rosita Hickey, 'The Evolving Role of the European Ombudsman in Context: The European Ombudsman's Perspective', chapter 5 in this volume.

[50] See Christian Linder and Pascal Lefèvre, 'The Relations Between the European Commission and the European Ombudsman', chapter 4 in this volume; and Dirk Detken and Laura Weemering, 'Transparency That Is Fit for Purpose: EFSA's Experience with the European Ombudsman and Proactive Transparency', chapter 13 in this volume.

[51] See Tanja Ehnert and Koen Roovers, 'The European Ombudsman's Role in Fostering Institutional Legitimacy', chapter 10 in this volume; and Mariolina Eiantonio and Danai Petropolou Ionescu, 'The European Ombudsman as a Good Administration 'Influencer': Revisiting Concepts, Methodological Challenges, and Promises Ahead', chapter 11 in this volume.

[52] See Anchrit Wille, 'The European Ombudsman as an Evolving EU Accountability Institution', chapter 1 in this volume; Harald Schumann, 'The Ombudsman – An Indispensable Source of Encouragement', chapter 3 in this volume; Sarah Tas, 'The Role of the European Ombudsman in Fostering Transparency

Emily O'Reilly described leading the EO as a form of art, like directing an orchestra: rather than a single right way to approach issues, one must find solutions that work for each case.[53] The paths to achieve different goals may be multiple and non-linear. As this brief overview demonstrates, the repeat battles and new challenges are many. The next section explains how this book attempts to collect many visions to approach them. We hope as editors that the result is a symphony of different voices and different issues, old and new, intertwined in an audible and visible whole.

III. THE ROUTE OF THIS BOOK: A SYMPHONY OF CHORDS AND SCALES

Over the last decade, the EO has increased its efforts to communicate its work and engage with citizens, institutions and independent experts, including on its own role. As one result of this endeavour, this book brings together leading voices from academia, civil society, EU institutions and the EO's office. It draws on their diverse experience in working with, and on, the EO to analyse the EO's work, and show different aspects and perceptions of the EO's work and influence. The collection highlights the diverse challenges, expectations, hopes and occasional fears that the EO faces in continuously carving out its unique role. Some of the issues showcase current advances that have been central to the EO's agenda across all three decades of its existence. Others demonstrate how the institution is responding to recent developments and new actors. Both display different stances on how the EO should develop and expand its work in the future.

Its roots lie in a conference on the 'Evolving Role of the European Ombudsman' jointly organised by the European University Institute's Department of Law and School of Transnational Governance in November 2022. The diverse perspectives that emerged are captured and expanded on in this edited volume. Its vision is to complement the emerging literature on the EO and Ombudsmen more broadly with stakeholder voices on its evolving and future strategies. Building upon existing doctrinal accounts on the institution and its functioning, this book zooms in on the EO's work with selected actors and on specific challenges and zooms out to the wider political and institutional ecosystem within which it operates.

First, this book places the EO within the wider EU accountability landscape, tracing its achievements and the limits of its role and its relationship with other EU institutions and public watchdogs. Second, it zooms in on the EO's increasingly proactive approach towards fostering the transparency, independence and accountability of EU institutions and persisting challenges. Third, it highlights the way the EO can act as an influencer of change within the Union going forward, proactively promoting transparency and good administration in new forms and contexts. To capture the multiple dimensions of the evolving role of the EO in these areas, each

and Accountability of EU Agencies: Zooming-in on Europol and Frontex', chapter 7 in this volume; and Onno Brouwer and Anne Friel, 'Barriers to Obtaining Information to Protect the Environment: The Role of the European Ombudsman', chapter 8 in this volume.

[53] Emily O'Reilly at EUI Conference on the Evolving Role of the European Ombudsman (November 2023, Florence), www.ombudsman.europa.eu/en/speech/en/163063.

of the three book sections combines two academic analyses with shorter views from practice – of civil society, EU institutions and bodies and – innovatively – from within the EO office. The chapters discuss evergreen battles of institutional legitimacy and cutting-edge ones on the digital and green transition. The EO's proactiveness and prospects form a common thread throughout the contributions.

Part I explores the evolving role of the EO. The part starts with a chapter by Anchrit Wille, which explores the position of the EO as an integral component of the broader EU accountability landscape. She analyses how the EO has effectively leveraged its flexible mandate on maladministration, non-binding powers and limited resources through a strategic and network approach. Nikos Vogiatzis' chapter discusses the limits and prospects of the EO as an institution, highlighting its increasingly proactive role. He points out the delicate balance the EO has to strike between individual redress and systemic inquiries in carving out its unique path. Accounts from practice detail how the EO increasingly engages with two key actors in their view: journalists and the European Commission. Harald Schumann depicts how the EO strengthens leading actors of this network – journalists –, providing an essential contribution to democratising the EU. He points to many outstanding issues, such as the struggle to access hidden information from EU institutions and bodies. Christian Linder and Pascal Lefèvre depict the regular interplay between the European Commission and the EO. They value the EO as a non-conflictual and easily accessible actor that pursues practical improvements in EU administration. Finally, Rosita Hickey concludes this part by showing how the EO office views its role of assisting individual complainants and ensuring good administration. She highlights how its success depends on continuous adaptations and constructive collaboration with both EU institutions and citizens, particularly in the context of its ever-growing mandate.

Part II spotlights the EO's role in fostering institutional legitimacy, with work on institutional transparency, independence and accountability remaining at the core of its mission to strengthen trust in EU institutions. Emilia Korkea-Aho opens this section with a chapter on the issue of revolving doors which became prominent under Emily O'Reilly's mandate. She argues that the conflicts of interest framework thereby used overlooks the role of the new employer, which can be better captured by distribution of expertise considerations. Sarah Tas showcases the EO's potential to illuminate the work of rapidly growing EU agencies, as a step towards accountability. To do so, the chapter explores the EO's work on two key agencies in the field of Justice and Home Affairs – Europol and Frontex. Coming from the practice of access to information, Onno Brouwer and Anne Friel recount challenges and progress in the struggle to access information to protect the environment in the spirit of the Aarhus Convention. Labelling the EO as a reliable forum for complainants, they call on it to take a bold and uncompromising approach in addressing inadequate institutional compliance to achieve systemic change. As a voice from civil society, Olivier Hoedeman showcases challenges of industry lobbying at the example of the Commission Regulatory Scrutiny Board, viewing the EO as a decisive factor in combatting undue influence. He calls for more resolute measures. From the inside, Tanja Ehnert and Koen Roovers depict the work and ambitions of the EO in the area. They highlight the agenda setting power of the EO and invite viewing it as independent from immediate results.

Part III further investigates how the EO facilitates change within the Union. This part starts with an inter-disciplinary piece from Mariolina Eliantonio and Danai Petropoulou Ionescu that discusses how to conceive and research the soft influence of the EO. They call upon us to look beyond the rate of compliance with EO recommendations, proposing alternative methods to capture the understudied and hard-to-capture influence of the EO. Exploring potentials in the future extent and limits of the EO mandate, Moritz Schramm proposes for the EO to proactively supervise private online platforms' speech governance. He argues that the EO could help EU authorities in safeguarding that platforms comply with public values beyond ceremonial rituals. Dirk Detken and Laura Weemering share the European Food Safety Authority's experience in collaborating with the EO. One field where they argue that the EO can shape meaningful proactive transparency is risk analysis. Aidan O'Sullivan concludes this section with a perspective from the EO office on its role in driving improvements to EU administration. He depicts key challenges the EO has faced and strategies it has devised to overcome them.

There are inevitably also limitations to the approach adopted in this book: given the large number of stakeholders the EO engages with, the editors could only give voice to a selection, leaving others such as the European Parliament outside. We hope that the result nevertheless gives both a broad overview and concrete insights into the work of the EO and the challenges it currently facing and will likely soon face.

Despite its limited resources and non-binding power, the EO is a crucial actor in promoting transparency and accountability in EU administration. As it continues to push for proactive transparency of legislative and administrative process, limits to revolving doors and undue influence and solutions for complainants in individual grievances, new challenges emerge from the *agencification*[54] and states of crisis from the digital and environmental arenas. This book collects different perspectives on the EO and its future role, highlighting challenges, developments, strategies and potentials for the road ahead. The EO is thereby less limited by its broad mandate for good governance than the EU institutions, bodies and agencies are. To scrutinize public-private cooperation, the focus of the EO should lie on the role and decisions of the public actors, the reviewing of national–EU cooperation and the cooperation with national Ombudsmen through the European Network of Ombudsmen. Cooperation with all stakeholders, from civil society to institutions, emerges as its core strength. If it continues to nourish this soft power and its attention for the individual grievances of EU citizens and residents as well as systemic issues such as transparency of documents and accountability of new bodies as they spring up, such as the Commission Regulatory Scrutiny Board and of AI being used by the EU public administration, it will continue to shape the legitimacy of EU institutions throughout the coming decades. The end of the third mandate as EO signifies the end of the beginning of the accountability road; it stretches long and weaving ahead. The office of the EO and its future incumbents are well placed to lead the way.

[54] *Agencification* means the proliferation of EU agencies and delegation of powers to them, see for example Ellen Vos, 'EU Agencies, Common Approach and Parliamentary Scrutiny' Study for the European Parliamentary Research Service on *EU Agencies, Common Approach and Parliamentary Scrutiny* (2018) and Morten Egeberg and Jarle Trondal, 'Agencification of the European Union administration – Connecting the Dots' (2016) *TARN Working Paper 1/2016*.

Part I

The Evolving Role of the European Ombudsman

1

The European Ombudsman as an Evolving EU Accountability Institution

ANCHRIT WILLE

I. ADVOCATING GOOD GOVERNANCE AND TRANSPARENCY

IN THE SHIFTING landscape of the European Union's governance, media headlines echo the voice of the European Ombudsman (EO), marking its advocacy for good governance: 'EU Ombudsman asks Council to join transparency register',[1] 'Ombudsman demands transparency on human rights abuses in EU-Turkey deal',[2] 'Ombudsman investigates "revolving doors" at ECB',[3] 'EU watchdog: failure to find VDL-Pfizer texts is "wake-up call"',[4] and 'European Ombudsman: Qatargate exposed a weak ethical culture – this must change'.[5] Collectively these news snippets illustrate the EO's active engagement in addressing maladministration within the European Union.

The headlines signify the EO's firm commitment to transparency, accountability and ethical governance. The EO has built a strong reputation as a good administration advocate. While the EO traditionally investigates individual complaints, it has increasingly taken on a proactive role in addressing systemic issues and shaping the behaviour of EU institutions toward greater openness and accountability.[6]

This chapter explores the evolved powers and performance of the EO over the past three decades, tracing its shift from a mere complainant-oriented role to a more systemic and influential accountability institution within the European Union. To understand the nature and implications of the EO's evolution, the chapter focuses

[1] *Euractiv*, 18 December 2017.
[2] *Euractiv*, 20 January 2017.
[3] *Politico*, 18 May 2022.
[4] *Politico*, 14 July 2022.
[5] *Financial Times*, 8 June 2023.
[6] HC Hofmann, 'The Developing Role of the European Ombudsman' in HC Hofmann and J Ziller (eds), Accountability in the EU: The Role of the European Ombudsman (Cheltenham, Edward Elgar, 2017) 1–27; N Vogiatzis, *The European Ombudsman and Good Administration in the European* Union (London, Palgrave Macmillan, 2018); A Wille and M Bovens, 'Watching EU Watchdogs Assessing the Accountability Powers of the European Court of Auditors and the European Ombudsman' (2022) 44(2) *Journal of European Integration* 183–206.

on the EO's evolving formal powers, its shift in network and organisational capabilities, and its proactive involvement in relevant account-holding activities. The analysis provides insight into the EO's dynamic response to challenges of maladministration, and the evolving impact of its actions on EU governance, contributing to the 'ombudsmanisation' of the broader accountability landscape.

II. THE 'OMBUDSMANISATION' OF THE EU'S ACCOUNTABILITY LANDSCAPE

The EO, the European Parliament, the Court of Justice and the European Court of Auditors have woven a dense web of accountability relationships around the EU executive in the past decades. Establishing these institutions for administrative, political, legislative and financial accountability, has contributed to the development of an accountability landscape.[7] Instituting procedures, and mechanisms aimed at establishing democratic accountability at the EU level, indicates how the EU is in constant constitutional development.

Two significant dynamics have shaped the trajectory of accountability in the EU and defined the contours of this evolving landscape.[8] The first trend is the parliamentarisation of the EU, empowering the European Parliament, which has progressively gained the capacity for deliberation, representation, and accountability within the EU. This process of parliamentarisation signifies a gradual evolution towards a system of governance at the European level that mirrors parliamentary democracy in a nation-state context.[9] The European Parliament has systematically sought to maximise its prerogatives and account-holding powers, achieved through an incremental process.[10] This involves the EP using newly acquired powers to propose an expansive interpretation of the rules, thus further expanding its role beyond the formal prerogatives given to the institution in political and technocratic appointments,[11] financial supervision, economic governance[12] and account-holding activities.[13]

A second development is the 'judicialisation' of EU politics.[14] European integration also encouraged the spread of a distinct 'juridified' mode of governance

[7] A Wille, 'The Evolving EU Accountability Landscape: Moving to an Ever Denser Union' (2016) 82(4) *International Review of Administrative Sciences* 694–717.

[8] A Wille, 'The EU's Accountability Landscape' in GJ Brandsma (ed), *The Handbook of EU Public Administration* (Cheltenham, Edward Elgar, 2024).

[9] H Van der Veer and S Otjes, 'A House Divided Against Itself. The Intra-institutional Conflict about the Powers of the European Parliament' (2021) 59(4) *JCMS: Journal of Common Market Studies* 822–38.

[10] A Héritier, KL Meissner, C Moury and MG Schoeller, *European Parliament Ascendant: Parliamentary Strategies of Self-Empowerment in the EU* (Cham, Palgrave Macmillan, 2019).

[11] MG Schoeller and A Héritier, 'Driving Informal Institutional Change: The European Parliament and the Reform of the Economic and Monetary Union' (2019) 41(3) *Journal of European Integration* 277–92.

[12] B Rittberger, 'Integration Without Representation? The European Parliament and the Reform of Economic Governance in the EU' (2014) 52(6) *JCMS: Journal of Common Market Studies* 1174–83.

[13] A Héritier, 'The Increasing Institutional Power of the European Parliament and EU Policy Making' (Working Paper No. 01/2017). Institute for European Integration Research; Rittberger (n 12); CC Montero, FG De León and GH González, 'Pragmatism and the Limits to the European Parliament's Strategies for Self-empowerment' (2021) 9(3) *Politics and Governance* 163–74.

[14] A Stone Sweet, 'The European Court of Justice and the Judicialization of EU Governance. Living Reviews in EU Governance' (2010) available at SSRN: https://ssrn.com/abstract=1583345 or http://dx.doi.org/10.2139/ssrn.1583345.

with an emphasis on enforcing legal norms through transparent legal rules and procedures and broad access to justice, empowering private actors to assert their legal rights.[15] Judicialisation has played a transformative role in the EU governance framework, fostering increased transparency and accountability in policy-making. This shift towards judicial involvement has not only elevated these principles but has also bolstered the authority and influence of the courts within the EU. It has empowered the courts, making them more potent actors in shaping and overseeing EU policies.

In tandem with these processes of parliamentarisation and judicialisation, a concurrent trend can be observed in the European Union, which I term 'ombudsmanisation'. This term denotes a gradual shift towards a governance system that incorporates principles akin to those upheld by ombudsman institutions. Much like parliamentarisation embodies democratic values and judicialisation reflects the role of the rule of law, ombudsmanisation reflects a movement toward open government and mechanisms for citizens to address maladministration.[16]

This ombudsmanisation is a trend that started in the twentieth century, when the concept of an independent ombudsman, which was first developed in Sweden in 1809, spread to many other jurisdictions. As numerous countries have developed towards the strengthening of democratic principles and the protection of citizen's rights, the spread of ombuds institutions worldwide has been noteworthy. However, their roles, mandates and scopes of intervention vary significantly from one country to another, influenced by distinct political, institutional and historical contexts.[17]

At the EU level, this process started in the 1970s with proposals for the creation of a European ombudsman, as a run-up to the Treaty of Maastricht.[18] The term refers to the increasing prominence and influence of an ombudsman-like entity, such as the EO, within the broader framework of accountability mechanisms in the EU. As the EU administration became more complex and the number of legal acts increased, the EO aimed to enhance the protection of citizens' rights and interests in the Union by offering an alternative route to administrative litigation.[19] The establishment of the EO in 1995 gave EU citizens the right to submit complaints about the increasingly complex administration and the growing number of legal acts issued in the EU.

The development of the EU accountability landscape is thus closely linked to the evolution of European citizenship.[20] EU citizens, residents of a Member State or organisations have the right to appeal to the Ombudsman for investigations into maladministration by EU institutions. This can include administrative irregularities, unfairness, discrimination, abuse of power, failure to respond, refusal of

[15] RD Kelemen and SK Schmidt, S. K. (2012) 'Introduction – the European Court of Justice and Legal Integration: Perpetual Momentum?' (2012) 19 *Journal of European Public Policy* 1–7.

[16] KE Zuegel, E Cantera and A Bellantoni, 'The Role of Ombudsman Institutions in Open Government', OECD Working Papers on Public Governance, No. 29 (Paris, OECD Publishing, 2018), https://doi.org/10.1787/7353965f-en, at 9.

[17] ibid.

[18] Hofmann (n 6) 2.

[19] A Tsadiras, 'Of Celestial Motions and Gravitational Attractions: The Institutional Symbiosis between the European Ombudsman and the European Parliament' (2009) 28(1) *Yearbook of European Law* 435.

[20] Hofmann (n 6) 2–3, P Zawadzki, 'Origin of the European Ombudsman' (2021) 19(1) *Miscellanea Historico-Iuridica* 443–59.

information or unnecessary delays, making it a recognised 'political right of European citizenship'.[21]

A. Three Dimensions of Accountability Power

Ombudsmanisation of the EO signifies a trend where an institution with characteristics similar to an ombudsman office plays an increasing role in overseeing and addressing issues related to administrative conduct, transparency and responsiveness within the EU. The EO's constitutional role, its activities and contributions to transparency and good governance are extensively described in the scholarly literature,[22] are an indication of this development. It indicates how the EO's role in the EU's landscape has shaped accountability.

Ombudsmanisation is a dynamic process and presumes that the ombudsman institution has built up over time accountability power.[23] Accountability power refers to an institution's capacity to hold executive actors accountable.[24] Three key factors shape this accountability power: (1) its formal authority to hold the executive accountable, (2) the organisational and network resources available for this task and (3) the implementation of relevant account-holding activities. To understand the position and performance of the EO in the broader landscape, it is essential to describe the empowerment along these three dimensions of accountability power.

First, it begins with getting insight into the establishment of the formal powers of an accountability institution to enable its operation. The creation of the different accountability institutions in the EU has shaped the institutional capacity for holding the executive to account.[25] The authority of these accountability institutions relies on formal powers granted by laws, treaties, regulations, decrees or statutes. These powers establish obligations for executive bodies to be accountable to the (new) accountability forums. Independence and investigative capabilities are crucial

[21] Vogiatzis (n 6) 74.

[22] P Magnette, 'Between Parliamentary Control and the Rule of Law: The Political Role of the Ombudsman in the European Union' (2003) 10 *Journal of European Public Policy* 677–694; C Harlow and R Rawlings, 'Promoting Accountability in Multilevel Governance: A Network Approach' (2007) 13(4) *European Law Journal* 542–62; K Kourtikakis, 'Imitation and Supranational Politics: Some Lessons from the European Ombudsman and the European Court of Auditors' (2010) 2(1) European Political Science Review 27–48; P Kostadinova, 'Improving the Transparency and Accountability of EU Institutions: The Impact of the Office of the European Ombudsman' (2015) 53(5) *JCMS: Journal of Common Market Studies* 1077–93; C Neuhold and A Năstase, 'Transparency Watchdog: Guarding the Law and Independent from Politics? The Relationship between the European Ombudsman and the European Parliament' (2017) 5(3) Politics and Governance 40–50; Silvia Kotanidis, 'The European Ombudsman: Reflections on the Role and its Potential', European Parliamentary Research Service (EPRS) PE 630.282 – November 2018; M Inglese and T Binder, 'The European Ombudsman' in David Levi-Faur and Frans van Waarden (eds), *Democratic Empowerment in the European Union* (Cheltenham, Edward Elgar, 2018) 85–100; Vogiatzis (n 6); T Erkkilä, *Ombudsman as a Global Institution: Transnational Governance and Accountability* (Cham, Palgrave Macmillan, 2020); M Spoerer and R More O'Ferrall, R. (2022). 'The European Ombudsman's Role in Access to Documents' (2022) 23(2) *ERA Forum* 253–66.

[23] HC Hofmann and J Ziller (eds), *Accountability in the EU: The Role of the European Ombudsman* (Cheltenham, Edward Elgar Publishing, 2017); Wille and Bovens (n 6).

[24] M Bovens and A Wille, 'Indexing Watchdog Accountability Powers: A Framework for Assessing the Accountability Capacity of Independent Oversight Institutions' (2021) 15(3) *Regulation & Governance* 856–76; Wille and Bovens (n 6).

[25] Wille (n 7).

attributes of these institutions. Treaty changes, notably the Maastricht[26] and Lisbon[27] Treaties, have laid a solid foundation for the EU accountability landscape. Relevant questions for examining the EO's formal accountability powers are: to what extent has the EO institutional independence and the discretion to investigate anything that falls within its mandate? Has it the statutory power to obtain information and to question officials? Has the EO formal powers to sanction actors in case of maladministration? And has the EO expanded its powers and competencies by leveraging legal ambiguities?

Second, organisational powers are vital for an accountability institution. A robust system of checks and balances requires accountability forums not only to possess formal authority but also to have the organisational capacity to effectively exercise these powers. This includes having the necessary resources, such as adequate budgets, qualified personnel, professional networks, strong leadership and the capacity to implement their accountability powers by working together.[28] Relevant questions to analyse these powers are: does the EO have the necessary resources to implement its formal powers? Does it have budgets and qualified personnel, and is it embedded in relevant networks? Does it operate based on a clear mission and strategy that is linked to achieving accountability? And has it modified the organisational parameters for reaching its goal?

Third, the actual exercise of these powers is of utmost importance. Simply examining formal rules and organisational capacity is insufficient; it is crucial to complement them with tangible outcomes. The effectiveness of accountability institutions depends on how they interpret and fulfil their mandates, the initiatives they undertake and their efficacy in exercising their powers. Effective accountability also involves going beyond traditional oversight and actively engaging in the executive's policymaking and decision-making processes.[29] By employing innovative approaches, accountability institutions can enhance their relevance, credibility, and impact on executive policies and programmes. Does the EO make use of its de jure powers and do its recommendations and reports lead to a follow-up by the EU executive? Does the EO make creative use of its powers to become visible and relevant in the political and policy arenas?

Getting insight into the empowerment process of the EO can contribute to an understanding of the ombudsmanisation of the EU landscape. The subsequent sections of this chapter examine the EO's evolution along these three dimensions of accountability power.

III. THE EO'S EVOLVED FORMAL POWERS

The effectiveness of accountability mechanisms is intrinsically tied to the formal powers of accountability institutions, and here the EO. Its accountability power

[26] Maastricht Treaty, TEU or Union Treaty: Treaty on European Union, 7 February 1992, 1992 OJ (C191) 1, 31 ILM 253.

[27] Treaty of Lisbon Amending the Treaty on European Union and the Treaty Establishing the European Community, 13 December 2007, 2007 OJ (C306) 1.

[28] Bovens and Wille (n 24).

[29] ibid.

depends first of all on the legal framework, mandate and authority bestowed upon the EO to hold executive institutions accountable. Questions surrounding institutional independence, discretionary investigative authority within its mandate, statutory powers to acquire information, interrogate officials and the capacity to impose sanctions in cases of maladministration have been pivotal for developing the accountability prowess of the ombudsman. These formal powers are not static; rather, the 'ombudsmanisation' of the EU reflects the EO's proactive efforts to actively expand its formal powers.

A. Legal Framework

The legal foundation for the EO's role and responsibilities can be found in Article 228 of the Treaty on the Functioning of the European Union (TFEU) and Article 43 of the Charter of Fundamental Rights of the European Union. The European Parliament also established the status and duties of the EO in a Statute.

The main objectives of the EO, as established by the Maastricht Treaty in 1992, are first, to improve the protection of citizens and legal persons in connection with cases of maladministration by EU institutions, saying that the EO has to check complaints from individuals; and second, to enhance openness and democratic accountability in the decision-making and administration of the EU's institutions. The EO's task is to provide supervisory oversight over the administration in general and to help improve its quality. It is not restricted to responding to complaints but can act on its own initiative, meaning that the EO can also check things even if it didn't get a complaint. This makes the institutional scope of the ombuds review very broad.

In 2021 the European Parliament adopted a Regulation laying down the new Statute of the EO, which codifies many office working practices. The update of the existing Ombudsman's Statute, last amended in 2008 (before the Lisbon Treaty came into force) further strengthened the Ombudsman's formal role and effectiveness. Over time, the Ombudsman's mandate has been expanded to cover all EU institutions, bodies, offices and agencies.

B. The EO's Independence

The EO's independence from executive bodies, explicitly safeguarded by the Treaty and the Statute, is designed to ensure impartiality when addressing complaints related to executive maladministration.[30] The EO must fulfil its role effectively, especially in investigating complaints against EU institutions and promoting good administrative practices. In the words of Nikiforos Diamandouros, the second officeholder: 'independence is vital to my credibility as an Ombudsman'.[31]

[30] Hofmann (n 6) 6; Vogiatzis (n 6) 77.
[31] Vogiatzis (n 6) 77.

A pivotal aspect of the EO's independence is its relationship with the European Parliament (EP). Operating as a parliamentary ombudsman, the EP holds exclusive authority over the EO's appointment, reappointment and potential dismissal by the Court of Justice of the European Union (CJEU). Additionally, it establishes rules outlined in the EO's Statute, actively participates in investigations and receives the EO's reports. The Committee on Petitions annually reports on the EO's activities. It ensures that the EO is also subject to a certain amount of oversight.

But it also creates a rather ambivalent relationship. While most ombudsmen in Europe lack the authority to oversee parliament, the European Ombudsman possesses this power.[32] The EP is potentially subject to the investigations of the EO in instances of alleged maladministration, as with any other EU body or agency.[33]

This ambivalence is also visible in the EO's nomination and election procedure. The election of the Ombudsman by the EP, the body that is directly representing EU citizens, is to contribute to the Ombudsman's legitimacy.[34] Yet, the appointment and reappointment processes are tethered to parliamentary terms and political majorities, introducing a risk of politicization.[35] Emily O'Reilly's reappointment in 2019 exemplifies the potential challenges. While her initial election in 2013 and subsequent reappointment in 2014 garnered substantial support, the 2019 process faced complexities. O'Reilly, known for her confrontations over transparency issues, encountered resistance. Competing against four other candidates, O'Reilly navigated a rigorous campaign. A public hearing before the Parliament's petitions committee and multiple voting rounds ensued, culminating in her securing 320 out of 600 votes for a new five-year mandate.

Despite the democratic nature of this process, the inherently political nature of the nomination and election process introduces considerations that could compromise the EO's autonomy. It is illustrative that O'Reilly has become more audacious in her second term, unburdened by concerns about reappointment. The need to navigate politically and find support for the (re)appointment can weaken the officeholder's ability to maintain full independence and impartiality. Similar to courts and auditors, the EO's role as an independent institution may necessitate an approach that puts less weight on the competition of several candidates to safeguard its autonomy and impartiality.

The independence of the EO is not only embedded in its formal structures but is also actively reinforced through how it functions in practice.[36] Tsaridis points out that over time the EO has become a significant player in providing non-judicial protection.[37] Research by Neuhold and Nastase indicates that the EO bolsters its

[32] ibid 79.

[33] To illustrate, after the corruption scandal, dubbed 'Qatargate' led to the arrests of several MEPs in December 2022 on suspicion of taking bribes, the EO called upon the European Parliament president to deliver on transparency reforms.

[34] Vogiatzis (n 6) 74.

[35] Every nomination requires backing from a minimum of 40 MEPs, originating from at least two Member States, and the successful candidate will be determined by the majority of votes cast anonymously.

[36] Vogiatzis (n 6) 80.

[37] Tsadiras (n 19).

autonomy from the European legislature by effectively playing the role of a transparency watchdog.[38] Also, the creation of a separate budget for the Ombudsman in 2000, distinct from the European Parliament's budget, has played a role in detaching the Ombudsman from direct control by Parliament.[39]

C. Investigative and Sanctioning Powers

The Ombudsman's investigative powers include the right to access any documents or information necessary for the investigation, and to interview EU officials and members of staff. According to the Statute of the Ombudsman, officials and other servants of the EU institutions are obliged to provide testimony upon the Ombudsman's request, although they are not required to take an oath as in court proceedings.

However, the institution has limited powers when it comes to imposing sanctions. If the EO identifies deficiencies in the activities of the administration, it lacks the authority to impose sanctions or obligations on individual officials or institutions. Although the decisions and recommendations of the Ombudsman do not carry legally binding force, the EU institutions and bodies have generally demonstrated a strong inclination to comply with the Ombudsman's proposed solutions and recommendations. One of the reasons for this compliance might be found in the exercise of its accountability powers.

D. The European Ombudsman's Open Mandate and Own-Initiative Opportunities

Two formal conditions have created a legal leeway for developing a proactive role for the EO. First, central to the Ombudsman's mission is the concept of 'maladministration', a term with broad implications. This encompasses instances where a lack of accountability or transparency, negligence or compromised integrity in administrative decision-making and the implementation of EU procedures could adversely affect citizens. It extends beyond a mere assessment of the legality of administrative actions. The Treaties, however, intentionally refrain from explicitly defining 'maladministration', affording the EO a significant role in delineating the scope of its mandate. This latitude has empowered the Ombudsman to conduct investigations and propose advancements within the domain of this open concept of maladministration.[40]

Second, the EO's executive oversight responsibility over the EU administration is based on the power, granted in Article 228 (1) TFEU and Article 2 of the EO Statute, to enter into own-initiative investigations. These powers are not only helpful when there's a public interest in clearing up and improving a situation, but also in cases

[38] Neuhold and Nastase (n 22), cf C Neuhold, 'Monitoring the Law and Independent from Politics? The Relationship between the European Ombudsman and the European Parliament' in H Hofmann and J Ziller (eds), *Accountability in the EU: The Role of the European Ombudsman* (Cheltenham, Edgar Elgar, 2017) 53–74.

[39] Vogiatzis (n 6) 81.

[40] Hofmann (n 6) 11–16.

where individuals might find it hard to make a complaint, or based on information from whistle-blowers. These initiatives are a strong tool, especially when lots of complaints point to a bigger problem, or when people might not have the ability or knowledge to complain, like in areas such as immigration and asylum policies. It enables the EO to provide a broader supervisory oversight over the EU administration in general.

In essence, the ongoing evolution of the EO's formal powers reflects a dynamic process within the legal framework, further empowering the institution to effectively ensure accountability within the European Union.

IV. THE EVOLVED ORGANISATIONAL POWERS OF THE EO

An effective ombudsman system extends beyond the mere possession of formal powers to oversee the executive; it crucially hinges on its evolving organisational capacities to implement these powers. It needs to be equipped with the necessary resources to effectively translate its formal powers into tangible actions. This means having budgets, qualitative personnel, and integration into pertinent networks. By adopting a longitudinal lens, we explore how the EO continually evolves, ensuring its organisational power aligns with the challenges of accountable governance. How have the organisational powers of the EO evolved?

A. Personnel, Office Organisation and Mission

The organisation of the EO has evolved since its creation in 1992 to reflect the changing demands of the EU that the Ombudsman deals with. When the EO was first established, it had a small staff of around 10 people. In 2022, the EO had a budget of over 12 million euros and a staff of 73 full-time equivalents (FTE), which is relatively small compared to many national ombudsmen.[41] For instance, the Dutch National Ombudsman had a staff of 186 FTE (about 210 staff employees during the same period and a budget of 23 million euros in 2022). However, the EO's caseload is limited because most complaints are lodged at the national level, as the implementation of EU policies largely falls under the responsibility of member states. Additionally, the EU administration is smaller in size compared to national bureaucracies. Around 60,000 EU civil servants and other staff serve the 450 million Europeans.[42] There are fewer than 33,000 civil servants in the EU Commission.[43] This is a relatively small number – the French Finance Ministry has around 140,000 staff for a population of over 67 million.

The Office has a highly qualified and multilingual staff that can deal directly with complaints about maladministration in most official EU languages and raise

[41] European Ombudsman Annual Report 2022, www.ombudsman.europa.eu/en/publication/en/167855.

[42] https://european-union.europa.eu/institutions-law-budget/institutions-and-bodies/types-institutions-and-bodies_en.

[43] https://commission.europa.eu/about-european-commission/organisational-structure/commission-staff_en#key-figures-on-european-commission-staff.

awareness about the Ombudsman's work throughout the EU. Taking into account its small size, the Office has a balanced geographical distribution in 2022, with 18 EU nationalities represented among staff.

In addition to the growth in numbers, the profile and expertise of the staff have also changed over time. Today, the EO employs staff with diverse nationalities, backgrounds and expertise, including lawyers, public policy experts, communication specialists and administrative staff. As the EO's mandate has expanded to cover a wider range of issues and areas of focus, such as revolving doors and human rights, the institution has also invested in building the necessary expertise and knowledge within its staff to effectively address these issues.

The EO has also embraced digitalisation and modern technologies to improve its efficiency and effectiveness. For example, the EO now uses online platforms and tools to facilitate the submission and handling of complaints, and it has developed a robust digital communication strategy to engage citizens and stakeholders across the EU.

Since 2014, the EO outlined its objectives through a comprehensive strategy document titled 'Towards 2019', enumerating four key priorities for five years. The mission of the EO serves as a pivotal tool for strategic direction and empowerment. Building upon the success and lessons learned, the EO formulated a new strategy in 2020, titled 'Towards 2024', providing a continued roadmap for its mandate. This strategy is meticulously articulated and systematically broken down into strategic objectives. To operationalise this strategic vision, the EO utilises an Annual Management Plan (AMP) along with several key management documents. These documents play a vital role in guiding and managing the office's activities in alignment with the overarching mission statement. Together, the mission, strategy and management documents form a cohesive framework for the EO to effectively navigate its responsibilities and pursue its objectives. It also helps to set an example by embracing open government principles in its operations and building up its institutional identity.

In short, the organisation and the staff working for the EO, and its mission have changed significantly over the past decades, reflecting the evolving role and responsibilities of the institution.

B. Leadership: An Effective and Empathetic Manager of Change

The Office of Ombudsman is a personal one. The success of the EO relies heavily on the quality and individual approaches of the persons appointed to the position and their ability to build relationships. As leaders of the organisation, they set the tone for the work and need to embody the values that underpin their investigations. They are the public face of the work and without the power to make binding recommendations, they must be able to influence EU decision-makers.

Since its establishment in 1992, the EO has had several different leaders who have each brought their approach and priorities to the role (see Table 1). Throughout its 30-year existence, the EU Ombudsman has undergone significant transformations as an institution, with each successive Ombudsman focusing on distinct aspects of maladministration.[44]

[44] Hofmann (n 6) 3–4; Kotanidis (n 22) 4.

Table 1 The different approaches of the EO officeholders

Period	Officeholder	Focus	Results
1995–2003	**Jacob Söderman from Finland**	He promoted transparency and openness in the EU institutions and ensured that citizens had access to information.	He placed particular emphasis on the legal dimensions of complaints, introducing the European Code of Good Administrative Behaviour as a flexible instrument of 'soft law'.
2003–2013	**Nikiforos Diamandouros from Greece**	He expanded the Ombudsman's mandate to cover all EU institutions, bodies, offices and agencies. And he widened the scope of maladministration to include areas beyond mere illegality and transparency concerns.	He prioritised the development of strategic relationships with other EU institutions, such as the European Parliament and the European Commission, to enhance the Ombudsman's impact.
2013–2024	**Emily O'Reilly from Ireland**	She has embraced a more proactive political role, undertaking high-level inquiries of great political sensitivity. These inquiries aim to enhance the visibility and openness of decision-making processes within the EU.	She has continued to strengthen the Ombudsman's role in promoting transparency and accountability in the EU and has emphasised the importance of engaging with citizens and stakeholders. She has also focused on modernising the Ombudsman's procedures and making its work more accessible to the public.

The first EO, Jacob Söderman from Finland, started in 1995. He established the institution and laid the groundwork for its future work. His central contribution was ensuring that the institutions respected their obligations by careful handling of complaints.[45] Nikiforos Diamandouros from Greece succeeded Söderman in 2003. In 2013, Emily O'Reilly became the first woman to hold the position of EO, was re-elected in 2014, and then re-elected for a second full term in 2019. She has adopted a more 'political' approach to her role, believing that the mission of the EO extends far beyond being merely a complaint handling body.[46] She sees the EO as playing a vital role in fostering democracy and driving change by promoting accountability and transparency in European institutions. Her broader understanding of the EO's purpose is advocating for transparency, accountability and good governance within the European Union.

Each of the three European Ombudsmen appointed thus far had considerable prior experience as national ombudsmen in their respective Member States. This pattern underscores the professionalisation of the role. Apart from Söderman, they did not

[45] Hofmann (n 6) 3; Kotanidis (n 22).
[46] Hofmann (n 6) 4.

have a political background and instead pursued careers as academics or journalists before assuming the role of national ombudsmen. Their ability to build relationships is crucial, and as leaders of the organisation, they not only set the tone for the work but must also represent the values underpinning its investigations. It implies that the EO has a history of adhering to ethical standards and good governance practices and that there should be no record of misconduct, corruption or any behaviour contrary to the principles the ombudsman promotes. It also involves not only talking about these principles but personifying them in day-to-day decision-making and communication, sharing relevant information with stakeholders, including employees and being transparent about the institution's activities. The success of the EO office is linked to its effective personal leadership. Despite the potential for a new EO to introduce adjustments in approach, the historical transitions between successive EOs have been remarkably seamless up till now. This cohesion is also attributed to the consistent institutional identity cultivated over its 25-year history.

C. Networking Power

Effective oversight relies increasingly on mutually supportive networks of accountability partners, and the EO has established strong inter-institutional linkages. In addition to the main office in Strasbourg, the EO has had a second office in Brussels since 2017, which enables it to be closer to the EU institutions and to carry out its work more efficiently. Having an office close to the main EU institutions offers strategic advantages for the EO, including improved access, visibility, networking opportunities and a better understanding of the EU's decision-making processes, all of which contribute to the effective functioning and impact of the EO in promoting transparency and accountability within the EU.

The EO plays a clear role in the system of parliamentary fire alarms.[47] The EO as a parliamentary ombudsman has very close relations with the European Parliament, and in particular with the Committee on Petitions presents her inquiries in committee meetings and actively participates in parliamentary hearings and workshops on topics related to EU administration, fundamental rights and access to documents. The EO reports and advises, but when push comes to shove, the EO can only enforce accountability indirectly by referring its findings to the EP. If the institution implicated in a case of maladministration refuses to comply with and rectify the Ombudsman's recommendations, the EO has the option to issue a special report to Parliament. It highlights the issue and could potentially lead to a resolution by Parliament. A balance needs, however, to be struck between developing sustainable dialogue and long-term relations with political stakeholders without being tied to the political ambitions of EU politicians, as this could lead to compromised independence and impartiality of the Ombudsman.

The work of the EO concentrates mainly on the supranational level. Since the implementation of EU law largely falls within the jurisdiction of national authorities,

[47] cf MD McCubbins and T Schwartz, 'Congressional Oversight Overlooked: Police Patrols Versus Fire Alarms' [1984] *American Journal of Political Science* 165–79.

the EO cannot address alleged infringements in such cases. Instead, complaints from EU citizens regarding potential breaches of EU law by national authorities are referred to the respective national ombudsmen. A large number (in 2022 two-thirds) of the complaints received do not fall within the EO's mandate, mostly because they did not concern the work of the EU administration. The first ombudsman recognised the problems of a mandate limited to the EU institutions and created an informal network of around 100 ombuds offices and similar bodies in Europe meant to exchange information on the EU administration, law, and policy, and to share best practices. The EO coordinates this informal European Network of Ombudsmen (ENO). Through parallel investigations, ENO members work together to look into issues that involve the EU administration and national or regional administrations. An example is an inquiry in 2015 into national authorities' compliance with human rights obligations when using EU migration policy funds.[48]

In conclusion, the European Ombudsman's dynamic adaptation of its organisational powers reflects a strategic evolution aimed at enhancing its efficacy and influence within the complex framework of EU accountability.

V. THE EXERCISE OF ACCOUNTABILITY POWER

Much of the accountability power of the EO depends on how it interprets and exercises its mandate, on the initiatives it undertakes and on the effectiveness of carrying out its powers. The exercise of powers by the EO constitutes a dynamic and multifaceted dimension that significantly influences its accountability impact. Beyond the implementation of de jure powers, the EO's ability to interpret and creatively deploy its mandate shapes the extent of its influence. How has the EO's use of its prescribed powers evolved and did it undertake initiatives that transcend the conventional boundaries of its powers?

A. From Reactive to a Proactive Role

The exercise of the EO's accountability powers is marked by a dynamic interplay of both reactive and proactive roles. To start with its reactive function, the EO diligently examines complaints brought forth by citizens, residents, companies or associations, aiming for consensual resolutions. There are more than 2,000 complaints each year but over two-thirds do not fall within her mandate, mostly because they do not concern the work of the EU administration. The number of inquiries opened has shown relative stability within the EO's mandate, fluctuating between approximately 200 and 500 over the past 25 years. Notably, in 2018, the EO saw heightened activity with 490 inquiries, surpassing previous years and even exceeding the peak observed in 2012 (see Figure 1). Subsequently, the post-coronavirus years witnessed a decline in this elevated volume.

[48] CASE SI/1/2015/MHZ.

An inquiry can lead to a finding of maladministration. The Ombudsman has no binding powers to compel compliance with its rulings; that is, it has no formal instruments to enforce a change in the behaviour of an EU institution or body that has committed misconduct, nor does it have sanctions, it can only make a recommendation.[49]

Figure 1 Number of inquiries opened by the EO 1996–2022

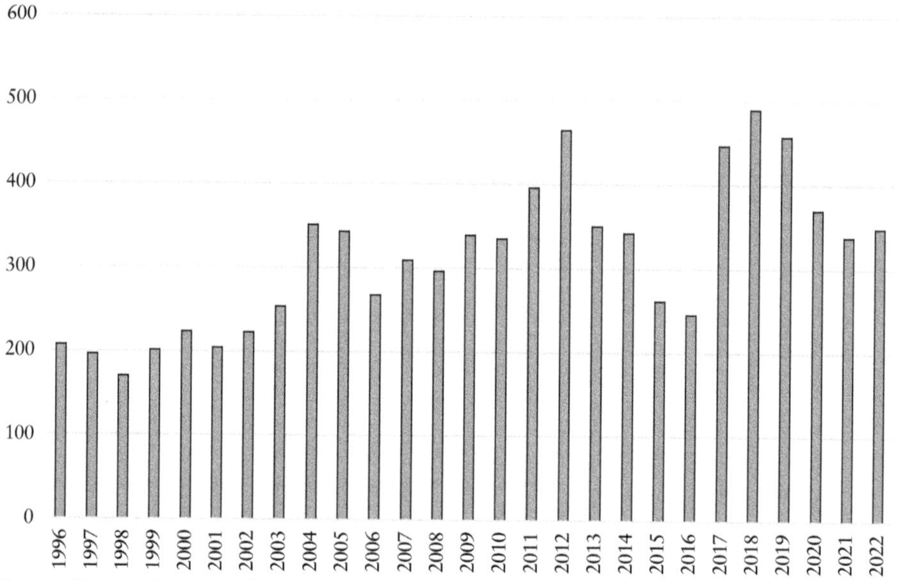

Source: The annual reports of the EO from 1996–2022.

Yet, EU institutions are bound to respond to these recommendations within a stipulated three-month timeframe. In cases where recommendations are not embraced, the EO issues a formal 'finding of maladministration'. Importantly, even in scenarios where explicit maladministration is not pinpointed, the EO remains empowered to provide suggestions for system improvement.[50]

At the same time, the EO assumes a proactive stance by initiating broader strategic inquiries and initiatives. This proactive role allows the Ombudsman to launch investigations at its discretion, responding to suspicions of maladministration stemming from complaints or other sources. The focus spans specific areas of concern, and through these initiatives, the EO identifies opportunities for EU institutions to enhance their accountability and transparency. Figure 2 shows a rise in the frequency of own-initiative inquiries since 2010, aimed at addressing systemic irregularities in the EU administration and increasing the institution's impact and visibility. This signifies a notable shift from previous years when the tool was employed more cautiously, as evident in earlier instances of own-initiative inquiries.

[49] P Zawadzki, 'Origin of the European Ombudsman' (2020) 19(1) *Miscellanea Historico-Iuridica* 443–59.
[50] Hofmann (n 6) 17.

Figure 2 Number of own initiative inquiries by the EO 1996–2022

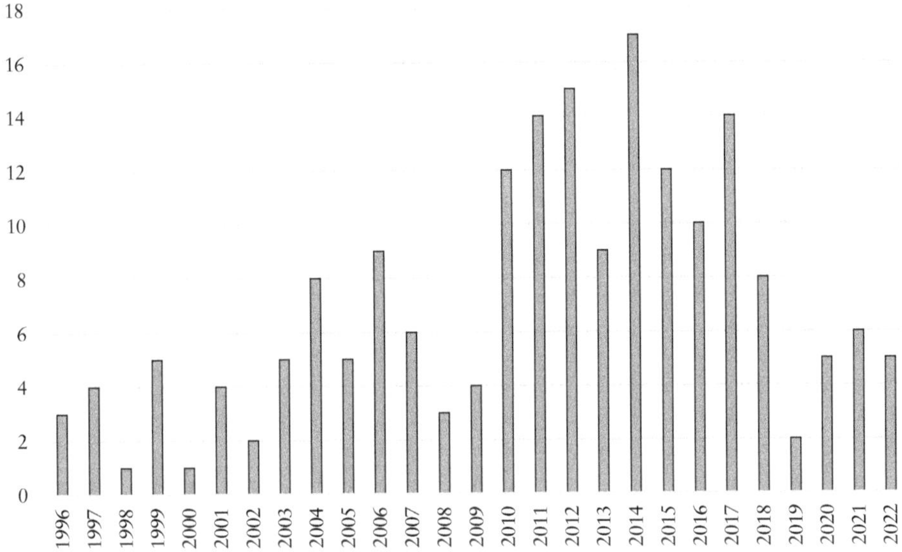

Source: The annual reports of the EO from 1996–2022.

The trend of the increased number of own-initiative inquiries started under the second EO and continued under the third ombudsman O'Reilly. In certain cases, the EO opts to launch an own-initiative inquiry after receiving numerous admissible complaints regarding the same issue, indicating a potential systemic problem.[51] Additionally, the EO may start own-initiative inquiries without a complaint when it becomes aware of potential maladministration through internal research, monitoring, or follow-up to previous inquiries.[52]

Starting from 2019, there has been a decline in the number of strategic inquiries conducted by the EO. Interpreting the numbers in Figure 2 should be approached with caution, as no data indicates the 'origin' of these inquiries. Also, during this period, the EO started to employ the lighter version called the strategic initiative. This involves addressing potential systemic issues within the EU's administration without necessarily initiating a full inquiry. Strategic initiatives are mostly letters sent to the EU administration, setting out observations, or gathering information on administrative practices.[53]

The expansion of the EO's own-initiative inquiries has witnessed a notable transformation in its thematic scope. Initially centred around traditional administrative matters like staff regulations and access to documents, these inquiries have evolved to embrace a broader array of contemporary topics. This shift is marked by the EO's proactive engagement with issues concerning fundamental rights, ethical

[51] An example is EPSO OII, OI/1/2023/VS.

[52] An ambitious example of such an inquiry was examining how the Commission and the ECB manage 'revolving doors' moves of its staff.

[53] This practice of strategic initiatives is included in the new Implementing Provisions (Article 8(2)).

considerations, transparency in negotiation processes and addressing challenges linked to the 'revolving doors' phenomenon. This transformation signifies a departure from conventional administrative concerns towards a more comprehensive and strategic approach to the evolved dynamics of EU governance.

B. Effectiveness and Impact

Effecting change within the EU administration requires identifying but also actively addressing shortcomings to promote good administration. The EO has demonstrated considerable effectiveness, as evidenced by acceptance rates detailed in its annual reports. Acceptance rates reflect the Ombudsman's success in eliciting positive responses from administrative bodies to proposals (solutions, recommendations and suggestions). In 2021, the EU institutions demonstrated satisfactory cooperation with the Ombudsman in 79 per cent of cases, positively responding to 26 out of 33 proposals aimed at rectifying or improving administrative practices.[54]

However, gauging the impact of the Ombudsman's work requires a nuanced perspective. While the acceptance rate provides a snapshot of institutional responses at a specific point in time, the transformative influence of the Ombudsman often unfolds gradually as EU institutions adapt to evolving norms of good administration. The annual report of 2022 highlights instances of positive change resulting from Ombudsman inquiries, including enhanced accountability in decision-making, increased transparency and ethics in lobbying, improved access to documents, greater legislative transparency and strengthened protection of fundamental rights.

The EO has successfully influenced the behaviour of EU institutions, motivating them to adopt more accountable practices. Three developments have facilitated this trend toward transparency advocacy: the EO positioning itself as a standard setter, employing soft power strategies and actively seeking the spotlight.

i. Standard-Setting: From Firefighting to Fire Prevention

Through its reports and systemic investigations, the EO identifies systemic issues and root causes of maladministration. A key aspect of this evolution is the EO's role in addressing these issues by articulating and promoting norms of good administration, aiming to prevent the recurrence of such problems. By actively offering guidance and advice, by promoting ethical standards, and good governance principles, the EO seeks to forestall issues before they emerge.

Examples of this are the development of the 'European Code of Good Administrative Behaviour', the creation of a set of guidelines that help the EU institutions to provide a more effective complaints-handling process, and a list of 'Dos and Don'ts' for EU officials interacting with lobbyists.[55]

[54] Annual Report European Ombudsman 2022 (n 41).

[55] CASE SI/7/2016/KR – www.ombudsman.europa.eu/en/publication/en/79435.

ii. The Politics of Soft Power

The EO has gained power through exercising soft power, which involves influencing others through persuasion and advocacy rather than coercion or force. In the absence of sanctioning powers, the EO relies on softer strategies, such as public exposure, moral suasion and recommendations, to exert influence and seek redress for maladministration. Soft power covers shaping preferences and behaviour by building positive relationships, promoting shared values and leveraging credibility.

The EO strategically uses soft power strategies, such as meetings, conferences and seminars, to share best practices, to promote transparency and accountability in the EU institutions and bodies and to facilitate dialogue and cooperation between stakeholders. For example, the EO uses special ceremonies, such as those announcing the recipient of the EO Award for Good Administration, not only to recognise and celebrate instances of exemplary administration.[56] It also serves as an occasion to build a narrative that underlines its commitment to values as transparency, public access to documents and upholding ethics standards.

iii. Seeking the Spotlight

An alternative way in which the EO gains impact is through the organisation of public communication. To engage a broader audience, the EO employed various communication channels such as extensive use of social media platforms, press releases and news articles, and introduced a periodic newsletter called the EO Express, delivering updates on important inquiries, activities, events and speeches. The number of social media followers on Instagram, LinkedIn and Twitter increased. Backed by a Communication Unit of almost 10 communication officers, the EO actively enhances its visibility among institutional stakeholders and the general public by ensuring the accessibility and reader-friendliness of its publications. Annual press conferences conducted by the Ombudsman highlight the Office's notable investigations and findings, contributing to a strategic approach aimed at capturing media attention, as illustrated in Figure 3. While the EO has seen an increase in attention from EU-focused media over the past decade, it remains an ongoing effort to extend this visibility to a broader audience through national media platforms.

The inquiries conducted by the EO are increasingly high-profile cases that attract public attention. Examples include the investigations into Barrosogate, about former Commission president Barroso's appointment to Goldman Sachs in 2018,[57] and the personnel policy of the European Central Bank in 2022.[58] Both are part of a broader monitoring effort by the Ombudsman to assess how the EU administration deals with issues related to 'revolving doors' – the movement of individuals between public and private sector roles. The EO leveraged these cases to sustain ongoing

[56] www.ombudsman.europa.eu/en/publication/en/172204.
[57] Case SI/9/2016/PD.
[58] Case OI/1/2022/KR.

Figure 3 Media attention to the EO 2000–2022 (Number of articles per year about the EO on EURACTIV)

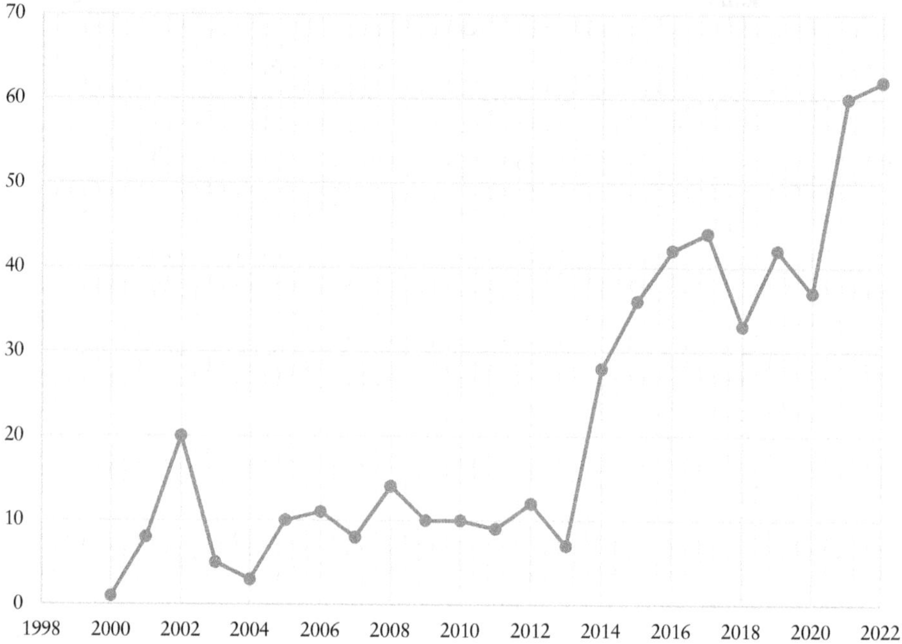

media attention, with headlines such as 'Brussels "becoming like Washington" for revolving doors'[59] and 'Watchdog calls for tougher curbs on "problematic" revolving doors'.[60] In another instance, the EO issued recommendations regarding the preservation of text messages after a controversy known as 'Delete-gate'. As part of a strategic initiative, in parallel to the complaint-based inquiry, the EO investigated how EU institutions and bodies record text and instant messages.[61] With this distinctive niche role, the EO not only tries to maintain and cultivate audience support and raise awareness about the importance of good governance within the EU. But with this, it also carves out a specialised and unique position for itself within the broader landscape of accountability institutions in which the EO focuses on specific and targeted areas of operation, addressing maladministration and promoting good governance.

In summary, using soft power strategies, engaging in transparency advocacy and seeking the spotlight, have enabled the EO to shape the policy agenda, influence decision-making processes and mobilise public opinion. By extending its influence and impact, the EO has played a significant role in shaping the EU accountability landscape.

[59] *EUOBSERVER*, 13 September 2022.
[60] *EUOBSERVER*, 18 May 2022.
[61] Case SI/4/2021/MIG.

VI. SHAPING ACCOUNTABILITY: THE EVOLVED POWERS OF THE EO

In its first annual report in 1995, the EO writes: 'The Ombudsman's primary duty … is to deal with the complaints that are addressed to him'.[62] In nearly 30 years of institutional development, the EO has transitioned from predominantly addressing individual complaints to actively contributing to the improvement of governance quality. This transformation of the EO is part of the broader ombudsmanisation of the EU, and is particularly evident in the growing influence and empowerment of the EO, manifesting across three crucial dimensions of power: formal, organisational and the exercise of powers.

In terms of its formal powers, the open definition of maladministration in the Treaties, in combination with the powers granted in Article 228 of TFEU and the EO Statute to enter into own-initiative investigations has provided flexibility for EO officeholders to shape accountability in innovative ways. The adoption of the Statute by the EP in 2021 has formalised certain existing practices. The ongoing evolution of the EO's formal and informal powers reflects a dynamic process within the legal framework, further empowering the institution to ensure accountability within the European Union effectively.

In terms of its organisation, the EO has effectively leveraged limited resources through a strategic approach that emphasises organisational and network development. Despite that its mandate is limited to EU institutions, the first EO office-holder took the initiative to establish a network of ombudsmen, including national ombudsmen and similar bodies in Member States, to address complaints related to the implementation of EU law. This collaboration with national ombudsmen facilitates the resolution of cross-border issues and promotes cooperation between EU institutions and national authorities. This sensible approach has allowed the EO to optimise its impact and enhance its effectiveness despite resource constraints.

In terms of the exercise of its powers, by using effective tools such as conducting investigations and employing soft power strategies, the EO has been able to take a proactive role. The identification and investigation of systemic issues in EU governance culminate in comprehensive findings outlining deficiencies in administration. These systemic investigations and recommendations present opportunities for making a greater impact than managing individual cases alone. By going beyond its traditional formal mediation role and actively engaging with the EU administration as a quasi-standard setter, the EO can enhance its influence on the EU accountability agenda and make a meaningful difference by formulating recommendations for systemic change. The office actively promotes best practices, facilitates institutional learning and disseminates professional standards, administrative norms and codes of conduct, which has further elevated the relevance of the EO.

The EO, in contrast to the European Court of Justice, lacks binding authority. The EO relies on persuasive measures, including publicised investigations and critical recommendations aimed at EU institutions, to hold them accountable. These actions are intended to expose and pressure non-compliant institutions publicly. Additionally,

[62] European Ombudsman Annual Report 1995, www.ombudsman.europa.eu/en/publication/en/3468, 11.

the EO's investigatory functions often depend on the cooperation of the institutions being investigated. If an institution fails to address identified maladministration, the EO relies on the Parliament to consider and act upon the reports. In Hofmann's words: 'The EO's contribution to maintaining the "integrity" of decision-making through their persuasive powers and their ability to raise public exposure and awareness through their reports and decisions'.[63]

The main drawback of the complaint-based system for initiating ombuds-review is its reliance on widespread awareness among European citizens. Only when citizens, who may be impacted by maladministration, are aware of the existence, accessibility and potential influence of the EO as an institution, will they submit complaints. The EO's own-initiative investigations serve therefore as a valuable tool for raising awareness of the EO.[64]

Gradually, the EO has become an integral component of the evolving landscape of accountability institutions, positioning itself as an advocate for good governance and transparency. Ombudsman institutions have become part of the democratic frameworks of most countries in the EU.[65] The opportunity for 'holding executive power to account' has shown the development of different accountability institutions in the EU – court, parliament, auditor and ombudsman. In this context, the EO has contributed to the 'ombudsmanisation' of the EU accountability framework. This trend, alongside parliamentarisation and judicialisation, has played a pivotal role in shaping the accountability structures within the European Union.

[63] Hofmann (n 6) 26.
[64] ibid.
[65] Zuegel et al (n 16).

2

The Evolving Proactive Role of the European Ombudsman

NIKOS VOGIATZIS*

I. INTRODUCTION

When Emily O'Reilly was elected European Ombudsman (EO) by the European Parliament in 2013, one of the issues she wished to emphasise upon assuming office was the proactive dimension of the office and the need to enhance impact and visibility. Thus, she stated that '[o]ne of [her] proactive roles as Ombudsman [was] to highlight citizens' concerns and help bridge the wide gap between them and the EU institutions', and also that 20 years after the establishment of the office (at the time) it was 'time to re-think its focus, with an eye to enhancing its impact and visibility'.[1] As one of the key aims of this volume is to provide an assessment of the evolution of the office, taking into account in particular the development of the mandate under the current office holder, there is no doubt that the visibility of the office has been enhanced, and that this has been achieved especially through wider use of the EO's proactive powers.

Although providing an exhaustive definition of proactive work would be a challenge when referring to ombuds offices, not least because mandates and practice differ considerably across institutions,[2] one can perhaps provide certain examples of such work at the outset to clarify the focus of this chapter. One prominent example would be the use of own-initiative inquiries; that is, inquiries that do not commence as a response to a specific complaint that the office has received. Another would be awareness-raising, including through the use of communication activities or via publication of standards of good administration. Contrasting *proactive* to *reactive* work can also help understand further the former: as noted above, in the reactive aspect of their work the ombuds office would respond to a specific complaint.

* The author would like to thank two anonymous reviewers for comments on an earlier version. The usual disclaimer applies.

[1] European Ombudsman (EO) Press release No 14/2013, 'Emily O'Reilly begins work as European Ombudsman' (2013).

[2] On this point see, for example, OECD Working Paper on Public Governance No 29, 'The Role of Ombudsman Institutions in Open Government' (2018) 4–8.

Reactive work is often associated with the role of courts – as they have to decide the case that is being put before them.

In exploring the evolving proactive role of the EO, the next section will focus on some broader considerations underpinning the proactive work of ombuds offices, drawing in particular on principles developed at international and European levels and relevant literature. The following section will briefly address the legal framework surrounding the Ombudsman's proactive work, while also providing some remarks on its historical development. Then, the next and main part of the chapter will explain how the proactive work of the office has evolved, in line with the broader title (and theme) of this edited volume. The penultimate section will address what can perhaps be termed as 'the other side of the coin', namely whether there might be limits or challenges in attributing that much focus on proactive work. The last section will offer some concluding remarks.

II. THE PROACTIVE ROLE OF OMBUDS OFFICES: BROADER CONSIDERATIONS

The possibility of an ombuds office to act proactively (as opposed to reactively) is considered one of the advantages of this accountability mechanism, especially when compared to courts. Thus, the International Ombudsman Institute (IOI)[3] in its guidance concerning the establishment, development or reform of ombuds offices has pointed out inter alia that their powers should include 'undertak[ing] investigations on his or her own initiative' as '[o]n occasions, the Ombudsman will be made or become aware of possible maladministration where no complaint has been made'.[4] Reasons for the use of proactive powers 'can include a reluctance on the part of complainants to come forward for fear of negative consequences or because the people concerned do not have ready access to the Ombudsman'; while benefits that '[s]uch investigations often consider systemic issues and ensure that the Ombudsman can be effective in tackling poor administration and improving public services'.[5] Nevertheless, there are still ombuds offices that do not benefit from the power to undertake own-initiative inquiries.[6]

The subsequent paragraphs will address some of the principles developed at the international and European levels, as well as in specialised institutes focused on the work of ombuds offices. These principles serve various purposes, including the following: they may codify or clarify existing practices as they have emerged in a number

[3] As is noted on its website (see www.theioi.org/the-i-o-i), the IOI 'is the only global organisation for the cooperation of more than 200 independent Ombudsman institutions from more than 100 countries worldwide. [It] is organised in six regional chapters (Africa, Asia, Australasia & Pacific, Europe, the Caribbean & Latin America and North America). In its effort to focus on good governance and capacity building, the IOI supports its members in a threefold way: training, research and regional subsidies for projects.'

[4] International Ombudsman Institute, 'Developing and Reforming Ombudsman Institutions: An IOI Guide for Those Undertaking these Tasks' (2017) 6.

[5] ibid.

[6] One example is the Parliamentary and Health Service Ombudsman in the UK, even though the office has supported a reform towards obtaining own-initiative powers. See, for example, Peter Tyndall, Caroline Mitchell and Chris Gill, 'Report of the Independent Peer Review of the Parliamentary and Health Service Ombudsman' (2018) in particular p. 32.

of jurisdictions; while also encouraging certain jurisdictions to adjust their standards accordingly (for example, when a reform of an ombuds office is being considered and then implemented). One may start with the (generally positively assessed) Venice Principles on the Protection and Promotion of the Ombudsman Institution,[7] developed under the aegis of the Council of Europe. It should be noted that the Council of Europe has contributed to the 'strengthening' of ombuds institutions since the 1970s,[8] starting with the development of principles of good administration via recommendations of the Committee of Ministers.[9] The Venice Principles were produced in 2019 by the Venice Commission, which – as is known – is the organization's advisory body on constitutional matters that fall within the remit of the organisation (in particular, rule of law, democracy and human rights).[10] A key word here is 'promotion': Principle 12, for example, states that the 'mandate of the Ombudsman shall cover prevention and correction of maladministration, and the protection and promotion of human rights and fundamental freedoms'.[11] This shows that 'promotion' is crucial to a proactive approach as it signifies work that – again – does not necessarily depend on reacting to a specific complaint. Crucially, Principle 16 states that the 'Ombudsman shall have discretionary power, on his or her own initiative or as a result of a complaint, to investigate cases with due regard to available administrative remedies'. As is shown below, the EO has made significant use of the own-initiative inquiry, which is generally considered a fundamental feature of the proactive role of ombuds offices. It may also be noted that the Venice Principles are more extensive in terms of scope than UN General Assembly Resolution 72/186[12] (which also encompasses national human rights institutions and mediators). That Resolution underlines the role of ombuds offices in the protection and promotion of human rights, in particular, but also in 'promoting good governance in public administrations, as well as improving their relations with citizens, and in strengthening the delivery of public services'.[13]

In addition, as one would expect, the aforementioned International Ombudsman Institute has developed several best practice papers that touch, directly or indirectly, upon the ombuds' proactive work. A broader paper on improving effectiveness of ombuds offices and the quality of public administration more generally explains, for example, that systemic recommendations may be made only where systemic problems

[7] Venice Commission, 'Principles on the Protection and Promotion of the Ombudsman Institution' (2019) CDL-AD(2019)005. For a general discussion and comparison with the Paris Principles on National Human Rights Institutions see Luka Glušac, 'A Critical Appraisal of the Venice Principles on the Protection and Promotion of the Ombudsman: An Equivalent to the Paris Principles?' (2021) 21 *Human Rights Law Review* 22; Dawid Sześciło and Stanisław Zakroczymski, 'From Paris to Venice: The International Standard of the Ombudsman's Independence Revisited' (2021) 25 *International Journal of Human Rights* 1819.

[8] Glušac (n 7) 24.

[9] See further Ulrich Stelkens and Agnė Andrijauskaitė (eds), *Good Administration and the Council of Europe: Law, Principles, and Effectiveness* (Oxford, Oxford University Press, 2020).

[10] See, among others, Angelika Nußberger and Júlia Miklasová, 'Council of Europe as the Guardian of Democracy: The Venice Commission' in Daniel-Erasmus Khan et al (eds), *Democracy and Sovereignty: Rethinking the Legitimacy of Public International Law* (Leiden, Brill, 2023) 269.

[11] On the role of ombuds and human rights more generally see Linda Reif, *Ombuds Institutions, Good Governance and the International Human Rights System* (Leiden, Brill/Nijhoff, 2021).

[12] UN Resolution 72/186, 'The role of the Ombudsman, mediator and other national human rights institutions in the promotion and protection of human rights', 19 December 2017.

[13] ibid, 2.

have been identified in the investigation and that a good working relationship with the administration, as well as follow-up monitoring, may be practice that improves effectiveness.[14] This is linked to proactive work as (and this also applies to the EO) systemic recommendations usually arise from own-initiative or strategic inquiries (the terminology that the EO uses is a matter that is returned to below). Another paper that is more closely associated with the scope of this chapter concerns own-initiative investigations: this paper discusses, among others, the added value but also the challenges of these investigations.[15] For example, it is noted that such an investigation may provide an 'early response to issues of concern'; 'bring attention to significant matters of public interest'; and be a 'useful tool to generate discussion on policy and legislative issues'.[16] The key challenge has rightly been identified in that paper: it pertains to resources and the need to balance systemic work with dealing with individual complaints: as underlined therein, 'an "own initiative" investigation should never serve to detract from the Ombudsman's role in remedying individual complaints'.[17] This matter is returned to in subsequent sections of the chapter.

If we now turn to the literature on ombuds' proactive work, it may generally be observed that the significance of such work is increasingly being recognised. Thus, proactive 'techniques' may be especially important in instances where individual complainants are 'unwilling or unable to complain'.[18] Moreover, it is a function associated with the 'learning perspective' of accountability.[19] An interesting study has found that, generally, the offices under examination implemented in their practice the theoretical advantages of own-initiative inquiries.[20] Other studies point to the need for independence (which should underpin every aspect of the work of ombuds offices) and point inter alia to criteria that have been established in order to decide which issues merit an own initiative investigation.[21] Proactive work is not solely confined to the launch of own initiative inquiries. In some cases this may take the form of producing codes of good practice and other standards or principles of good

[14] International Ombudsman Institute, 'Securing effective change: How to make recommendations that bring about sustainable improvement to public administration' (2017) available at: www.theioi.org/publications/ioi-best-practice-papers.

[15] International Ombudsman Institute, 'Own initiative investigations' (2018) available at: www.theioi.org/publications/ioi-best-practice-papers.

[16] ibid, 3.

[17] ibid.

[18] Trevor Buck et al, *The Ombudsman Enterprise and Administrative Justice* (Farnham, Ashgate, 2010) 148. Groups that may be included here are 'generally vulnerable groups such as minors, undocumented immigrants and those from the most economically disadvantaged sectors'; see Laura Díez, 'The Use of Own-Initiative Powers by the Ombudsman' in Marc Hertogh and Richard Kirkham (eds), *Research Handbook on the Ombudsman* (Cheltenham, Edward Elgar, 2018) 354, at 370.

[19] Buck et al (n 18) 48. The authors draw here on Mark Bovens et al, 'Does Accountability Work? An Assessment Tool' (2008) 86 *Public Administration* 225.

[20] Díez (n 18). As the author explains (at 370) these advantages pertain to: dealing 'in a much broader and more complete manner with a whole series of problems that might arise'; focusing on issues that may not necessarily be brought to their attention; addressing the needs of vulnerable groups; correcting maladministration 'resulting from situations of great social repercussion that occur unexpectedly'.

[21] Maaike de Langen et al, 'Effectiveness and Independence of the Ombudsman's Own-Motion Investigations: A Practitioner's Perspective from the Netherlands' in Hertogh and Kirkham (n 18) 373. The authors (at 379) refer to some of the criteria underpinning this choice, including the size of the problem, who is affected, the added value of the ombuds office – among others. Similar criteria have also been developed by the International Ombudsman Institute and other scholarly and practitioner accounts.

administration.[22] In the EU case, for example, the EO has produced the European Code of Good Administrative Behaviour.[23] Another example that can be mentioned, in this respect, is the 'Principles of Good Administration' by the UK Parliamentary and Health Service Ombudsman, which (like the EU case) can also serve as an indication of expectations from the respective administration(s) under scrutiny.[24]

In terms of models or typologies that have been devised to explore or assess the different functions of ombuds offices, one would need to refer to the well-known distinction by Harlow and Rawlings on 'fire-fighting' and 'fire-watching',[25] with some commentators adding 'fire-prevention' to underline proactive work that may not necessarily stem from information gathered from previous complaints.[26] In the first comprehensive study on the EO, Heede explored different models of ombuds offices, before elaborating on the (now well-known) distinction between 'redress' and 'control' models (with the latter more closely associated with 'fire-watching').[27] The power to conduct own-initiative inquiries was deemed to fall under control models, as in this case ombuds offices 'perform the control function, regulating the way the state authorities apply standards'.[28] Although Heede and other commentators acknowledge variations between the models (and, in reality, ombuds schemes may combine 'control' and 'redress' features) one can deduce that proactive work (which includes, but is not confined to, own-initiative inquiries) is more closely associated with the 'control' function of an ombuds office in improving standards within the administration, identifying systemic issues and acting on behalf of the public interest.

The struggle to classify ombuds offices and other (eg, data protection or audit) offices in the traditional separation of powers (which has tended to distinguish between the legislative, executive and judicial branches) has led commentators to propose a fourth branch, often called the 'integrity branch'.[29] Acting proactively to improve administrative standards as an accountability mechanism is a function that cannot be dissociated from this 'fourth branch' doctrine, which may now be regarded as widely accepted. Of course, one might object that the EU (and, indeed, many or

[22] Nikos Vogiatzis, *The European Ombudsman and Good Administration in the European Union* (Basingstoke, Palgrave Macmillan, 2018) 33.

[23] The Code can be accessed at: www.ombudsman.europa.eu/en/publication/en/3510.

[24] Parliamentary and Health Service Ombudsman, 'Principles of Good Administration' (2009) available at: www.ombudsman.org.uk/about-us/our-principles/principles-good-administration.

[25] Discussion of these notions can be found in the latest edition of Carol Harlow and Richard Rawlings, *Law and Administration* (Cambridge, Cambridge University Press, 2021) 561. Harlow had already underlined the potential of ombuds offices in improving administrative practice in Carol Harlow, 'Ombudsmen in Search of a Role' (1978) 41 *Modern Law Review* 446.

[26] Rick Snell, 'Australian Ombudsman: A Continual Work in Progress' in Matthew Groves and HP Lee (eds), *Australian Administrative Law: Fundamentals, Principles and Doctrines* (Cambridge, Cambridge University Press, 2012) 100, at 106.

[27] Katja Heede, *European Ombudsman: Redress and Control at Union Level* (Alphen aan den Rijn, Kluwer, 2000).

[28] ibid, 96. She interestingly observed (at 112) that there was no general discussion about the type of ombuds the EU office would be, which resulted in an antithesis between the aims of establishment (improving democracy and bringing citizens closer to the EU, ie control function) with the Treaty text (a primarily redress-focused ombuds modelled in accordance with the Danish plan).

[29] James Spigelman, 'The Integrity Branch of Government' (2004) 78 *Australian Law Journal* 724; Mark Tushnet, *The New Fourth Branch: Institutions for Protecting Constitutional Democracy* (Cambridge, Cambridge University Press, 2021).

most other jurisdictions) do not follow the traditional separation of powers model – but where the EO features or should feature in discussions around the EU principle of 'institutional balance'[30] is a matter that cannot be pursued further here.

Having outlined the proactive work of ombuds offices in broader terms, the next section will focus on the EU office and briefly address the legal framework surrounding its proactive work. It will also provide a brief overview of its historical development.

III. THE LEGAL FRAMEWORK SURROUNDING THE EUROPEAN OMBUDSMAN'S PROACTIVE WORK

That the EO's work is not confined to examination of individual complaints is, first and foremost, stipulated by the EU treaties (and has been so since the establishment of the office by the Maastricht Treaty as will be shown below – although a fuller exposition of the mandate and its development cannot be undertaken here[31]). Thus, Article 228(1) TFEU confirms that the EO can conduct also own-initiative (or strategic, as referred to more recently) inquiries. Crucially, the new Statute of the EO (Article 3(3)) underlines the Ombudsman's competence to act on behalf of public interest with a view to addressing systemic problems.[32] As noted elsewhere, although this competence is not new, the fact that it is explicitly provided for and elaborated upon in the newer version of the Statute may well be viewed as recognition of the significant work that has been undertaken, in this respect.[33] Proactive work is mentioned as well in the other key reference text for the EO, the Implementing Provisions – this matter will be returned to in the next section of the chapter.

The EU courts have also underlined the significance of the EO's power to conduct own-initiative inquiries. A full survey of the jurisprudence of the Union courts regarding the EO cannot be undertaken here (even if the number of relevant cases is not high). However, two interesting paragraphs from Advocate General Geelhoed's Opinion in

[30] See Art 13 TEU, and also, among others, Paul Craig, 'Institutions, Power and Institutional Balance' in Paul Craig and Grainne de Burca (eds), *The Evolution of EU Law* (Oxford, Oxford University Press, 2021) 46; Merijn Chamon, 'The Institutional Balance, an Ill-Fated Principle of EU Law?' (2015) 21 *European Public Law* 371. On the EO and institutional balance some brief remarks are also provided in Nikos Vogiatzis, 'The European Ombudsman in the EU's Administrative and Institutional Framework' in Gijs Jan Brandsma (ed), *Handbook on European Union Public Administration* (Cheltenham, Edward Elgar, 2024) 203, at 206.

[31] On which see, among others, Vogiatzis (n 22); Herwig CH Hofmann and Jacques Ziller (eds), *Accountability in the EU: The Role of the European Ombudsman* (Cheltenham, Edward Elgar, 2017); Ian Harden, 'Article 43' in Steve Peers et al (eds) *The EU Charter of Fundamental Rights: A Commentary* (Oxford, Hart Publishing, 2021) 1173; The European Ombudsman: *Origins, Establishment, Evolution: Commemorative Volume Published on the Occasion of the 10th Anniversary of the Institution* (Office for Official Publications of the EU, 2005).

[32] This provision is worded as follows: 'The Ombudsman may conduct own-initiative inquiries whenever he or she finds grounds, and in particular in repeated, systemic or particularly serious instances of maladministration, in order to address those instances as an issue of public interest. In the context of such inquiries, he or she may also make proposals and initiatives to promote administrative best practices within Union institutions, bodies, offices and agencies'.

[33] Nikos Vogiatzis, 'The New Statute of the European Ombudsman and Transparency' Open Government in the EU blog (2021) available at: www.eu-opengovernment.eu/?p=2787.

Lamberts[34] may be added here – not least because this was the case in which the EU judiciary provided the first comprehensive overview of the EO's mandate, in the context of its examination of the Ombudsman's non-contractual liability.

> The fact that [the EO] has the power to [carry out own-initiative inquiries] indicates that the Ombudsman is to be regarded as an administrative body, rather than as comparable to a court or tribunal. I would observe, however, that that power is in addition to the power to act upon complaints, rather than a second primary duty, as is clear from the background to the body of Ombudsman, the Ombudsman's own view that his primary duty is to deal with complaints, and the operation of the Ombudsman in practice. … In short, the Ombudsman does not offer any legal protection in the proper sense. The Ombudsman is to be regarded as an administrative body whose task – primarily via complaints – is to identify in the public interest instances of maladministration by the Community institutions and to help to put an end to that maladministration. It is also appropriate for that task that the Ombudsman is appointed by the European Parliament and that he is required to submit to Parliament an annual report on his inquiries.[35]

One can certainly raise objections with regard to some of the points of the preceding paragraphs or at least the way they were formulated (it is, for example, very disputable that the Ombudsman 'does not offer any legal protection in the proper sense'). In any case, much has changed since the time of that Opinion (2003), not only in terms of the Ombudsman's priorities (after all, the Opinion refers to the first Annual Report of 1995) but also in terms of the case law of the Union courts on the EO's liability.[36] What is certainly not outdated is the observation that the EO is not a court but performs a different, yet complementary – in the opinion of this and other authors[37] – function within the EU legal order.

As noted above, while the new Statute introduced a specific provision on own-initiative inquiries, this competence is not new: it was explicitly provided for in the Maastricht Treaty as well as the first Statute of the EO.[38] Examples of important own-initiative inquiries undertaken by Söderman can be found in his reflective account of the early years of the office.[39] Interestingly, the otherwise antagonistic Committee on Petitions of the European Parliament (PETI), especially in the years prior to the establishment of the EO,[40] was supportive of the EO's own-initiative work from the start.[41] Accordingly, in 1998, in its report on the EO's Annual Report, PETI noted

[34] Case C-234/02 P, *European Ombudsman v Frank Lamberts*, EU:C:2004:174.

[35] Opinion of AG Geelhoed in Case C-234/02 P, *European Ombudsman v Frank Lamberts*, EU:C:2003:394, paras 62–63.

[36] Most notably, Case C-337/15 P, *European Ombudsman v Staelen*, EU:C:2017:256.

[37] See also Milan Remac, *Coordinating Ombudsmen and the Judiciary: A Comparative View on the Relations between Ombudsmen and the Judiciary in the Netherlands, England and the European Union* (Antwerp, Intersentia, 2014); Michal Krajewski, *Relative Authority of Judicial and Extra-judicial Review: EU Courts, Boards of Appeal, Ombudsman* (Oxford, Hart Publishing, 2021).

[38] Art 3(1) of Decision of the European Parliament of 9 March 1994 on the regulations and general conditions governing the performance of the Ombudsman's duties, 94/262/ECSC, EC, Euratom.

[39] Jacob Söderman, 'The Early Years of the European Ombudsman', in *Commemorative Volume* (n 31) 83.

[40] Jean-Pierre Jarry, 'The European Parliament and the Establishment of a European Ombudsman: Twenty Years of Debate, 1974–1995' (2015) *European Parliament History Studies* PE 538.885.

[41] Eddy Newman, 'The Policy-Relationship between the European Ombudsman and the European Parliament's Committee on Petitions' in *Commemorative Volume* (n 31) 143, at 153–55.

that 'own-initiative inquiries can pinpoint administrative irregularities with political implications'.[42]

More generally, the practice of the two previous office holders (especially Nikiforos Diamandouros) certainly encompassed work that was not confined to own-initiative enquiries but had a proactive dimension to it. To mention just a few examples, Diamandouros started the expansion of the EO's communication team, engaged more widely with external stakeholders (including ombuds offices beyond the EU), while rewarding compliant EU institutions and bodies with a 'star case exemplifying best practice' in the Annual Reports.[43]

The above remarks are significant because they can put in context praise of or criticism for (depending on one's perspective) the EO's more prominent proactive work undertaken by the current office holder. This will be addressed in subsequent sections of this chapter.

IV. THE EVOLUTION OF THE EUROPEAN OMBUDSMAN'S PROACTIVE WORK

The purpose of this section is to explain that, under the current office holder, Emily O'Reilly, the proactive work of the EO has evolved. As subsequent paragraphs will demonstrate, this concerns both the volume and the subject matter of strategic inquiries, as well as further initiatives that underline strategic work. The shift of focus on own-initiative inquiries upon the commencement of her first term was promptly noted in literature that was produced around that time[44] and later on.[45] This was also clearly emphasised in the 2014 Annual Report:

> When Emily O'Reilly took office as European Ombudsman in October 2013, she announced that she would use her own-initiative power to investigate systemic problems in the EU administration more strategically. The Ombudsman wants to ensure that her office's work becomes more relevant to the major concerns of ordinary European citizens and residents. To that end, she appointed an Own-Initiative Investigation Co-ordinator to steer the strategic own-initiative investigations, in collaboration with colleagues, for speedy and effective delivery.[46]

A. 'Strategic' Inquiries and Initiatives

Changes in the terminology that is being used also carry some significance. The most notable of these has been, of course, the use of the term 'strategic inquiries' instead of own-initiative inquiries. This term is not to be found in the EU Treaties or the

[42] Report on the annual report on the activities of the European Ombudsman in 1997 (C4-0270/98).

[43] Nikos Vogiatzis, 'Communicating the European Ombudsman's Mandate: An Overview of the Annual Reports' (2014) 10 *Journal of Contemporary European Research* 105, at 120–22.

[44] See, for example, Vogiatzis (n 22) 22.

[45] See, for example, Krajewski (n 37) ch 6.

[46] European Ombudsman, Annual Report 2014, 7.

Statute of the EO.[47] That being said, what constitutes a strategic inquiry is not clearly established. According to the Ombudsman's website, the latter 'carries out strategic investigations on her own initiative, which aim to draw attention to matters of public interest and look into wider systemic issues affecting the EU institutions and the democratic decision-making process'.[48] In addition, and crucially, there is now a separate category titled 'strategic initiatives' which concerns instances in which the Ombudsman may not open a formal inquiry but pursue systemic priorities via other means, such as seeking clarifications from EU institutions or raising issues directly with them.[49] Recent examples include the strategic initiative on how the EU Agency for Asylum 'complies with its fundamental rights obligations and ensures accountability for potential violations'[50] or the initiative concerning the transparency and accountability of the Recovery and Resilience Facility.[51] The above is clearly evidence of the evolution of proactive work: by attributing the term 'strategic' to inquiries and by establishing a new type of intervention in the form of strategic initiatives, the EO has clearly signalled an intention to try to bring about systemic change in the EU administration.

Strategic initiatives may give greater discretion to the Ombudsman but this does entail certain challenges as well, especially from the point of view of procedural safeguards for complainants and the EU institutions concerned. While exchanges of letters and other communications were not entirely uncommon prior to the establishment of 'strategic initiatives', the emphasis of this type of work, alongside the loose (if non-existent) regulation of its operation, may give the impression that the Ombudsman has an unduly broad procedural and substantive mandate to pursue their own agenda and priorities. This matter is returned to below, where the limits of proactive work are considered.

In order to provide further clarity on some of the issues that the current office holder has been dealing with),[52] it may be useful to mention here a number of high-profile own-initiative or strategic inquiries. These are, of course, non-exhaustive examples – but they illustrate not only proactive work, but also its evolution – in the sense that they do not necessarily refer to traditional areas of administrative activity (or malfunction) but could be viewed, at least by some, as potentially engaging with certain policy choices or the political work of the EU institutions. One could refer to the inquiry concerning the transparency of trilogues;[53] the Commission's role in the European citizens' initiative (ECI);[54] and the follow-up strategic initiative concerning

[47] Regulation (EU, Euratom) 2021/1163 of the European Parliament of 24 June 2021 laying down the regulations and general conditions governing the performance of the Ombudsman's duties, OJ L 253.

[48] See: www.ombudsman.europa.eu/en/strategic-issues/strategic-inquiries/all-strategic-inquiries.

[49] See: www.ombudsman.europa.eu/en/strategic-issues/strategic-initiatives; see also thematic paper 'Own-initiative inquiries', available at: www.ombudsman.europa.eu/en/thematic-paper/en/84478.

[50] See SI/4/2022/MHZ.

[51] See SI/6/2021/PVV.

[52] Many of these issues will, of course, be returned to in other chapters of this volume.

[53] See OI/8/2015/JAS.

[54] See OI/9/2013/TN.

the revision of the ECI Regulation;[55] various 'revolving door' cases;[56] and the fundamental rights obligations of Frontex – among others.

B. Interplay between Strategic Work and Individual Complaints

While transparency and ethical administration have no doubt constituted a priority for O'Reilly, it would appear useful to remind the reader that not all high-profile cases stem from an own-initiative or strategic inquiry. In other words, a case that may attract publicity and varied responses (and occasionally criticism as well) may as well stem from the submission of an individual complaint. A key example, in this respect, was the Ombudsman's investigation into the appointment of Martin Selmayr as the Commission's Secretary-General, which resulted from two complaints received by the office.[57] Of course, given the publicity of the case, the Ombudsman's keen interest in ethical matters and the interest and participation of the European Parliament in developments around that appointment, it cannot be precluded that the Ombudsman inevitably might have been involved in one way or another. It could also be argued that the more the EO pursues proactive work concerning (including raising awareness about) ethical standards, the more it is likely that individual complainants wishing to raise high-profile issues may contact the office. Be that as it may, the fact remains that some investigations which are widely debated and discussed result from individual complaints. Another example relates to the complaint by a journalist against the Commission further to its refusal to grant access to text messages between the Commission President and the CEO of a pharmaceutical company on the purchase of COVID-19 vaccines).[58]

If the Ombudsman finds that there has been no maladministration, but still feels that guidance can be issued to EU institutions as to the appropriate standards of good administration, this may be viewed as a proactive initiative, even when it takes place on the occasion of an inquiry resulting from an individual complaint. This should serve as a reminder that the boundaries between reactive and proactive work are not always clear-cut, especially in extra-judicial avenues such as ombuds and similar offices that can be characterised by a great degree of flexibility in their operation. For example, the activation of own-initiative inquiries in the past was greatly informed by a high volume of complaints received by the office. It should be noted, however, that more recently the dependency on the volume of complaints in order for strategic work to be launched has decreased. Conversely, the flexibility of the mandate can enable the Ombudsman to address guidance to all institutions and offices upon the conclusion of the investigation of a specific complaint. This could be viewed as proactive work given that these (additional) institutions were not part of the initial enquiry

[55] See SI/6/2017/KR.

[56] Such as OI/1/2021/KR concerning the Commission's handling of 'revolving doors' moves of its staff members.

[57] Joint Cases 488/2018/KR and 514/2018/KR, available at: www.ombudsman.europa.eu/en/decision/en/109855.

[58] Case 1316/2021/MIG, available at: www.ombudsman.europa.eu/en/decision/en/158295.

(but the Ombudsman may – proactively – anticipate that the issues raised would be of relevance to them as well). A recent example of such guidelines was the publication of 'practical recommendations' regarding the 'recording of text and instant messages sent/received by staff members in their professional capacity'.[59] This followed another case (launched after a complaint) in which the Ombudsman examined a request for public access to text messages sent by the then President of the European Council to heads of state and government (and in which no maladministration was found).[60]

C. Emphasis on Proactive Work in the Strategy

The latest strategy 'Towards 2024' echoes the focus on systemic work and the need to operate under pressures stemming from limited resources, which is a perennial challenge for the office. For example, one objective is to achieve 'lasting impact on the EU administration' via trusted leadership in areas relevant to the Ombudsman's mandate.[61] In addition, one of the priorities for 'real-life relevance' to European citizens is to 'continue to help people who seek redress and to identify proactively and research areas of key importance to European citizens and residents for possible systemic inquiries and initiatives'.[62] The wording of this objective already indicates the emphasis on systemic work.

D. Beyond Strategic Inquiries

Proactive work is not confined to strategic inquiries, but also extends to the adoption of Codes, communication initiatives, good practice guidance addressed to the EU institutions – among others. The Ombudsman may also publish and share broadly consultations on matters that could form the basis of a strategic inquiry. In such cases, she becomes a vehicle for public participation. For example, one of the latest calls has concerned transparency and participation in environmental decision-making, and contributions were invited and received on challenges related to both transparency and participation, mainly by civil society organisations.[63] This dialogue with civil society is highly desirable and verifies, once again, the privileged relationship between the Ombudsman and NGOs working on EU transparency and related issues.[64]

Flexibility and creativity are necessary features of an effective ombuds office: the investment in communication and outreach[65] throughout O'Reilly's tenure serves as evidence that the above features were quickly realised. In that regard, the Award for

[59] Case SI/4/2021/MIG, available at: www.ombudsman.europa.eu/en/publication/en/158302.
[60] Case 1219/2020/MIG. This case is mentioned in the background to the strategic initiative.
[61] European Ombudsman strategy: 'Towards 2024' – Sustaining Impact (2020) available at: www.ombudsman.europa.eu/en/strategy/our-strategy/en.
[62] ibid.
[63] See: www.ombudsman.europa.eu/en/public-consultation/en/160313.
[64] Peter Bonnor, 'When EU Civil Society Complains: Civil Society Organisations and Ombudsmanship at the European Level' in Stijn Smismans (ed), *Civil Society and Legitimate European Governance* (Cheltenham, Edward Elgar, 2006) 141.
[65] On which see also Vogiatzis (n 30) 211.

Good Administration enables the Ombudsman to proactively reward institutions and bodies (or specific departments thereof) for work that has a positive impact on citizens.[66] Receiving an 'award' from the Ombudsman is something that many institutions and bodies are keen to highlight in their social media presence and elsewhere. This is also evidence of the good working relationship that has been established, at times; and the fact that *some* parts of the EU administration are more prepared than others to view the Ombudsman's recommendations in a more constructive fashion, rather than as mere criticism against their work.

A further possibility arising from the Ombudsman's proactive dimension of the mandate is that it enables the latter to identify broader issues, debates or challenges concerning the work of the EU administration and take appropriate steps, to that effect. This type of work may take a more deliberative turn than a usual 'inquiry': even if it starts as an exchange of views on matters of common concern, it can inform the future work of the office and of course the practice of the EU institutions without the need to respond to a specific inquiry. A recent example will illustrate this point: mindful of the challenges that Artificial Intelligence (AI) poses already to any administration, the Ombudsman opened a strategic initiative in June 2021 'concerning the impact of artificial intelligence on the EU administration and public administrations in the EU'.[67] This initiative was preceded by a 'European Network of Ombudsmen' (ENO) webinar 'on AI and e-government in public administration'.[68] The Ombudsman's opening statement is indicative of the approach outlined above, namely to initiate a conversation about an ever-increasing challenge: '[i]n recent years, artificial intelligence (AI) has permeated every aspect of our lives, from the trivial to the highly consequential, such as decision making related to medical diagnoses or social security benefits'.[69] Of course, the initiative was crucially informed as well by the proposed 'Artificial Intelligence Act'.[70] It involved the participation of certain national ombuds offices, as well as the European Commission and the European Data Protection Supervisor. It concluded with 'a set of *observations* on the potential implications of AI on public administrations, and the role that ombudsman institutions could play to this end'.[71]

E. Initiatives within the Network

The evolution of proactive work is also evidenced via initiatives that have recently been undertaken in the context of the ENO.[72] In addition to the EU office, this

[66] For further details on the 2023 awards see: www.ombudsman.europa.eu/en/event/en/1493.

[67] See SI/3/2021/VS.

[68] ibid, para 2.

[69] ibid, para 1. At para 4 of the closing report, the Ombudsman explained that '[t]he purpose of this strategic initiative was to keep ENO members informed about these important developments at EU level and to help prepare the European Ombudsman's Office for potential future work in this area, notably in terms of dealing with possible complaints alleging maladministration by EU institutions'.

[70] European Commission Proposal for a Regulation of the European Parliament and of the Council laying down harmonised rules on Artificial Intelligence (Artificial Intelligence Act) and amending certain Union Legislative Acts, COM(2021) 206 final.

[71] See www.ombudsman.europa.eu/en/case/en/59538 (emphasis added).

[72] See further on the ENO Carol Harlow and Richard Rawlings, 'Promoting Accountability in Multilevel Governance: A Network Approach' (2007) 13 *European Law Journal* 542.

network brings together national and regional ombuds offices from EU Member States, candidate countries, other European Economic Area countries, as well as the Committee on Petitions of the European Parliament.[73] Of the initiatives undertaken within the network, the so-called parallel inquiries stand out as an example of proactive work.[74] In such cases (which may also be termed 'parallel initiatives') the EU office and participating national ombuds offices may look into matters of common interest that involve both the EU and national or regional administrations.[75] Recent parallel inquiries have concerned Frontex's complaint mechanism for fundamental rights breaches;[76] and the Commission's monitoring of EU Structural and Investment funds to 'ensure they are used to promote the right of persons with disabilities to independent living and inclusion in the community'.[77] Although a fuller assessment of parallel inquiries would probably necessitate a separate study, what can be noted here is that such inquiries are indeed instances of proactive work, not only because it is generally the EU office that initiates them, but also (and perhaps relatedly) because the network more broadly is rather informal and loose in its operation,[78] which means that there is no legal obligation on the EU office to take such steps.

Overall, the evolution of the Ombudsman's proactive work (which, as already stated, can be characterised by a significant degree of creativity) can be viewed as a positive development. To return to O'Reilly's aims when she assumed office, one of the clear implications of being more proactive especially on salient issues is that increased visibility (within and beyond the EU's institutional setting) and relevance for the office have been achieved. That being said, the next section considers some of the challenges (or limitations) that could arise when the office actively pursues systemic change in the EU.

V. ARE THERE ANY LIMITS TO THE PROACTIVE APPROACH OF THE EUROPEAN OMBUDSMAN?

To begin with, it should be noted that the issue of whether there could be limits to the Ombudsman's proactive work is not a matter that has arisen only in relation to initiatives undertaken by the current office holder, Emily O'Reilly. For example, in 2005 and shortly after assuming office, the second office holder, Nikiforos Diamandouros, while underlining the significance of proactive work, also in terms of its educational and legitimacy-enhancing value, also pointed out that 'the employment of proactive working methods inevitably involves the risk that officials might doubt whether

[73] See: https://eno.ombudsman.europa.eu/home.html.

[74] The other prominent form of cooperation is the 'EU queries' scheme, on which see Natasa Athanasiadou and Nikos Vogiatzis, 'The EU Queries: A Form of Extra-Judicial Preliminary Reference in the Field of Maladministration?' (2021) 22 *German Law Journal* 441.

[75] It may be reminded, in this respect, that the European Ombudsman's competence does not extend to the national level but only covers alleged instances of maladministration by the EU institutions, bodies, offices and agencies, even when national or regional authorities implement EU law.

[76] See Case OI/5/2020/MHZ, available at: www.ombudsman.europa.eu/en/case/en/57955.

[77] See Case OI/2/2021/MHZ, available at: www.ombudsman.europa.eu/en/case/en/58464.

[78] On this point see also Athanasiadou and Vogiatzis (n 74).

the ombudsman's actions are truly necessary and justified'.[79] What Diamandouros was perhaps implying was the risk of alleged activism and/ or allegations that the Ombudsman exceeds the boundaries of their mandate.

The first issue to be considered, in this respect, pertains to procedural guarantees for complainants and the respective EU institutions. Regarding the aforementioned distinction between 'strategic inquiries' and 'initiatives', it is interesting to note that the new Implementing Provisions of the EO do not refer directly to 'strategic initiatives'.[80] However, they appear to allude to them under Article 8 (which concerns, more generally, the own-initiative inquiries). The most relevant provision (which does not feature in the 2008 or 2016 versions of Implementing Provisions) seems to be the second paragraph of the said article, which states that the Ombudsman

> may, outside the scope of inquiries, contact the institutions in writing, in order to raise awareness, share observations or gather information on administrative practices. Within the limits of Article 1(3) of the Statute and in accordance with Article 3(3) thereof, the Ombudsman may decide to conduct own-initiative inquiries following such contacts with the institutions.

Crucially, however, the third paragraph of Article 8 of the latest (adopted) Implementing Provisions (which did *not* feature in the draft Implementing Provisions published on the Ombudsman's website[81]) inter alia points to procedural safeguards as it states that '[t]he procedures applicable to inquiries opened following a complaint shall apply to own-initiative inquiries under paragraphs 1 and 2 of this Article to the extent that they are relevant to those inquiries'. It is understood that Article 8(2) of the new Implementing Provisions was proposed by the EO with a view to formalising the use of strategic initiatives. If so, the overall structure of Article 8 can be viewed as a compromise between formalising strategic initiatives but also reminding the EO that the procedural framework underpinning these should be robust and not deviate from other inquiries. That being said, the proviso 'to the extent that they are relevant to those inquiries' is unclear but does give some discretion to the EO.

In this respect, it is of interest that, unlike earlier versions of the Statute, the new Statute (Article 18) outlines the 'minimum' provisions that should be included in the Implementing Provisions (which are adopted by the Ombudsman but after consultation of the European Parliament, the Council and the European Commission), as follows: '(a) procedural rights of the complainant and the Union institution, body, office or agency concerned; (b) receipt, processing and closure of complaints; (c) own-initiative inquiries; and (d) follow-up inquiries'. This can be viewed as an effort to somewhat confine the discretion of the Ombudsman in these fields. The wording of the Statute appears to suggest that more elaboration on the procedural rights of complainants and the EU institutions (and the European Ombudsman process, more generally) was deemed desirable, at least by the three institutions that participate in

[79] Nikiforos Diamandouros, 'Reflections on the Future Role of the Ombudsman in a Changing Europe' in *Commemorative Volume* (n 31) 217, at 234.

[80] Decision of the European Ombudsman adopting Implementing Provisions (2023) available at: www.ombudsman.europa.eu/en/legal-basis/implementing-provisions/en.

[81] See: www.ombudsman.europa.eu/en/document/en/161393.

the consultation for the Implementing Provisions. As such, procedural safeguards are brought to the fore especially when steps are taken that are not envisaged as such in the documents outlining the Ombudsman's functions, such as 'strategic initiatives'.

Authors have pointed out (also via empirical research) that O'Reilly's views appear to have been that undue procedural formality may impede upon the efficiency of the investigation. To address this, procedures were envisaged that would give greater discretion to case-handlers and could result in an ad hoc participation of the complainant and/or the institution concerned in every stage of the process.[82] This has raised concerns within several EU institutions and bodies about the need to fully respect the right to be heard (according to the same account, some members from within the EO's office expressed at the time doubts as well as to whether such expedited practice would be compatible with the Statute).[83] This issue does not concern specifically the proactive work of the Ombudsman – but it certainly encompasses it. When the Ombudsman decides to 'write' to the EU institutions outside the context of an inquiry to seek information, for example, lack of clarity around the procedural framework applicable therein may raise concerns within the EU institutions and undermine the success of the Ombudsman's initiatives as well.

Another line of criticism that has emerged in recent years – and was reflected, to some extent, also in debates around the time of O'Reilly's re-election – was that the Ombudsman has been, at times, unduly activist or even 'political'. According to another study that has also included interviews with staff members, there would appear to be two sets of allegations: first, an undue focus on strategic inquiries and initiatives and second, an overall approach that seemed to depart from (at least in critics' views) the predominantly legal approach of earlier years.[84]

However, in discussions as to whether an unduly activist approach to the mandate has recently been pursued, the flexibility of the Ombudsman's mandate needs to be noted. More recently, there was an opportunity to confine further (via the revision of the Statute) the EO's mandate. However, such efforts did not materialise, not least because not everyone working within the EU institutions is of the view that a more active Ombudsman is necessarily an undesirable development. In addition, when an EU institution (eg, the Council[85]) disputes the Ombudsman's competence to inquire into a specific area, this is not, in and of itself, evidence that the Ombudsman has actually overstepped the boundaries of the mandate. These considerations should not be understood as implying that criticism against the EO may not be warranted where appropriate: but rather, that a plethora of factors need to be taken into consideration in the assessment of the work of each office holder.

Lastly, the question can be posed as to whether the Ombudsman's findings or recommendations in an inquiry should differ depending on whether such inquiry

[82] Krajewski (n 37) 174–78.

[83] ibid, 179–80.

[84] Tero Erkkila, *Ombudsman as a Global Institution: Transnational Governance and Accountability* (Basingstoke, Palgrave Macmillan, 2020) ch 6. At 184, and with reference to further literature, it is claimed that 'there is a potential trade-off between the new political edge of the institution and the objectivity, consistency and legality of its decisions as perceived by other EU institutions'.

[85] One example (of many) is the Ombudsman's inquiry into the transparency of trilogues.

stems from a complaint or from the own initiative of the office. Leaving aside the distinction between 'inquiry' and 'initiative', once an inquiry is opened, there is nothing to suggest that its origin should mandate the procedure or the outcome. Article 8(3) of the new Implementing Provisions seems to confirm this. The same applies to the findings and recommendations, even if the inquiry raises high-profile issues. In that sense, the Ombudsman might start an 'initiative' to ascertain whether there are grounds to open an 'inquiry'.

VI. CONCLUDING REMARKS

Earlier sections have underlined that the significance of proactive work for ombuds offices is recognised in the literature, international texts and best practice guides. With some benefit of hindsight and taking into account the undeniable fact that the profile of the office has increased over the last decade,[86] it is difficult to criticise the decision that was adopted around 2014 to attach greater significance to proactive work, including via own-initiative or strategic inquiries. Was that priority exercised in an optimal way? Opinions by academic commentators may differ here depending on one's views about specific high-profile cases. However, flexibility is (and has always been) a key feature of the Ombudsman's mandate. Indeed, as Soderman observed in the 1997 Annual Report, 'the open ended nature of the term [maladministration] is one of the things that [distinguish] the role of the Ombudsman from that of a judge'. If so, office holders may take full advantage of the opportunities that are offered by open-ended, loosely defined terms, such as 'maladministration'.

Another point that naturally follows from the flexibility of the office is that significant discretion is granted to each office holder as to how the role will evolve. For example, there might be some holding the view that Soderman was very formalistic/legalistic, Diamandouros customer-service focused and – as noted above – O'Reilly rather activist or political. In reality, none of the office holders advanced *only one* particular dimension of the role, and it is entirely possible that once the time for O'Reilly's succession comes, the new office holder might wish to (simply put) try something else. That is not to suggest that the Ombudsman should not respect the boundaries of the mandate: when that does not happen, criticism is, of course, appropriate. Instead, what is argued here is that the assessment of each office holder should not take place with reference to a particular vision of an ombuds office that each assessor may have.

Overall, therefore, and as the title of this edited volume indicates, the role and institutional presence of the Ombudsman has evolved over the last years; so has her proactive work, as this chapter has sought to demonstrate. Does that set a precedent for future office holders (in the sense that the essence of the role has somewhat changed, with *that level* of proactiveness now being an indissociable aspect of the Ombudsman's functions)? Not necessarily – as was mentioned above, openness is required when setting expectations from (and then assessing the work of) offices as flexible as this one.

[86] See also Vogiatzis (n 30) 210.

There would appear to be awareness, within the office, that an impression might have been given at times that only strategic work constitutes the priority. For example, in the aforementioned thematic paper of 2017 it was stated that 'in the absence of a complaint (that by its very nature helps legitimise a decision to inquire into a matter), a particular effort is needed to explain why the EO chooses to pursue an [own-initiative inquiry]'; and, later on:

> The central function of the EO will therefore remain the hundreds of inquiries conducted each year through which the EO resolves payment disputes in EU projects, obtains documents, rights wrongs and remedies injustices suffered by individual complainants. The fact that the EO does not typically open more than a few large-scale [own-initiative inquiries] per year can be seen as a way to seek to strike the right balance between the dual functions.[87]

Indeed, the key issue is whether a reasonable balance can be achieved between pursuing systemic work and providing redress (by devoting due attention and resources) to individual complainants, whose case may not necessarily raise high-profile issues. If that balance is achieved, ambition, creativity and proactive initiatives fully align with a modern understanding of an extra-judicial office that wishes to be impactful and relevant to EU citizens and residents. Let us not forget that the right to complain to the EO is part of the provisions on Union citizenship, and also features in the EU Charter of Fundamental Rights.

[87] Thematic paper (n 49).

3

The Ombudsman: An Indispensable Source of Encouragement

HARALD SCHUMANN

If journalists want to meet their professional standards and obtain comprehensive information in order to report critically on what is happening in the institutions of the European Union (EU), they usually have to fight hard for access to information and documents. For in many cases, the responsible officials feel far more obliged to the power interests of their political leadership and the national government apparatuses than to the citizens and their legally enshrined right to participate in democratic legislation. As a result, they usually hide much more than is legally allowed.[1]

This applies to both the European Commission and the Council of the EU, as well as to their subordinate authorities. And even the leadership of the European Parliament and its administration frequently and arbitrarily refuse to answer legitimate questions from the media. Yet it is absolutely clear that without information from independent journalists and the media, the democratic participation of citizens guaranteed by the EU Treaties is not possible. Those who are not informed cannot form a well-founded opinion and certainly cannot exert any influence. Nevertheless, journalists constantly encounter resistance in this task. Commissioners, directors-general and heads of departments usually only pay lip service to transparency. In reality, they constantly conceal it.

In this environment, the very existence of the European Ombudsman institution is a blessing. With high expertise, and a journalist herself, she is aware of the importance and challenges of journalistic work. Journalists can rely on her and her team to understand the citizens' right to participation, enshrined in Article 10 of the Treaty on European Union, as the mandate for the media and journalists: We have to deliver the necessary information, and we can only do that if we get it.

[1] Arts 1 and 10(3) of the Treaty on European Union, and related case law of the Court of Justice of the European Union and inquiries by the European Ombudsman. See also Harald Schumann, 'EU court forces access to files of Europe's most important lawmaker', *Investigate Europe*, 26 January 2023, www.investigate-europe.eu/posts/eu-court-forces-access-to-files-of-europe-most-important-lawmaker, and Harald Schumann, Sigrid Melchior and Thodoris Chondrogiannos, 'Emily O'Reilly, EU Ombudsman: "The Council Should Record the Member States' Positions"', *Investigate Europe*, 2 December 2020, www.investigate-europe.eu/posts/emily-oreilly-eu-Ombudsman.

But this does not work if those responsible do not fulfil their duty. This constant denial of information is common practice especially in the central body of European legislation, the Council of the EU.[2] There, the representatives of the national governments – usually not elected and not known by name – negotiate the texts of future laws as if they were international treaties, that is to say, according to the rules of diplomacy. As a result, they practice maximum secrecy.

Sometimes this leads to bizarre consequences. This is exemplified by the fate of the directive on the introduction of 'country-by-country reporting' about the tax payments of transnational companies.[3] Once transposed into national law, it will force transnational companies from 2024 onwards to report publicly on their tax payments, turnover and number of employees, differentiated according to individual states. The aim was to make the tax avoidance of large corporations visible since 2015 and thus put them under pressure to pay taxes where they generate their profits and not in tax avoidance countries such as Ireland, Luxembourg and the Netherlands or their affiliated operetta states in the Caribbean. According to the Commission's estimates, this tax avoidance costs the state coffers of the EU countries up to 70 billion euros a year, which corresponds to almost half of the annual EU budget.[4]

This proposal was stuck in the Council for five years because a blocking minority of 13 states prevented its adoption against the will of the vast majority of the EU Parliament. At the head of this alliance was the German government. At least that is what the German media reported correctly. But no one investigated which other governments made common cause with the Germans. And without journalistic intervention, it would have remained that way until today. It was only when the cross-border journalism team of *Investigate Europe*[5] (to which the author of this article belongs) revealed that the Social Democrats from Portugal and Sweden were also playing the game of the corporate lobby, contrary to their election promises, that things started to move. Under pressure from his own party colleagues in parliament, who referred to the press reports, Portugal's economy minister had to change his position. The Austrian Parliament later followed suit and in May 2021, six years after the bill was introduced, the Council and the EU Parliament finally helped it become law.

While this result flatters us journalists, it documents the undemocratic nature of the structures in the Council. It should not depend on the commitment of a few journalists whether or not an urgently needed EU law comes into force.

And comparable cases usually do not have such a good ending. Since 2013, more than a hundred important laws have failed in the Council due to a blocking

[2] Harald Schumann, Sigrid Melchior and Juliet Ferguson, 'Behind Closed Doors: Secret Deals in the Council of the EU', *Investigate Europe*, 8 December 2020, www.investigate-europe.eu/posts/behind-closed-doors-secrets-in-the-council.

[3] Directive (EU) 2021/2101 of the European Parliament and of the Council of 24 November 2021 amending Directive 2013/34/EU as regards disclosure of income tax information by certain undertakings and branches, [2021], OJ L 429.

[4] R Dover, B Ferrett, D Gravino, E Jones and S Merler, 'Bringing Transparency, Coordination and Convergence to Corporate Tax Policies in the European Union', Study commissioned by the European Parliamentary Research Service, September 2015, www.europarl.europa.eu/thinktank/en/document.html?reference=EPRS_STU(2015)558773.

[5] Paulo Pena, 'Unblocking Portugal – the Secret Votes Behind Corporate Tax Transparency', *Investigate Europe*, 27 March 2020.

minority organised by influential lobby groups, without EU citizens ever hearing a word about them.[6]

Against this backdrop, Ombudsman O'Reilly's frequently made plea on the subject carries great weight: The EU citizens 'cannot exercise their right to participate in the democratic life of the Union', she concluded in 2018 after her investigation into Europe's most powerful institution, the Council.[7] The national officials involved systematically keep secret which national government represents which position. That is why, according to O'Reilly, 'it is virtually impossible for citizens to find out how a European law came into being'. But this 'undermines their right to hold their elected representatives to account' and 'aims at the very heart of the EU's legitimacy', O'Reilly has repeatedly warned.

This has an effect. Since then, the responsible officials in the Council know that they must expect to have to give the Ombudsman all the information they deny journalists. The latter only have to lodge a corresponding complaint with her.

When the financial system slips into crisis, all sources of credit dry up and the central banks have to step in as lenders of last resort. The Ombudsman has a similar function. When faith in freedom of information and democratic standards is lost, journalists and citizens lose heart. In such a situation, a capable Ombudsman is a source of encouragement of last resort – and helps those affected not to give up.

Our Investigate Europe team has also used this successfully. In March 2021, we requested all documents from the Member States' negotiations on the Digital Markets Act from the Council Secretariat in order to be able to report on this important law. In doing so, we also specifically asked for the so-called 'working documents', in which demands and comments of the individual Member States are mentioned. However, the officials of the Council administration refused access because, according to the Member States, this would be detrimental to the ongoing negotiations at this point in time.

We objected to this because one of the fundamental tasks of journalists in a democratic society is to report on ongoing legislative procedures and to present the arguments of the various legislative actors to the citizens. As many as seven governments agreed with this opinion, but the majority of those in power in the EU Member States do not care about press freedom when they legislate behind closed doors. That is why we complained to the Ombudsman.

The latter finally stated three months later that these are 'clearly legislative documents to which the highest standards of transparency must apply'.[8] According to 'established case-law', 'the preliminary nature of the deliberations in Council working groups on a Commission proposal' in no way justifies the Council's claimed exception to this requirement. Rather, a legislative proposal is 'by its very nature intended to be discussed and debated, and public opinion is perfectly capable of understanding

[6] See Legislative Observatory of the EP, https://oeil.secure.europarl.europa.eu.

[7] Decision in strategic inquiry OI/2/2017/TE on the transparency of the Council legislative process, 15 May 2018.

[8] Recommendation on the Council of the European Union's refusal to give full public access to documents related to negotiations on the draft 'Digital Markets Act' (case 1499/2021/SF), 28 February 2022.

that the author of a proposal may subsequently change its content', O'Reilly quoted a relevant ruling of the European Court of Justice.[9]

By then, the Council had already given in to the pressure and had sent the requested documents. This was much too late for reporting on the draft law. But the warning shot was fired nonetheless. Since then, the Council Secretariat has sent many 'Working documents' even during the ongoing negotiations on a draft law.

The institution of the Ombudsman strengthens us journalists and thus makes an indispensable contribution to the democratisation of the EU. However, the road to truly overcoming the democratic deficit of the Union is still long. Member States' governments still unscrupulously use every crisis to spend billions of euros of taxpayers' money at EU level without parliamentary control and to negotiate central legislative projects behind the backs of their voters and citizens. Decisions they could never take at national level, because there the Parliaments defend their power and would never waive their right to control the budget.

But at EU level it happens again and again. This was the case during the euro crisis and the uncontrolled exercise of power in the crisis states by means of the troika of International Monetary Fund, European Central Bank and Commission. It was so during the Covid-19 pandemic and the looting of state coffers for secret deals with the pharmaceutical industry, which was shamelessly given profit margins of almost 2,000 per cent beyond all democratic control. Additionally the allocation of the more than 700 billion euros of the Recovery and Resilience Facility is decided by the Commission without scrutiny by the European Parliament. This is an invitation for corruption and mismanagement.

And it is happening again now in the face of the war in Ukraine, where EU states are once again using undemocratic methods to defend Ukrainian democracy. This is illustrated by the non-transparent allocation of funds to the arms industry and in the Orwellian-style so called European Peace Facility.[10] This is a joint fund of the EU states for the financing of arms exports, which is administered by the Council and the Commission, but was deliberately set up outside the usual EU legal system and operates beyond any democratic control. Thus, the EU governments redistribute among themselves around 10 billion Euros without any parliamentarian even being able to see who exactly gets how much for which arms deliveries to Ukraine. But where so much money flows without external control, corruption and abuse are almost certain.

Asked about this, Ombudsman O'Reilly told us in March 2022:

> People will want to know exactly what the EU is doing in this area – how money is being spent, what kind of projects are foreseen, how policy is changing. The EU administration should anticipate this interest and make more information proactively available. My office will follow developments in this area closely.

In November 2023, the Ombudsman opened an own-initiative inquiry into how the Commission ensures that there are no conflicts of interest with external experts who assist it in evaluating projects under the European Defence Fund.[11] This inquiry is yet to be concluded.

[9] ibid, para 22.

[10] Apostolis Fotidiadis and Nico Schmidt, 'The European Peace Facility, an Unsecured Gun on EU's Table', *Investigate Europe*, 29 March 2022, www.investigate-europe.eu/posts/european-peace-facility-controversy.

[11] Case OI/5/2023/KR, opened on 10 November 2023.

4

The Relations between the European Commission and the European Ombudsman

PASCAL LEFÈVRE AND CHRISTIAN LINDER*

I. INTRODUCTION

An observer with occasional interest in EU affairs might have the impression that relations between the European Ombudsman (EO) and the European Commission (Commission) were tense or a source of constant disagreement.[1] And yet, as will be demonstrated in this chapter, the relations between the Commission and the three Ombudsmen, who have held this office so far, have always been good, constructive, based upon mutual trust and respect and beneficial for European citizens.

Disagreements between the two institutions are in fact rare,[2] and are most of the time merely the expression of two self-confident independent institutions with different roles and constraints. This chapter intends to zoom in to the EO's role over the Commission, highlighting some of the most prominent decisions taken.

II. THE COMMISSION: IN VOLUME THE BIGGEST 'CLIENT' OF THE OMBUDSMAN

The Commission is the main addressee of the EO's inquiries and initiatives (62.81 per cent out of 398 inquiries in 2023, 57.1 per cent out of 348 inquiries in 2022).[3]

* The information and views set out in this chapter are those of the authors and do not necessarily reflect the official opinion of the institution.

[1] Elena Sánchez Nicolás, 'Watchdog slams Commission on BlackRock "green rules" deal' *euobserver* (Brussels, 25 November 2020) euobserver.com/news/150175.

[2] Maladministration was found only 7.3 per cent of all inquiries (including those concerning the Commission) closed by the European Ombudsman in 2023. European Ombudsman, Annual Report 2023, 19 March 2024, 23.

[3] European Ombudsman, Annual Report 2024, 19 March 2024, 20.European Ombudsman, Annual Report 2023, 25 April 2023, 18.

As the EO acknowledges, this is not surprising, as the Commission is the largest EU institution with 32,000 staff members, more than 40 different departments and most of the direct administrative contacts with citizens, businesses and associations.[4] Inquiries on access to documents issues are nowadays, by far, the most numerous, but other transparency issues are also very frequently addressed, as will be seen below.

However, closing decisions with a finding of 'maladministration' are rare: only between 1 and 7 per cent of the cases, depending on the year.[5] This is a clear indication that a positive and dynamic dialogue prevails, and that, in the context of an inquiry, the Commission does take into account most of the proposals, suggestions, and recommendations submitted by the EO, the acceptance rate being 81 per cent in 2023,[6] despite their non-binding character. In the remaining cases, the Commission is bound by legal constraints, the need to avoid undesired spill-over effects from an individual case to general practice or simply does not agree with the EO's conclusions. But even if the Commission disagrees in a concrete case, it does not necessarily mean that the EO's work does not have an impact. In some cases, the EO's influence becomes visible only later. The EO's recommendation may raise awareness about a particular issue, and trigger further internal reflection and subsequent changes in regulation or practice. The right of an administration to disagree is inherent to the non-binding nature of the EO's powers and an advantage for the cooperation between the EO and the EU administration. An Ombudsman with binding decision-making powers would fundamentally change the institutional setup, create a contentious procedure, and would interfere not only with the independence of the EU institutions and bodies, such as the Commission but also with its own, specific role in the institutional balance of the EU. This is particularly true in areas where the EO does not deal with administrative issues but also looks into broader policy issues, for example with regard to legislation or international negotiations. This approach relies on the willingness of administrations actively to seek solutions to problems and to put themselves into question.

The numbers detailed above demonstrate the general quality of the administration, the Commission's openness to follow the EO's 'friendly advice', but also the practical impact and success of the EO's work over the Commission. The EO welcomed the Commission's responses in several cases. It for example reacted very positively to the Commission's announcement that it would start publishing details about Commissioners' travel expenses every two months, by stating that this constitutes 'a very positive step towards greater transparency in this area'.[7] Another inquiry where the Commission followed the EO's recommendation concerned a request for

[4] European Commission, 'Commission staff', commission-europa-eu.eui.idm.oclc.org/about-european-commission/organisational-structure/commission-staff_en.

[5] European Ombudsman, Annual Report 2023, 19 March 2024, 23; European Ombudsman, Annual Report 2022, 25 April 2023, 21; European Ombudsman, Annual Report 2021, 18 May 2022, 33; European Ombudsman, Annual Report 2020, 18 May 2021, 34.

[6] European Ombudsman, Annual Report 2023, 19 March 2024, 25.

[7] Decision in cases 562/2017/THH and 1069/2017/THH on the Commission's handling of a large number of requests for access to documents concerning Commissioners' travel expenses, 16 November 2018, para 20.

public access to correspondence exchanged with Member State authorities concerning the distribution of medical masks, which did not meet the required quality standard, in the context of the Covid-19 crisis.[8] The Commission had identified 135 documents in total and had given wide public access to the documents. However, the complainant took issue with the Commission's refusal to give access to (parts of) 12 documents and, specifically, its reliance on the need to protect the commercial interests of the manufacturer concerned. The EO issued a recommendation asking the Commission to reconsider its decision to refuse public access to (parts of) the 12 documents at issue.[9] Considering the changed circumstances since the complainant had submitted his request, the Commission accepted the requested disclosure of nearly all remaining documents.[10]

Overall, 2366 complaints were registered by the EO in 2023, amongst them 398 inquiries were officially opened.[11] Most of the remaining complaints did not fall under the EO's mandate. Given the number of interactions between the EU administration and citizens, economic operators or associations, these numbers do not, in our view, indicate significant general problems in the EU administration.

III. THE COMMISSION'S INTERNAL WORKINGS: THE JOURNEY OF AN OMBUDSMAN COMPLAINT

When the EO launches a complaint-based or own-initiative inquiry, she can request information, a reply, a meeting, an inspection or a hearing. Deadlines depend on the circumstances of the case (from some days in a 'fast-track procedure'[12] to three months) and justified extensions can be requested (maximum twice one month).[13]

If the Commission must take a formal position, the reply is prepared by the lead and associated services concerned by the matter. The Legal Service, the Secretariat-General, which coordinates all procedures and, if the decision has budgetary consequences, the Directorate-General for Budget must be consulted as well as the relevant Members of the Commission. The agreement of the Member in charge of the file and the Member in charge of the relations with the EO is required during the adoption procedure (written empowerment procedure).

[8] How the European Commission handled a request for public access to documents concerning the quality of medical masks distributed during the COVID-19 pandemic 790/2021/MIG, decision on 25 May 2022.

[9] Recommendation on how the European Commission handled a request for public access to documents concerning the quality of medical masks distributed during the COVID-19 pandemic (790/2021/MIG), 5 November 2021.

[10] Reply from the European Commission to the recommendation of the European Ombudsman on how the European Commission handled a request for public access to documents concerning the quality of medical masks distributed during the COVID-19 pandemic (790/2021/MIG), 7 April 2022.

[11] European Ombudsman, Annual Report 2023, 19 March 2024, 12.

[12] www.ombudsman.europa.eu/en/access-to-documents/fast-track.

[13] Art 5(3) of Regulation (EU, Euroatom) 2021/1163 of the European Parliament of 24 June 2021 laying down the regulations and general conditions governing the performance of the Ombudsman's duties (Statute of the European Ombudsman) and repealing Decision 94/262/ECSC, EC, Euratom [2001] OJ L 253/1.

If a complaint concerns minor issues, such as a lack of reply, the EO's services may ask for a direct reply to the complainant. In that case, there is no inter-service consultation in the Commission and no empowerment procedure. Deadlines are overall shorter. The EO's services close the inquiry once the matter is settled.

Meetings and inspections are frequent and have proven useful to help clarifying or closing cases at an early stage. A report is established by the EO's services and sent to the Commission and the complainant.

Following a positive trial period with the Commission, the EO introduced, in 2018, a 'fast-track procedure' for access to documents complaints, allowing a handling of requests within a very short period (provision usually within five working days of the (unredacted) documents requested by the complainant, speeding up of the adoption of confirmatory decisions, etc).[14] This new approach has proven to be mutually beneficial, and was therefore extended to other institutions.

EO inquiries may be closed in several ways. There may be either a closure of an inquiry with or without any further request (meeting, inspection, formal position, etc), a closure with a solution proposal (for example, disclosure of documents to the complainant by the Commission) or suggestions for improvement or recommendations of specific actions or finally a closure with or without a finding of 'maladministration'.

IV. MUTUAL TRUST AND CONSTRUCTIVE COOPERATION: AN EFFICIENT FORUM FOR ACCOUNTABILITY

The main areas of the EO's Commission-related inquiries and initiatives are transparency (namely access to documents, transparency of the decision-making process, international negotiations, Covid-19 crisis management, expert groups, accessibility to websites and online tools); ethics and conflicts of interest issues (such as codes of conduct for Members of institutions, Staff Regulations for EU staff, the so-called 'revolving doors' phenomenon, advisory boards, interactions with lobbyists and stakeholders), fundamental rights (for example, human rights clauses in international agreements, rights of persons with disabilities, discriminations, boarder management controls); grants, contracts and tenders (namely payments, rejections of costs, information and tender documents, selection of tenderers); and late or lack of replies (so-called 'failure to reply' inquiries).

This section zooms in on recent examples of investigations launched by the EO with the Commission, which illustrate the variety of topics addressed. First, in 2021, the EO launched a strategic own-initiative inquiry into how the Commission implements its rules on 'revolving doors'.[15] She made several proposals to ensure a more systematic and effective approach to dealing with former staff members moving to the private sector or people moving from the private sector into the Commission.[16]

[14] www.ombudsman.europa.eu/en/access-to-documents/fast-track.

[15] Decision on how the European Commission manages 'revolving door' moves of its staff members (OI/1/2021/KR), 16 May 2022. See also the contribution of Emilia Korkea-Aho in this volume.

[16] ibid.

The EO's aim is to strengthen the prevention of situations such as the lobbying of former colleagues or inappropriate access to confidential information. The Commission pledged to put in place many of the EO's proposals.[17] These included asking the person moving to the private sector to provide more information about the organisation they are going to, and more detail about the nature of their new job. In 2021, the EO requested details of decisions that the Commission had taken related to staff moving to the private sector. She indicated that the inquiry covered economically important departments as well as the Cabinets of Commissioners and the Legal Service. The aim was to assess the decision-making process and how this process could be improved. In 2022, the Commission noted with satisfaction that the EO had not found any instance of maladministration in the 100 Commission decisions that her team had examined.[18] It also noted that the EO had welcomed the improvements made by the Commission since her last inquiry on the issue. Nevertheless, the EO asked the Commission to forbid certain jobs temporarily if risks cannot be offset or restrictions cannot be enforced, and to publish decisions on staff members' new jobs faster. The Commission replied, notably, that, as regards occupational activities after leaving the service, it was well aware of the possibility to forbid an activity and that it used the full range of restrictions and conditions available to it to safeguard its legitimate interests, in line with primary law, the provisions of Staff Regulations[19] and of the Commission decision on outside activities and assignments and on occupational activities after leaving the Service.[20] It considered that, as a result, its current practice was both proportionate and robust. As regards outside activities during leave on personal grounds, the Commission indicated that, since 2021, it had been implementing a more restrictive approach thereto, compliant with the provisions of the Staff Regulations. Concerning the publication of staff members' new jobs, the Commission stressed, amongst others, that it strictly followed the provisions of Article 16(4) of the Staff Regulations as regards information on post-service occupational activities of former senior staff members. These rules provide for the publication of an annual report on former senior managers' cases involving lobbying or advocacy vis-à-vis their former institution on matters for which they were responsible during their last three years in service.

Second, activities of Commissioners were also monitored by the EO who welcomed the responses from the Commission in several cases, notably when the Commission announced that it would start publishing details about Commissioners' travel

[17] Reply from the European Commission on implementation of the European Ombudsman's suggestions resulting from the second own-initiative inquiry on the revolving doors phenomenon OI/3/2017 AB-NF, 20 January 2022.

[18] Comments of the European Commission on a closing decision from the European Ombudsman concerning strategic inquiry OI/1/2021/KR on how the European Commission manages 'revolving door' moves of its staff members, 9 June 2023.

[19] Regulation No 31 (EEC), 11 (EAEC), laying down the Staff Regulations of Officials and the Conditions of Employment of Other Servants of the European Economic Community and the European Atomic Energy Community [1962] OJ P 045.

[20] Commission Decision of 29.6.2018 on outside activities and assignments and on occupational activities after leaving the Service(C(2018) 4048 final).

expenses,[21] and when it extended the period during which former Commissioners must notify new professional activities to the Commission.[22]

Third, the transparency of international negotiations is another regular issue. For example, for two years, the EO monitored the Brexit negotiations and praised the generally high level of transparency.[23] She asked the Commission and Council to maintain these standards in any future negotiations on the relationship between the EU and the UK. She stressed that positive steps by the Commission's Brexit Taskforce included the publication of over one hundred negotiating documents, making the Chief Negotiator's calendar publicly available, and meeting only registered lobbyists. She added that the Taskforce had a transparent working process. Some years ago, the EO initiated an inquiry on the transparency and public participation in relation to the Transatlantic Trade and Investment Partnership (TTIP) negotiations, which notably led to the publication of the EU negotiating directives. In this context, she also asked the Commission to ensure that the public can follow the progress of these talks and contribute to shaping their outcome. The Commission confirmed that it is building on its more proactive approach to publishing TTIP documents and outlined the full range of actions it has taken to inject greater transparency into the negotiations.[24] The EO welcomed the fact that the Commission had engaged positively with her in this area of key importance to citizens. She applauded the fact that the Commission was leading by example and was convinced that the ambitious transparency agenda it had set for TTIP augured well for future trade and investment negotiations.[25]

Finally, the transparency of decision-making is another frequent topic, for example in relation to the role of expert groups established by the Commission,[26] the inclusion of gas infrastructure projects in the EU's list of 'Projects of Common Interest' (PCIs)[27] – cross-border energy infrastructure projects meant to help achieve EU energy and climate policy objectives or in relation to the Recovery and Resilience Facility (RRF),[28] a temporary instrument that is the centrepiece

[21] Decision in cases 562/2017/THH and 1069/2017/THH on the Commission's handling of a large number of requests for access to documents concerning Commissioners' travel expenses, 16 November 2018, para 20.

[22] European Ombudsman, 'Ombudsman welcomes proposals to strengthen Commissioner ethics and transparency rules' (press release no 8/2017).

[23] Strategic Initiative with the European Commission on the negotiations on the UK withdrawal from the EU (SI/1/2017/KR).

[24] Own-initiative inquiry on transparency and public participation in relation to the Transatlantic Trade and Investment Partnership ('TTIP') negotiations (OI/10/2014/RA), decision on 6 January 2015.

[25] European Ombudsman, 'Ombudsman commends Commission for progress on transparency in TTIP negotiations' (press release no 6/2015).

[26] Decision of the European Ombudsman in her strategic inquiry OI/6/2014/NF concerning the composition and transparency of European Commission expert groups, decision on 14 November 2017.

[27] The European Commission's action relating to the drawing up of the EU list of 'Projects of Common Interest' in the energy sector (1933/2018/KR), decision on28 November 2019.

[28] Strategic Initiative on the transparency and accountability of the Recovery and Resilience Facility (SI/6/2021/PVV), decision on 12 September 2023; the European Commission's refusal to give public access to documents concerning the Swedish and the Danish national plans under the Recovery and Resilience Facility (925/2022/LDS), decision on 29 November 2022; the European Commission's refusal to give public access to documents concerning the French national plan under the Recovery and Resilience Facility

of NextGenerationEU, the EU's €800 billion temporary recovery instrument to support the economic recovery from the Covid-19 pandemic and build a greener, more digital and more resilient future.

The number of inquiries related to access to documents is the highest. They can concern individual cases but also general issues like the EO's practical recommendations on the recording of work-related text and instant messages,[29] where the Commission agreed to issue further guidance,[30] or general delays in handling requests for access to document which led to a 'Special Report' to the European Parliament.[31]

Despite the issues which attract media and political interest, one must not forget the many individual cases handled by the EO, such as in the area of contracts and grants where the cooperation between the EO and the Commission often helps finding a solution which does not attract public interest but is equally important for the persons concerned. For example, a German company turned to the EO after the Commission decided to recover around EUR 100,000 from it.[32] The company participated in an EU-funded project in Namibia, which aimed to develop the capacity of Namibia's national authorities to manage EU funds and programmes. The Commission recovered the money after an audit deemed costs related to personnel were ineligible, as some employees did not have the correct qualifications and some worked on public holidays, in breach of Namibian law. The EO pointed out that although the contract had recommended that employees have such qualifications, this was not a requirement. Following the EO's intervention, the Commission paid back €97,461 to the complainant. Equally, following the EO's intervention, the Commission revised its stance on costs incurred by a recipient of an EU grant for a water infrastructure project in Lebanon.[33] It agreed to accept as eligible the staff costs the complainant had submitted. Other cases also had a clear impact on the daily lives of people concerned. For example, the EO investigated a case where, following information received from staff members, she wrote to the European Parliament, Council and Commission asking them to inform her about their internal policies

(1129/2022/SF), decision on 27 October 2023; how the European Commission dealt with a request for public access to documents concerning the Dutch national plan under the Recovery and Resilience Facility (409/2023/OAM), decision on 16 March 2023; the European Commission's refusal to give full public access to documents related to the German plan under the Recovery and Resilience Facility (137/2023/SF), decision on 27 October 2023.

[29] The European Commission's refusal of public access to text messages exchanged between the Commission President and the CEO of a pharmaceutical company on the purchase of a COVID-19 vaccine (1316/2021/MIG), decision on 12 July 2022.

[30] Reply of the European Commission to the Recommendation from the European Ombudsman regarding the European Commission's refusal of public access to text messages exchanged between the Commission President and the CEO of a pharmaceutical company on the purchase of a COVID-19 (1316/2021/MIG), 27 June 2022.

[31] Special Report of the European Ombudsman in her strategic inquiry concerning the time the European Commission takes to deal with requests for public access to documents (OI/2/2022/OAM), 20 September 2023.

[32] The Commission's recovery of EUR 103,911.85 in the context of an EU-funded project in Namibia (279/2018/JN), decision on 7 August 2019.

[33] The decision by the European Commission to consider ineligible certain costs declared in the context of a grant contract with an NGO (1227/2021/LM), decision on 8 March 2022.

regarding the leave rights of staff members who become parents through surrogacy.[34] The staff members that contacted the EO had drawn attention to inconsistencies between the different EU institutions concerning those leave rights for staff members. The Commission replied that, since 2012, its standard practice had been to grant, on an *ad hoc* basis, 20 weeks of leave, the same as granted to staff becoming parents through adoption. It stated that it intended to formalise this practice.[35] The Council replied that it would follow the practice of the Commission,[36] while the Parliament said it was prepared to engage in inter-institutional dialogue to find a common approach to the matter.[37]

V. CONCLUSION

The EO has impact and is valued, by citizens, associations and businesses who turned to the EO, but also by the institutions, bodies, offices and agencies of the Union. The EO is an alternative to the right to submit petitions or to take an administration to the Court of Justice. It is a non-conflictual and easily accessible approach, also in terms of cost. The EO is not a judge, and decisions are not legally binding. Yet, it is the 'soft power' of the EO, which makes this office special and allows to find practical solutions to practical problems and to improve the administration of the Union.

The framework for the performance of the EO's duties has evolved since the 1990s and allows the EO to act on a strong legal basis, notably the new Statute of the EO adopted in 2021.[38] The EO is an important factor in the administrative structure of the EU and a major contributor to the administrative culture of the EU.

[34] The leave rights of certain staff members and the best interests of the child (SI/1/2019/AMF), decision on 1 October 2019.

[35] Reply of the European Commission in SI/1/2019/AMF concerning the leave rights of certain staff members and the best interests of the child, 14 June 2019.

[36] Reply of the General Secretariat of the Council in SI/1/2019/AMF concerning the leave rights of certain staff members and the best interests of the child, 28 June 2019.

[37] Reply of the of the European Parliament in SI/1/2019/AMF concerning the leave rights of certain staff members and the best interests of the child, 1 July 2019.

[38] Regulation (EU, Euroatom) 2021/1163 of the European Parliament of 24 June 2021 laying down the regulations and general conditions governing the performance of the Ombudsman's duties (Statute of the European Ombudsman) and repealing Decision 94/262/ECSC, EC, Euratom [2001] OJ L 253/1.

5

The Evolving Role of the European Ombudsman in Context: The European Ombudsman's Perspective

ROSITA HICKEY*

I. INTRODUCTION

THE EUROPEAN OMBUDSMAN (EO) was established as part of the citizenship of the Union, which very much informs its role and functions, as well as the way in which, ideally, the EU administration should engage with the EO's findings.

The Maastricht Treaty did not restrict the EO's competence to complainants' personal grievances caused by maladministration. The mandate extends beyond administrative acts addressed to individuals, broadly covering instances of 'maladministration in the activities of the Union institutions, bodies, offices or agencies'.[1] In the three decades since the EO was established, the Union has embarked on an ever-expanding range of activities, from authorising chemical substances to vaccine procurement on a massive scale. It is hardly surprising then that the EO has also been called upon to deal with complaints and inquiries in these hugely important areas.[2]

Given its link with EU citizenship, it was only logical for the EO to be particularly attentive and responsive to the concerns expressed by individual citizens. At the same time, it is surely also an honest reflection of what was intended for this

* I would like to thank Peter Dyrberg, Inquiries and Process Expert, for his help in preparing my speaking points for the Florence seminar, as well as Natalia Chiner Ridaura, inquiries officer at the European Ombudsman's Office, for her help finalising this chapter which draws on that presentation. Any errors or omissions are mine.

[1] See Art 228(1) of the Treaty on the Functioning of the European Union, as well as Art 1(3) of Regulation (EU, Euratom) 2021/1163 of the European Parliament of 24 June 2021 laying down the regulations and general conditions governing the performance of the Ombudsman's duties (Statute of the European Ombudsman) and repealing Decision 94/262/ECSC, EC, Euratom [2021] OJ L 253.

[2] See, respectively, Decision in case 1606/2013/AN on how the European Chemicals Agency applies rules concerning animal testing, 11 September 2015, and Decision on how the European Commission dealt with a request for public access to documents concerning the negotiations for the procurement of COVID-19 vaccines (case 2206/2021/MIG), 18 July 2022.

institution that the EO deals with matters of wider public importance which many of the 'activities of the Union institutions, bodies, offices or agencies' are bound to amount to. With a naturally shifting focus, the EO seeks to both help individual complainants – in areas like recruitment,[3] grants and contracts[4] – and ensure that the EU administration works properly when it comes to matters as diverse as banking supervision[5] and risk management of chemicals.[6]

This chapter sets out how, ideally, the EU institutions should respond to and engage with the assessments and findings of the EO. It then describes the context in which successive EOs have done their work and how this might have impacted on how the EO has evolved as an institution. Finally, it touches on areas the EO is likely to have to ready itself for, in the future.

II. HOW THE EU INSTITUTIONS ENGAGE WITH EO FINDINGS

The EO's ability to pursue its goals effectively is greatly impacted by how EU institutions engage with its findings. The EO has no binding powers and cannot overturn administrative decisions. The EO can, however, invite institutions to revisit them. In order to live up to the reasonable expectations of citizens and encourage them to turn to the EO, EU institutions should be receptive to EO findings.

An Ombudsman inquiry is not like being before the Court of Justice. Before the Court, an institution is expected to defend a decision at all costs. With the Ombudsman, institutions may be invited to revisit decisions, if the EO takes the view that things could have been done better. The institutions should be open to considering such invitations. Even if they ultimately disagree, they should not, from the start, take a position that in essence denies the very possibility of an Ombudsman solution or say that legally the institution is barred from considering the Ombudsman's invitation to revisit the issue.

In a case concerning public access to declarations of interest of members of its Regulatory Scrutiny Board, the Commission said during the inquiry that 'it considers its reply was legally and factually correct at the point in time it was taken and does not see any reason to adopt a new decision'. Thankfully, the matter did not stop there and the Commission showed a willingness to engage by accepting an alternative proposal the Ombudsman had put forward.[7]

An institution should always take into account developments that have taken place between the moment when the facts giving rise to the complaint occurred and

[3] Further information on this area of the EO's work is available at: www.ombudsman.europa.eu/en/areas-of-work/recruitment-issues.

[4] Further information on this area of the EO's work is available at: www.ombudsman.europa.eu/en/areas-of-work/management-of-eu-funds.

[5] See Strategic Initiative SI/10/2016/EA on Transparency of the ECB's Supervisory Review and Evaluation Process, closed on 11 October 2016.

[6] See Strategic Inquiry OI/2/2023/MIK on the risk management of dangerous chemical substances by the European Commission, opened on 8 June 2023.

[7] See Decision on the European Commission's refusal to give full public access to declarations of interests by the members of its Regulatory Scrutiny Board (case 74/2023/MIK), 2 October 2023.

the time when the Ombudsman invites the institution to revisit the matter. That is one of the advantages of turning to the EO – its role involves seeking friendly solutions that can also take account of new circumstances, like the passage of time or developments in the relevant procedure. This is particularly relevant in public access cases when, for example, trade negotiations have ended or all follow up actions on an audit have been finalised.

While most EO cases gravitate around principles of good administration, at times the EO finds that an institution has not acted in compliance with the law. In one case,[8] in which the EO found that the position the European Personnel Selection Office (EPSO) took was 'wrong in law', she asked it to reconsider the complainant's administrative complaint, taking into account recent EU case law regarding the matter.[9] In its first reply to the Ombudsman, EPSO opted not to do so, stating that it derives from the principle of legal certainty that EPSO cannot revise its own decision on the complainant's administrative complaint, and that only the Court of Justice has the power to annul such a decision. The EO drew attention to the fact that, in principle, any EU authority can itself withdraw unlawful decisions. If the Court alone had the competence to verify that an administrative decision is legally sound and its content complies with the law, the Ombudsman would be deprived of its role as an alternative redress mechanism in such complaints. In its second reply, EPSO explained that its initial reply reflected an interpretation based on the specific factual context of the case and apologised for having given the impression of calling into question the Ombudsman's role as an alternative redress mechanism for individuals impacted by a decision on an administrative complaint. It agreed with the Ombudsman that while decisions of EU authorities, including replies to administrative complaints, may be annulled only by the EU Courts, this does not mean that the EU authority that issued the decision cannot itself withdraw a decision that is unlawful.[10] In a number of public access cases concerning the Council,[11] the Ombudsman inquiry team was informed that 'the confirmatory decision has not been challenged before the EU Courts', seemingly implying 'nothing for the Ombudsman to see here'. The EO would tend to disagree.

While Ombudsman procedures are inspired by court procedures, the EO should not simply emulate them, as its proceedings are meant to be less burdensome. Unlike court procedures, which are meticulously regulated, the EO's work is governed by a concise Statute and Implementing Provisions. The legislators have wisely kept the new Statute (revised in June 2021) to a minimum in terms of regulatory detail,

[8] See Recommendation on how the European Personnel Selection Office (EPSO) dealt with a complaint concerning a selection procedure for recruiting staff in the field of financial rules applicable to the EU budget (case 1656/2021/FA), 30 June 2023.

[9] See Cases T-554/19 *Spain v Commission* ECLI:EU:T:2021:554, [2021] and T-202/17 *Ana Calhau Correia de Paiva v Commission* ECLI:EU:T:2021:323, [2021].

[10] See Decision on how the European Personnel Selection Office (EPSO) dealt with a complaint concerning a selection procedure for recruiting staff in the field of financial rules applicable to the EU budget (case 1656/2021/FA), 28 February 2024, para 19.

[11] See Decision on the Council of the European Union's refusal to give full public access to documents related to negotiations on the draft 'Digital Markets Act' (case 1499/2021/SF), 27 June 2022, and Decision on the Council of the EU's refusal to give public access to documents concerning the ongoing negotiations on the taxation of digital services (case 1703/2021/AMF), 30 May 2022.

thus acknowledging the effectiveness of the EO's current working methodologies and safeguarding the procedural agility and flexibility that is the hallmark of the institution.

While, ultimately, disagreements may arise, institutions should as a matter of principle be ready to adhere to the EO's views and recommendations, in order to enable the EO to exercise its role effectively. They sometimes do not.[12] Although the institutions themselves often point to the EO as a remedy instance for citizens, for instance in staff cases or public access decisions, they may then go on to adopt a defensive attitude towards the EO. One must ask what signal this sends to citizens? Complainants are entitled to entertain reasonable confidence in the EU institutions' readiness to modify their position, in response to an Ombudsman finding. Otherwise, what would motivate them to expend time and energy complaining?

III. THE EO'S EVER-EXPANDING ROLE: HOW TO DEAL WITH THE CHALLENGES IT POSES?

Each successive European Ombudsman has faced their own challenges. The first Ombudsman, Jacob Söderman, who took office in 1995, was tasked with establishing the institution as a relevant and respected player among the other more settled EU bodies. He found a prominent role for the Office in handling complaints in the areas of public access, infringements, grants and contracts. He conceived of and set up what became known as the European Network of Ombudsmen; devised and promulgated the European Code of Good Administrative Behaviour and tackled discriminatory staff selection practices on grounds of age and gender.

One of the first challenges for P. Nikiforos Diamandouros was to ready the Office for the biggest enlargement of the EU when 10 new Member States joined in 2004. This saw an additional nine languages in which to handle a steep rise in complaints. The Office produced 'Public Service Principles' to help guide the EU civil service,[13] conducted major inquiries in areas as diverse as competition law[14] and clinical trial transparency,[15] and saw its first efforts to hold Frontex to account.[16] The second Ombudsman also placed a particular focus on assessing compliance with Ombudsman

[12] See Recommendation on issues related to how the European Border and Coast Guard Agency (Frontex) communicates with citizens in relation to its access to documents portal (Joined Cases 1261/2020/PB and 1361/2020/PB), 21 June 2022.

[13] European Ombudsman, 'Public service principles for the EU civil service', 19 June 2012, www.ombudsman.europa.eu/en/publication/en/11650.

[14] See Decision of the European Ombudsman closing his inquiry into complaint 1935/2008/FOR against the European Commission, 14 July 2009. This case concerned alleged procedural errors by the Commission during an anti-trust investigation of Intel.

[15] See Decision of the European Ombudsman closing his inquiry into complaint 2560/2007/BEH against the European Medicines Agency, 24 November 2010. This case concerned public access to clinical study reports and corresponding trial protocols for two anti-obesity drugs.

[16] See Decision of the European Ombudsman closing own-initiative inquiry OI/5/2012/BEH-MHZ concerning the European Agency for the Management of Operational Cooperation at the External Borders of the Member States of the European Union (Frontex), 12 November 2013. This case covered Frontex's Fundamental Rights Strategy, Codes of Conduct, the Fundamental Rights Officer, European Border Guard Teams, and Coordinating Officer, and the termination of joint operations and pilot projects.

proposals, recommendations and suggestions. An annual report addressing this essential metric[17] was produced, emphasising the point made above about showcasing the extent to which institutions are ready to accept the EO's findings.

Emily O'Reilly sought, from taking Office in 2013, to make the Ombudsman even more relevant, visible, impactful and efficient. Key to this was identifying and addressing systemic issues in the functioning of institutions, so that as many citizens as possible can benefit from the EO's work. The efforts to raise awareness about the EO's role has led to matters of significant public interest being raised in an increasing number of complaints, with this Ombudsman conducting inquiries in areas ranging from conflicts of interest[18] to the transparency of trade deals between the EU and other countries.[19]

In the pursuit of a transparent and accountable administration, the EO's role continues to expand over time, which poses a number of challenges. The EO has a broad mandate that covers instances of maladministration in the activities of Union institutions, but its resources are limited. As stated by the Ombudsman in her strategy 'Towards 2024': 'We are a small Office with a big mandate'.[20] The Treaty of Lisbon and the Charter of Fundamental Rights of the EU made complaining to the EO an individual fundamental right.[21] The character conferred by this development on the relationship between EU citizens and the EO raises a number of questions as regards the latter's discretion in its handling of complaints, not least of which is: how does one reconcile the fundamental right to turn to the EO with the EO's discretion as to whether it is justified to inquire into a complaint? Does such discretion concern solely the merits of the case, or does it extend to include external factors, such as the effective use of the Office's limited resources, or the fact that if there was maladministration, it is likely to be of no systemic relevance? The Office must simultaneously uphold the fundamental right of citizens to turn to the EO, while properly exercising its discretion to decide whether to open an inquiry. These are pivotal considerations for determining how the EO may deal with its broadening role.

Challenges have also arisen from the context in which the EO operates. Take now the European Commission, against which the vast majority of complaints are lodged. As set out by Emily O'Reilly in October 2023: 'In a blink, the European Commission has moved from a simple Commission under José Manuel Barroso, to a "Political Commission" under Jean-Claude Juncker and is now a self-styled "Geopolitical Commission" under President von der Leyen.'[22] The challenge for the EO is

[17] The first such report was produced in 2008. European Ombudsman, 'Study of follow-up given by institutions to critical remarks and further remarks made by the Ombudsman in 2006', 22 May 2008, https://www.ombudsman.europa.eu/en/doc/follow-up/en/3820.

[18] Further information about this area of work is available at: www.ombudsman.europa.eu/en/areas-of-work/ethical-issues.

[19] See Strategic inquiry OI/10/2014/RA on transparency and public participation in relation to the Transatlantic Trade and Investment Partnership ('TTIP') negotiations, closed on 6 January 2015.

[20] European Ombudsman, 'European Ombudsman strategy: "Towards 2024" – Sustaining Impact', 7 December 2020, www.ombudsman.europa.eu/en/strategy/our-strategy/en.

[21] See Art 43 of the Charter of Fundamental Rights of the EU.

[22] Emily O'Reilly, 'Global Ireland Summit – Key note speech on the Future of Europe', 24 October 2023, www.ombudsman.europa.eu/en/speech/en/176879.

'in decoupling and disentangling the "politics" – which is none of our business – from the "administration" which is, and which encompasses the fundamental values that should guide good government – trust, transparency and fundamental rights'.[23]

How the EU administration functions as it tackles issues of defence,[24] digitalisation and AI,[25] climate[26] and migration[27] will very much determine the types of complaints the EO receives. The EO has already had to tackle the challenges the Commission is facing to remain accountable in a timely manner as it takes on more and more tasks. This can be seen in the Special Report issued in September 2023 on the time taken by the Commission in dealing with requests for public access to documents.[28]

As the EU looks to enlarge and to reform, the EO's role to investigate instances of 'maladministration in the activities of the Union institutions, bodies, offices or agencies' will evolve accordingly. In a first instance, during the reform process itself: the extent to which citizens will be involved, and how, will be of immediate concern to the citizen's Ombudsman. How will the EO itself be affected as the EU looks again at its institutional architecture? There is no room for complacency.

IV. CONCLUSION

The EO fulfils its role of promoting good administration and safeguarding the rights of EU citizens by providing assistance to individual complainants and ensuring the proper functioning of the EU administration. Its ability to achieve these goals is dependent on the acceptance of EU institutions of its findings, as it lacks binding powers. It is therefore crucial that institutions become familiar with the role of the EO and engage with it accordingly.

Similarly, to perform effectively the EO must be vigilant about the environment in which it operates, standing ready to deal with matters of significant public interest that are brought before it, while never neglecting the individual complainants who exercise their fundamental right to complain.

[23] Emily O'Reilly, 'Speech at the University of Warsaw – The European Ombudsman in a geopolitical age: protecting fundamental rights and accountability', 27 September 2023, www.ombudsman.europa.eu/en/speech/en/175670.

[24] See Strategic inquiry OI/5/2023/KR on how the European Commission ensures that there are no conflicts of interest with external experts who assist it in evaluating projects under the European Defence Fund, opened on 10 November 2023.

[25] See Letter from the European Ombudsman to the European Commission on artificial intelligence and the EU administration, SI/3/2021/VS, 18 June 2021, www.ombudsman.europa.eu/en/doc/correspondence/en/144218. See also Strategic Initiative SI/4/2024/MIK on how the European Commission decides on and uses artificial intelligence, opened on 15 March 2024.

[26] See Decision on the European Commission's refusal to give public access to documents concerning the energy consumption and greenhouse gas emissions of the ceramics industry reported under the EU's emissions trading system (case 2000/2022/PVV), 19 December 2023.

[27] See Case 1418/2023/VS on how the European Commission monitors EU funds granted to Greece in the context of border management operations, opened on 7 November 2023.

[28] Special Report of the European Ombudsman in her strategic inquiry concerning the time the European Commission takes to deal with requests for public access to documents (OI/2/2022/OAM), 20 September 2023.

As the EU looks set to embark on what may prove to be a fundamental rethink of how it functions, the EO should stand ready to contribute, to handle the concerns that citizens raise and to adapt if needed.

Ultimately, the EO's success in fulfilling its aspirations, as envisioned by the Treaties, is contingent upon continued reflection, adaptation and constructive engagement with EU institutions and citizens alike.

Part II

The European Ombudsman's Role in Fostering Institutional Legitimacy

6

When the Doors of EU Administration Revolve: The European Ombudsman's Legacy and Future Action

EMILIA KORKEA-AHO

I. INTRODUCTION

THE MOVEMENT OF individuals between public and private positions has gained increasing attention in recent years, leading to calls for greater transparency and accountability. The European Ombudsman (EO), especially under the leadership of Emily O'Reilly, has been a vocal and focused advocate for measures addressing the revolving door phenomenon, to the extent that revolving doors has been described as her 'signature issue'.[1] The EO has conducted several inquiries into cases that raise concerns, made recommendations, and voiced support for the implementation of 'cooling-off periods'. These periods require departing officials to wait for a specified amount of time before taking up a new position.[2] In the Ombudsman's view, EU institutions do not take the issue seriously enough and should step up their efforts in actively reviewing and, if necessary, restricting, certain activities that give rise to concern.

People change jobs, and in most cases, this is business as usual. However, if a high-ranking public official or a government employee moves from a position in the public sector (government or regulatory agencies) to the private sector (corporations or industries regulated by government), the movement is referred to as 'revolving doors'.[3] The revolving doors phenomenon is often used to describe situations where a government employee leaves for a job in a company or an industry association (exit), but it also involves corporate executives accepting jobs in

[1] Politico EU, 2 March 2023, www.politico.eu/newsletter/politico-eu-influence/ukraines-russian-doll-lobbying-cancer-spat-spreads-qatar-flight-mode-2/.

[2] I discuss these cases in Section II.

[3] OECD, *Post-Public Employment: Good Practices for Preventing Conflict of Interest* (Paris, OECD Publishing, 2010) https://doi.org/10.1787/9789264056701-en.

government (entry).[4] The clear majority of the Ombudsman's 'case law' relates to exit situations, which is also the focus of this chapter.

While the revolving doors mobility may be a good thing both for an organisation and an individual,[5] it is not without risks. Scholars have voiced concerns that inside knowledge and personal connections within government can be exploited by individuals who take up positions as in-house staff for corporations, or as staff for hire within commercial lobbying firms.[6] Those who can afford to hire individuals with prior government experience will gain an unfair representational advantage, hurting the public interest idea of 'un-biased' political competition and raising concerns about undue influence. Revolving doors can also conflict with the legitimate interests of public administration if, for example, the departure of an official leads to confidential information being unduly disclosed or misused or a former staff member uses their friendships with ex-colleagues to lobby.[7]

Laws and regulations are designed to limit the damage of this practice. General rules exist on conflicts of interests and interest representation activities (lobbying), but also more targeted measures such as the adoption of 'notification' and 'cooling-off' periods. Departing officials need to notify their employer of their plans of change of employment while cooling-off periods require policymakers to move to corporate and consulting jobs only after a specified period of time (eg, one year) has passed since leaving their public position. The cooling-off period can be compensated by transitional allowances.

In the EU, most revolving door moves are regulated under Staff Regulations, which involve provisions on targeted measures such as notification and cooling-off periods in Article 16.[8] Former staff must, even after their employment, behave with integrity and discretion. All staff members must inform the institution of their intention to engage in an occupational activity. This notification period extends to two years after leaving the service. If the authority considers that there is a risk of a conflict of interest, it may forbid the staff member from accepting the job or give approval only subject to conditions such as bans on contacting former colleagues for lobbying purposes.[9] The authority must also impose a 12-month lobbying ban

[4] An example of a study that looks at both exit and entry situations through a 'bidirectional' approach, see A Chalmers, R Klingler-Vidra, A Puglisi and L Remke, 'In and Out of Revolving Doors in European Union Financial Regulatory Authorities' (2021) *Regulation & Governance* 1233.

[5] In the UK, Office for National Statistics (ONS) data shows workers who change jobs within a year of beginning a role have consistently higher hourly wage growth over those who stay, www.ons.gov.uk/employmentandlabourmarket/peopleinwork/earningsandworkinghours/articles/jobchangersandstayersunderstandingearningsukapril2012toapril2021/april2012toapril2021.

[6] DA Halpin and A Lotric, 'The Place of Political Experience in Lobbyist Careers: Decisive, Divergent or Diverse?' (2024) 63(1) *European Journal of Political Research* 192–213; J Broulík, 'Cultural Capture of Competition Policy: Exploring the Risk in the US and the EU' (2022) 45(2) *World Competition* 159–94; D Orchard, A Gouglas and H Pickering, 'Life after Whitehall: The Career Moves of British Special Advisers' (2023) *The British Journal of Politics and International Relations* 1–21.

[7] Keynote at PETI Workshop on Conflicts of Interest Achievements and Challenges for EU Institutions, 2 April 2019, www.ombudsman.europa.eu/en/speech/en/112005.

[8] Regulation No 31 (EEC), 11 (EAEC), laying down the Staff Regulations of Officials and the Conditions of Employment of Other Servants of the European Economic Community and the European Atomic Energy Community.

[9] According to Art 1(a)–(b), Staff Regulations apply to officials of the institutions, EU agencies, and a few other institutions including the EO and the European Data Protection Supervisor.

on its former senior officials in matters for which they were responsible during their last three years in the service.[10] There are distinct rules for EU Commissioners,[11] and since 2023, also for Members of the European Parliament (MEPs).[12]

In this chapter, I argue that the revolving doors phenomenon is complex, and its regulation needs to consider several aspects that are not always readily combined. The revolving doors mobility can create conflicts of interests and incur reputational damage, which speaks for efforts in actively reviewing and, if necessary, forbidding, certain moves. Yet, as the Ombudsman has emphasised, government employees, like others, have a constitutionally guaranteed right to work, and any restrictions should be evaluated against this right.[13] Besides the employee's (legal) rights, the pragmatic needs of the employer must also be considered. The lack of expertise in particular domains within the public sector has also emerged as a reason to insist on the positive impact of the revolving doors.[14] As employers, EU institutions defend revolving door moves arguing that 'revolvers' usefully transfer knowledge and expertise over siloed organisations. For instance, the European Central Bank (ECB) defended the authorisation granted to a staff member to take up employment with a private sector bank while on unpaid leave. It noted that its 'staff can develop their skillset by taking up positions outside the ECB' and that 'the experience that the staff member would gain while in the job would be of relevance to the ECB'.[15] The inference is that letting revolvers move benefits the society at large.

To address the revolving doors and its many often conflicting facets, I argue in this chapter that the EO has adopted three roles: umpire, institutional designer and trendsetter. I will first give an overview of EO's revolving doors 'case law' followed by a characterisation and discussion of the Ombudsman's three roles using concrete examples where the EO has assessed specific instances of revolving door moves. By looking at the EO's case law we can deepen our understanding

[10] ibid, Art 16.

[11] Code of Conduct provides for a two-year cooling-off period (three years for the former Commission President). Former Commissioners are obliged to notify the professional activities in which they intend to engage during this period. If the intended activity is linked to the Commissioner's former portfolio, the Commission can only give its approval after having consulted the Independent Ethical Committee. There is furthermore a two-year lobbying ban, which extends to three years for the Commission president, see Commission Decision of 31 January 2018 on a Code of Conduct for the Members of the European Commission. C/2018/0700. OJ C 65, 21.2.2018, 7–20.

[12] The EP bureau decided on a six-month cooling-off period following the end of MEP's mandate. During this period, former Members shall not engage in lobbying or representational activities with the EP. After this period, if former Members decide to engage in lobbying or representational activities with the EP, they will have to register in the Transparency Register and they will not be entitled to the access rights and facilities provided to them as former member, see Art 9 of Code of Conduct for Members of the European Parliament regarding Integrity and Transparency, www.europarl.europa.eu/pdf/meps/Code_Of_Conduct_20231101_EN.pdf.

[13] See n 7.

[14] S Yates and E Cardin-Trudeau, 'Lobbying "from Within": A New Perspective on the Revolving Door and Regulatory Capture' (2021) 64 *Canadian Public Administration* 301–19, 313.

[15] Decision on how the European Central Bank (ECB) deals with 'revolving door' cases (OI/1/2022/KR), www.ombudsman.europa.eu/en/decision/en/162341, paras 27 and 28. While the expertise that an ECB official gains from the private sector during unpaid leave may be valuable, it is contingent on the official returning to the ECB after the unpaid leave period concludes.

of the functioning and rationale of revolving doors regulation. Unlike lobbying transparency, the desirability of (stringent) revolving doors rules divide opinions,[16] rendering the EO's recommendations particularly helpful. Finally, I will offer some concluding remarks.

II. THE EO'S REVOLVING DOOR 'CASE LAW'

Below I describe the engagement of the EO with revolving doors and explain how the EO's approach evolved and intensified particularly during O'Reilly's two consecutive mandates. This will be illustrated by examples of specific actions taken by the Office. I have attempted to include all decisions addressing revolving doors irrespective of whether they have been given to complaints or undertaken as own-initiative inquiries.[17] This section thus shows how the EO's approach to revolving doors has evolved over time.

A. Early Engagements

The earliest mention on the EO's website of 'revolving doors' is from 2007. Greenpeace had published a study of chemicals lobbying,[18] referring to 'revolving doors' between the Commission and the chemical industry. The report defined this term as the tactic under which Commission officials and industry lobbyists were 'trading working places among themselves'. The study led to a heated exchange between the Commission and Greenpeace, the latter alleging that the Commission had made inaccurate, misleading and defamatory accusations in relation to the study issued. The Ombudsman at the time, P Nikiforos Diamandouros, concluded that the allegation had not been substantiated, but emphasised the importance of transparency in relation to lobbying activities exercised during the legislative procedure.[19]

A few years later, in a speech given on the occasion of the 'International Right to Know Day', on 28 September 2010, the EO Diamandouros mentions in passing the revolving doors of the Commission and the European Parliament as a concern.[20] The first complaint concerning specifically revolving doors was lodged with the EO in 2011. A German NGO alleged that the European Food Safety Agency (EFSA) had

[16] See n 6 (Orchard, Gouglas and Pickering).

[17] The search for references to revolving doors was conducted using the search function on the EO's website in November 2022 and updated to add more recent cases in September 2024.

[18] Toxic lobby, how the chemicals industry is trying to kill REACH, www.indymedia.be/files/toxic%20lobby.pdf.

[19] Decision of the European Ombudsman on complaint 2740/2006/TN against the European Commission, www.ombudsman.europa.eu/en/decision/en/3222. The EO noted that, viewed in the context in which it was used in the report, the term 'revolving doors' could reasonably be considered as questioning the integrity of Commission officials, justifying the Commission's strong reaction.

[20] European citizens' right to know – complaints about lack of transparency, 28 September 2010, www.ombudsman.europa.eu/en/speech/en/5314.

failed to address a conflict of interest arising from the move of an EFSA Head of Unit to a biotechnology company.[21] In a detailed examination, the EO concluded that EFSA had failed to ensure that its staff members are aware of their obligations to notify EFSA when moving to new jobs. Due to EFSA's poor record keeping, the details of the case remained unclear, but the staff member had allegedly notified EFSA of her new occupation four days after starting in a new job. Besides finding that EFSA had breached relevant procedural rules, the EO concluded that EFSA had not assessed a possible a conflict of interest, amounting to a substantive oversight. The EO noted how EFSA, according to its website, is 'committed to ensuring that Europe's food is safe', but that this mission is endangered due to EFSA 'tolerating' conflicts of interest. The EO concluded that 'EFSA did not carry out as thorough an assessment of the alleged potential conflict of interest of its former staff member as it could and ought to have carried out. This constituted maladministration'.[22] EFSA did not readily accepted the findings and defended many of its problems referring to this case being its first revolving door case. The EO regretted to observe how EFSA refused to accept that 'it had made a mistake',[23] or engage in sincere dialogue about steps to take in order to prevent similar incidents in the future. In the subsequent stages, the EO affirmed its findings and suggested detailed amendments to EFSA's rules.

Emily O'Reilly was appointed as EO in 2013, which also marked the year when the EO's office opened its first inquiry into how the Commission implements its rules concerning conflicts of interest in revolving doors cases.[24] The inquiry, prompted by complaints that Corporate Europe Observatory, Greenpeace, LobbyControl and Spinwatch submitted to the EO in 2012 and 2013, did not focus on any particular revolving door moves, but was based on a systematic review of the Commission files.[25] In the EO's conclusion, Article 16 of the EU Staff Regulations provides a strong legal basis for managing revolving doors, but the challenge – then and now – lies in making the most of the rules. The EO found weaknesses in how decisions, especially positive ones where the Commission approved a new job, were reasoned and documented. In particular, the EO recommended that decisions concerning senior officials' new occupations should be published online.[26] This recommendation was implemented by the Commission, which has since 2015 published summary information on decisions, but the frequency and specificity of information has remained a point of contestation between the EO and the Commission.

[21] Decision of the European Ombudsman closing his inquiry into complaint 775/2010/ANA against the European Food Safety Authority (EFSA), www.ombudsman.europa.eu/en/decision/en/50246.

[22] ibid, para 66.

[23] ibid, para 67.

[24] Note though that this inquiry was opened by her predecessor.

[25] Decision closing the inquiry based on complaints 2077/2012/TN and 1853/2013/TN concerning the European Commission's handling of the 'revolving doors' phenomenon, www.ombudsman.europa.eu/en/decision/en/71136.

[26] ibid, para 15(k).

B. Controversial Cases of Petite and Barroso

During her first mandate (2013/2014–19), Emily O'Reilly dealt with two high-profile revolving door cases. Michel Petite, a former Director-General of the Commission Legal Service, had been re-appointed by the Commission to its ad hoc ethical committee (which assesses the revolving door moves of former Commissioners) in December 2012. LobbyControl, Corporate Accountability International and Corporate Europe Observatory lodged a complaint with the EO about Petite's reappointment, drawing attention to the fact he had moved from the Commission to a law firm Clifford Chance in 2008.[27] The EO found that the Commission's reappointment of Petite as a chair created a situation where he would, in effect, be adjudicating on the future employment prospects of Commissioners who, on the basis of their current positions, had huge influence on matters of great consequence for his private clients. Since Petite had stepped down prior to the completion of the inquiry, the EO did not make recommendations to the Commission.[28]

Another case that generated a significant public concern related to former Commission President Barroso's appointment to Goldman Sachs within weeks after the then 18 months cooling-off period.[29] The Commission had consulted the ethics committee, which concluded that there were not sufficient grounds to establish a violation of the former Commission President's legal obligations under the treaties. The EO found that the Commission should have taken a formal reasoned decision, and its failure to do so constituted maladministration. This case had wider repercussions, because following the EO's decision, the Commission in 2018 updated the Code of Conduct for former Commissioners, extending, as suggested by the EO, the cooling-off period for former members to two years and three years for presidents. The EO also made several suggestions for improvement concerning the ethics committee – some of which (for example the committee's authority to act on its own initiative) remain unimplemented even today.[30]

C. Extending the Gaze Beyond the Commission

In 2017, the EO opened a follow-up inquiry.[31] This inquiry, like the 2012 inquiry, did not concern any specific revolving door move, but rather focused on the systemic

[27] N Nielsen, 'Tobacco Lawyer Steps Down from EU Ethics Panel', https://euobserver.com/eu-political/122580.

[28] Decision of the European Ombudsman closing her inquiry into complaint 297/2013/(RA)FOR against the European Commission, www.ombudsman.europa.eu/en/decision/en/52934.

[29] Q Aries, 'José Manuel Barroso's New Job at Goldman Sachs Angers EU', www.politico.eu/article/jose-manuel-barrosos-new-job-at-goldman-sachs-angers-eu/.; Decision of the European Ombudsman in the joint inquiry into complaints 194/2017/EA, 334/2017/EA, and 543/2017/EA on the European Commission's handling of post-mandate employment of former Commissioners, a former Commission President and the role of its 'Ethics Committee', www.ombudsman.europa.eu/en/decision/en/99946.

[30] See Commission Decision in n 11. The EO expressed her dislike for the term 'cooling-off period' and suggested the use of the term 'notification period', see n 29, para 15.

[31] Decision of the European Ombudsman in her strategic inquiry OI/3/2017/NF on how the European Commission manages 'revolving doors' situations of its staff members, www.ombudsman.europa.eu/en/decision/en/110608.

issues identified in the previous inquiry, excluding, however, issues arising from occupational activities taken up by former Commissioners and focusing solely on the members of the Commission staff.

The EO's analysis found that the Commission's management of revolving door situations fell short in two main respects. First, it was not publishing details about the instances of senior staff moving to another job in all cases (but only for those where it identified a potential for lobbying), and the information was only published once a year. The EO reiterated her past recommendation that the Commission should publish information on individual cases regularly. Second, she also recommended that if the Commission imposes conditions on a former staff member, then the person concerned should inform their future employer. A further proposal was that former senior staff's moves to the private sector be published directly on the Transparency Register.[32] These inquiry recommendations were early signs of her attempt to conceptualise the revolving doors as an issue extending to private sector employers.

Much of the EO's work had up until this point dealt with the Commission. This is logical because the Commission annually makes around 2 000 conflict of interest checks for incoming staff members, and around 400 checks for staff members who intend to take up employment outside the EU administration.[33] Furthermore, it was former Commissioners' revolving door moves that had raised significant concerns and generated complaints to the EO.

In 2017, the EO, however, extended her gaze beyond the Commission and organised a mapping exercise, approaching 15 institutions and agencies to ask them how they implement EU rules on revolving doors, as laid out in Article 16 of the Staff Regulations.[34] The replies depicted a picture of fragmentation, with some organisations having in place an extensive system for monitoring revolving doors, while others paid little to no attention to the matter.[35] The EO does not discuss the reasons for fragmentation, but her recommendations for institutions and agencies to adopt implementing measures that define 'senior staff', 'a fully effective lobbying and advocacy ban' and 'a procedure for notifying colleagues that a senior staff member has been placed under a lobbying and advocacy ban' implies that she is concerned about the lack of implementing measures. The effectiveness of the Article 16 procedure is diminished if institutions and agencies do not actively implement it. This involves ensuring that departing officials notify the appointing authority and monitoring their compliance with the imposed restrictions and conditions. In her conclusions, the EO finally recommends the publication of all revolving door cases and suggests that when the former staff member is moving

[32] ibid. The EO also suggested that when a former senior staff member is placed under a temporary lobbying ban, the Commission should inform that person's former colleagues within the institutions.

[33] Figures are from the decision in n 31.

[34] These were: EBA, Foreign High Representative, Data Protection Supervisor, EFSA, ECHA, Secretary-General of the Commission, CJEU, ECA, Aviation Safety Agency, EESC, EIOPA, Committee of Regions, EMA, ESMA and EP. The EO's inquiry does not elaborate on the selection of these.

[35] An overview of EU institutions' practices based on their replies to this strategic initiative and publicly available information can be found as an annex to the EO's report, www.ombudsman.europa.eu/en/doc/inspection-report/en/110521.

to an organisation on the Transparency Register for lobbyists, the information published on their case should include a link to the organisation's entry on the Transparency Register.[36]

In 2019, the EO returned to the Commission. This case concerned the Commission's refusal to grant public access to names contained in documents related to a corporate event attended by Commission officials and by a former Commission head of unit.[37] The complainant, a journalist, wished to get access to the information in the documents to investigate whether the former Commission head of unit, who had left the EU civil service to take up a position in a multinational company, had acted in accordance with his legal obligations not to lobby former colleagues. Despite the EO's recommendation to disclose the required documents, the Commission refused to disclose them, arguing that the complainant had provided only abstract and general references to possible wrongdoings by a former staff member and that such concerns could not justify disclosing the personal data to him. The EO found maladministration, noting that the Commission's lack of full public disclosure is not helpful in terms of public confidence in the management of revolving door situations.[38]

D. EU Agencies and Bodies under Scrutiny

While the first revolving doors complaint lodged with the EO concerned the European Food Safety Agency in 2011, much of the early 2010s revolving doors 'case law' focused on the Commission.

From the mid-2010s onwards, the EO began receiving more complaints concerning EU agencies and bodies. One of them related to the decision of the European Banking Authority (EBA) to allow its Executive Director to take up a position as CEO of a lobby group.[39] The EO found two instances of maladministration, concluding that EBA should have forbidden the move and withdrawn immediately its Executive Director's access to confidential information. She also made recommendations to avoid similar issues arising in future. Besides putting in place internal procedures, providing guidance to staff, and defining criteria for evaluating revolving door moves, the EBA should, where necessary, invoke the option of forbidding its senior staff from taking up certain positions after their term-of-office.[40] This is the first case where the EO discussed the balance between the need to protect the right to work and

[36] Report of the European Ombudsman on the publication of information on former senior staff so as to enforce the one-year lobbying and advocacy ban: SI/2/2017/NF, www.ombudsman.europa.eu/en/doc/inspection-report/en/110521.

[37] Decision in case 1794/2019/OAM on the European Commission's refusal to provide full access to documents relating to an event attended by Commission officials and by a former Commission head of unit, www.ombudsman.europa.eu/en/decision/en/136065.

[38] ibid.

[39] Decision in case 2168/2019/KR on the European Banking Authority's decision to approve the request from its Executive Director to become CEO of a financial lobby group, www.ombudsman.europa.eu/en/decision/en/135141.

[40] ibid.

the need to restrict that right to avoid conflicts of interest, or the perception thereof, emphasising the importance of careful scrutiny.[41]

The second case, which was an own-initiative inquiry, concerned the European Defence Agency (EDA).[42] In this case, like in the EBA case above, the EO held that EDA should have forbidden its former Chief Executive from becoming a strategic advisor at Airbus. While the EO's inquiry on the implementation of Article 16 demonstrated that many agencies had deficiencies in adopting implementing rules, the EDA case, decided five years later, brought to light how timidly EU agencies monitor revolving door conditions.[43] In its reply to the Ombudsman's question on how the EDA monitors and enforces the restrictions it imposed on the former Chief, the EDA said that it 'has neither the resources nor the competence to perform a systematic monitoring of post-employment conditions, beyond raising awareness and ensuring transparency on the conditions set'.[44] The EO reminded the EDA that the necessary prerequisite for authorising its staff's post-employment activity is the ability of the institution to impose credible conditions that effectively mitigate the risk of conflicts of interest.[45]

Apart from EBA and EDA, the European Investment Bank (EIB) and the ECB have also been scrutinised by the EO. In the former case, the EIB approved the request by its former Vice-President and Management Committee member to take up a post at Spanish company Iberdrola that had received loans from the EIB.[46] The EIB argued that the former Vice-President had not been involved in the negotiation and implementation of the financing agreements between the EIB and the company. What was unexpected in the case was that the complainants were two Members of the European Parliament. While the EO reprimanded the EIB for not properly managing the risk of conflicts of interest in the case at hand, it did not pursue the matter further given that the EIB had made improvements to its ethics rules.[47]

In the latter case into the ECB, the Ombudsman's inquiry assessed one specific case and reviewed 26 cases of requests by staff members to take up occupational activities, either while on unpaid leave or after finishing work with the ECB. In all but one of the files reviewed, ECB staff members moved to the private sector, including entities and banks that are under ECB supervision. The Ombudsman concluded that

[41] ibid, para 24.

[42] Decision in case OI/3/2021/KR on how the European Defence Agency handled the applications of its former chief executive to take on senior positions at Airbus, www.ombudsman.europa.eu/fi/decision/en/151826.

[43] In the 2022 report, the European Court of Auditors concluded that EU agencies should tighten their rules and controls to minimise the risk that managers and other senior staff who leave may take up private sector jobs that could put the integrity of the EU institutions at risk, www.eca.europa.eu/Lists/ECADocuments/AGENCIES_2021/AGENCIES_2021_EN.pdf.

[44] Recommendation on how the European Defence Agency handled the applications of its former Chief Executive to take on senior positions at Airbus (OI/3/2021/KR), www.ombudsman.europa.eu/en/recommendation/en/144268.

[45] ibid, para 30.

[46] Decision on how the European Investment Bank (EIB) handled the move of a former Vice-President to an energy utility company that had received EIB loans (1016/2021/KR), www.ombudsman.europa.eu/en/decision/en/158894.

[47] ibid.

the ECB should apply a more robust approach in relation to revolving door moves of its middle ranking and senior staff to private sector jobs.[48] Taking note of the ongoing revision of the ECB's Ethics Framework, the EO recommended enhancing the notification and cooling-off periods, lengthening the period during which lobbying is prohibited, and improving the monitoring of compliance. As in the agency cases, the EO emphasised that if risks cannot be mitigated or conditions monitored, the job move should not be authorised.[49]

In 2023, the EO found maladministration in how the EIB handled the move of one of its vice-presidents to become CEO of a 'national promotional bank' in Italy.[50] The former vice-president had participated in approving financing agreements between the EIB and the national promotional bank in the weeks before his appointment as its CEO despite advice from the EIB's chief compliance officer to avoid any business with the national promotional bank while his appointment procedure was underway.[51] The Ombudsman asked the EIB to strengthen the role of its ethics and compliance committee by giving its authority to impose measures to mitigate any potential conflicts of interest risks it identifies. The EIB should also make the committee's decisions on mitigation measures public shortly after their adoption.

E. Final Pushes?

In 2021, the Ombudsman completed a full circle and returned to the Commission by launching an own-initiative inquiry into how the Commission handles revolving doors cases among its staff. In the most extensive inspection to date, the Ombudsman investigated 100 personnel files related to decisions by the Commission on requests by senior and mid-level managers for approval of either new employment or unpaid leave in order to undertake another activity. The files covered a total of 14 Directorate-Generals in addition to all Commissioners' cabinets, the Commission's Legal Service, Secretariat-General, internal think tank and the Regulatory Scrutiny Board.[52] In its findings, the EO noted that the Commission risks undermining the integrity of EU administration without a more robust approach to the movement of staff to the private sector. Out of the 100 inspected decisions, the Commission had prohibited activities in only two cases, whereas, in the EO's assessment, more job moves should have been prohibited. While the EO acknowledged that the Commission had made improvements since the last Ombudsman inquiry, it still needs to do more. Specifically, the EO recommended that the Commission should forbid jobs temporarily if they pose risks that cannot be offset by restrictions or if restrictions cannot be credibly monitored and enforced, emphasising the Commission's consistent underperformance

[48] See Decision in n 15.

[49] ibid.

[50] Decision on how the European Investment Bank (EIB) Group handled the move of a former vice-president to become the CEO of a 'national promotional bank' (case 611/2022/KR).

[51] National promotional banks are financial intermediaries between the EIB and small-scale projects that benefit from EIB investments.

[52] Decision on how the European Commission manages 'revolving door' moves of its staff members (OI/1/2021/KR), www.ombudsman.europa.eu/fi/case/en/58428.

in this regard. Returning to previous inquiry recommendations, the EO once again urged the Commission to publish decisions on staff members' new jobs faster and more extensively. The EO's final recommendation concerned the role of the private sector, as the EO suggested that the Commission should make its approval of a new job conditional on the staff member obtaining a commitment from the new employer to publish any restrictions on its website. At a minimum, the Commission should require the (former) staff member to submit evidence that the imposed restrictions were shared with the new employer.[53]

The circle would not be complete without a look at the Commission's highest echelons, its Members. Following reports that the European Anti-Fraud Office (OLAF) had closed an investigation into a potential breach of ethics rules by a former commissioner Neelie Kroes in relation to post-mandate activities with transport platform Uber, the Ombudsman asked in January 2024 the Commission to clarify whether it has made any improvements to the Code of Conduct in light of the affair, once again raising the issue to the public debate.[54]

As the time of writing (September 2024), two investigations are ongoing, in addition to the pending review of the Commission's Members. First, the EO initiated an inquiry following a CSO complaint to investigate how Europol handled post-service activity requests from two former staff members. These individuals allegedly worked on matters related to preventing and combatting child sexual abuse online while at Europol, and their new roles appear to be connected to the same issue.[55] Former Europol officers moved to a U.S.-based non-profit,[56] which raises new public interest considerations. Is a move to a non-profit more legitimate than a move to profit-making entity? The second investigation is on familiar grounds, involving a former director from the Commission's competition department, who transitioned to a partner position at the Brussels office of a U.S. corporate law firm.[57] The EO seems particularly annoyed about the Commission withholding details about the move, while the law firm announces the new recruitment in its press release.

III. THE EO'S THREE ROLES

O'Reilly's early encounters, largely coinciding with her first mandate, with revolving doors were reactive, dealing with complaints submitted to her. Another feature, to a great extent dictated by the nature of complaints, is that the two defining cases of this early era (Petite and Barroso) concerned Commissioners and the system that the Commission had put in place for its members. The EO did not, however, neglect the mobility of EU staff, and in her first inquiry in 2012, she began drawing

[53] ibid, paras 43 and 44.

[54] Case SI/1/2024/KR, www.ombudsman.europa.eu/en/case/en/65721. The case has not been closed at the time of writing (September 2024). For the regulation of EU Commissioners' revolving doors, see L Avril and E Korkea-aho, 'Administration as usual? Revolving doors and the quiet regulation of political ethics', *Journal of European Public Policy*, https://doi.org/10.1080/13501763.2024.2410922.

[55] Case 2091/2023/AML, https://www.ombudsman.europa.eu/en/case/en/65144.

[56] Thorn is a 501(c)(3) non-profit organisation under the federal law of the United States, according to the Internal Revenue Code, dedicated to combating online child abuse.

[57] Case SI/5/2024KR, https://www.ombudsman.europa.eu/en/opening-summary/en/186549.

the Commission's attention to the importance of implementing Article 16 of Staff Regulations.[58] While her focus was primarily on the Commission, she also underlined that the implementation of Staff Regulations would concern not only EU institutions but also EU agencies, bodies and offices.

She also initiated a long – still ongoing – push to convince the Commission to regularly publish online all relevant information about senior EU officials, including their names, who leave to work outside the EU administration. In an effort to awaken the Commission to the rationale of revolving doors regulation, the Ombudsman noted how private companies would not allow their business secrets to exit with former employees, and it is simply 'sound business sense' for the EU institutions to take all necessary steps to avoid those potential harms.[59]

The EO's second mandate is characterised by themes familiar from her earlier work, but her focus both intensified and expanded. She continued by concentrating on the Commission, but rather than looking at the Commissioner level, she required the Commission to step up its efforts in controlling staff's revolving door moves. Particularly since the 2017 mapping exercise, the EO also paid more attention to other institutions and EU agencies, a development increasingly prompted by complaints from civil society. Another noteworthy feature is that the EO consistently made calls for making the respect for revolving door rules a matter for the private sector too.

When looking at the EO's revolving door 'case law' from a distance, two things stand out. First, the case law is predominantly from O'Reilly's mandate, suggesting that the revolving doors was not seen as a policy problem in the 2000s and early 2010s, something she worked to change. Second, while O'Reilly's case law appears consistent, systematically raising the same issues across complaints and inquiries, the case law on revolving doors reveals that O'Reilly has adopted three roles between which she alternates: umpire, institutional designer and trendsetter.

A. The Role of Umpire

The umpire role is evident in cases initiated by complaints from civil society, journalists or in some cases from parliamentarians. In such cases, the Ombudsman is asked to assess if the authority's decision, usually, to accept the job move has been correct and whether the authority's action or inaction constitute maladministration. While often finding that there has been maladministration, EU institutions and agencies are reluctant to acknowledge the EO's findings of maladministration directed towards them (e.g., EFSA, EDA, Commission (the journalist case), ECB).

The Ombudsman's umpire role lacks the normative bite or 'umph' and is not effective, because the conflicts of interest framework, which the EO's office uses to probe revolving door cases, is unclear.

[58] See n 25.

[59] Speech to the European Parliament Budget Control Committee – Address by the European Ombudsman, 18 March 2014, www.ombudsman.europa.eu/en/speech/en/53848.

The Ombudsman is not obligated to adhere to any specific benchmark, but it seems that conflicts of interest have become a benchmark due to the conceptualisation of revolving door cases in Article 16 of the Staff Regulations.[60] It lays down that if new activity, which an official intends to take up, is related to the work carried out by the official during the last three years of service and could lead to *a conflict with the legitimate interests of the institution*, the appointing authority may, having regard to the interests of the service, either forbid him from undertaking it or give its approval subject to any conditions it thinks fit.[61] Article 11 of the Code of Conduct for Commissioners on revolving door moves does not use the concept of conflict of interest.[62] Instead, it refers to the duty of integrity and discretion, which bounds former Commissioners even after they have left service. It is not conditional on any actual or potential risk of a conflict of interest. The ECB's Ethics Framework includes provision according to which 'members of staff … shall inform the Compliance and Governance Office if the nature of the occupational activity may lead to a conflict of interest with the professional duties of the member of staff'.[63]

If the above provisions specify the conflict of interest specifically in the revolving doors context, we should also inquire about how the conflict of interest is defined more generally, outside the revolving doors context. Interestingly enough, Staff Regulations do not provide a general definition of a conflict of interest. Laying down the rights and obligations of an official, Article 11, however, refers to it. When recruiting an official in the entry or ingoing mobility where staff members are recruited from the private sector, the appointing authority must examine whether the candidate has any personal interest such as to *impair his independence or any other conflict of interest*.[64] Article 2(6) of the Code of Conduct for Members of the Commission, as reformed in 2018, offers another possible way of defining a conflict of interest: 'A conflict of interest arises where a personal interest may influence the independent performance of their [Commissioner] duties'.[65] The ECB describes a conflict of interest as 'a situation where members of staff have personal interests

[60] Art 16 of Staff Regulations (emphasis added).

[61] According to Art 16 case law, the power of the employing institution to prevent a (former) official from exercising a post-service activity within two years of leaving is subject to two conditions, namely that the intended activity: 1) is related in any way to the activity of the official during their last three years of service, and 2) could lead to a conflict with the legitimate interests of the institution, see case F-86/13, *Van de Water v Parliament*, paras 46, 48 and 51. In a subsequent ruling, the Civil Service Tribunal clarified that it is sufficient that the envisaged activity can be perceived as giving rise to a (risk of) conflict of interest, see case T-667/18, *Pinto Teixeira v EEAS*, para 51. For both cases, see E Despotopoulou, 'Those Doors that Keep Revolving: Reflections on a Subject with Hardly any Case Law' (2021) 22 *ERA Forum* 643–53.

[62] See n 11.

[63] Point 0.2.8.1 of the Ethics Framework of the ECB, OJ C 204, 20.6.2015, 3–16.

[64] Art 11 of Staff Regulations (emphasis added). Anyone who applies for a job with the EU institutions has to inform them of any actual or potential conflict of interest. Future staff members do not need to provide a declaration of all of their interests, but only of those that may impair their independence and thus constitute a potential or actual conflict with the interests of the EU institution. Such potentially problematic interests may be financial or family interests, as well as interests related to previous employment. Conflicts of interest of incoming staff members were key to the EO's 2017 inquiry, see n 31.

[65] See n 11.

that may influence or appear to influence the impartial and objective performance of their professional duties'.[66]

The Ombudsman has also defined the conflict of interest. Noting that her definition is not 'exhaustive', she has argued that

> a conflict of interest exists when a person participates in a public authority's decision-making process despite the fact that he or she has a personal interest in the outcome of that process. A conflict of interest thus undermines a civil servant's independence and capacity to act only in the public interest.[67]

The EO's broad definition is similar to the one adopted in the Code of Conduct for Commissioners and the ECB's Ethics Framework, emphasising how the conflict of interest materialises in cases where a staff member's personal preferences influence her or his professional activities. In her investigations, the EO references and applies the applicable institutional definition, if available.

There are three issues with the EU's conflict of interest framework that consequently undermine the EO's umpire role based on them. First, there is no regulation within the EU defining a conflict of interest, leading to varying interpretations by institutions and agencies in the absence of a standardised definition across the board. Second, the relevant rules exhibit asymmetry. While the Staff Regulations generally lack a definition of a conflict of interest, they specify one concerning revolving doors. In contrast, the Code of Conduct for Commissioners take an opposing approach, offering only a general definition of a conflict of interest without applying it to revolving door rules. The ECB's Ethics Framework provide a definition of both.

Third, there is a lack of a common shared understanding of what constitutes a conflict of interest in the context of revolving door mobility. Is it the legitimate interests and reputation of the EU that we should be concerned with? Or is it a potential competitive advantage gained by a firm recruiting revolvers? Or both? What about moves into CSO sector? What other aspects should be included in the risk assessment? For example, recent literature underscores a shift in the Commission's dynamics, with increasing politicisation becoming a prominent factor.[68] Should the Commission's transformation into a more political institution impact the risk assessment and if so, in what way? Additionally, what about EU agencies, which, as noted by the EO herself, often operate in highly technical and specialised areas and rely on expert staff?[69] Are revolving doors riskier in agency environment than for instance within the Commission?

While the EO has not put forth any clarifications or modifications to the conflicts of interest framework, the Ombudsman is aware of the narrow focus of application of Article 16 of Staff Regulations as a basis for risk assessment.[70] Ever since the

[66] Point 0.2.1. of the ECB's Ethics Framework in n 63.

[67] See n 25, para 3; see also n 31.

[68] M Hartlapp, 'Politicization of the European Commission: When, How, and with What Impact?' in MW Bauer and J Trondal (eds), *The Palgrave Handbook of the European Administrative System. European Administrative Governance* (London, Palgrave Macmillan, 2015).

[69] See n 7.

[70] In scholarly literature, the risks of revolving doors are often associated with regulatory capture. There is no mention of regulatory capture in the EO's decisions and recommendations, a choice which is likely deliberate given the illegal nature of regulatory capture as corruption.

first decision made by the EO on revolving doors, the Ombudsman Diamandouros has stressed that 'the assessment of a potential conflict of interest in the context of a "revolving door" type of conflict is a complex exercise that requires a careful examination of the staff member's tasks and the envisaged activities in the intended employment'.[71]

B. The Role of an Institutional Designer

The EO's umpire role frequently comes to the forefront in cases where she is called upon to decide on a complaint. Her second role, that of an institutional designer, appears to primarily manifest in the EO's own-initiative cases, allowing her to evaluate institutional performance over an extended period and propose improvements. However, it is noteworthy that many umpire cases also encompass elements of institutional design. In the revolving door case involving EFSA, the EO engaged in detailed discussions about how EFSA should amend its code of conduct.[72] Similarly, in the complaint concerning the appointment of former Commission President Barroso at Goldman Sachs, apart from identifying maladministration, the EO provided numerous specific suggestions for enhancing the workings of the (then) ad hoc ethical committee.[73] In most instances, the institutions and agencies involved often acknowledge and put into practice the EO's recommendations for improvement, even if they may reject the EO's findings in relation to maladministration.

Her second role, that of an institutional designer, is predominantly evident in the EO's own-initiative cases. The EO's own-initiative inquiries afford her an opportunity to evaluate and influence institutional design, and I will highlight two examples. The first pertains to the publication of information on revolving door moves. The EO has consistently urged the Commission, in particular, to disclose decisions related to the job transitions of its senior officials. However, both the Commission and other institutions and agencies have been slow to act, citing concerns related to personal data protection. In this context, the EO is supported by the European Data Protection Supervisor's Guidelines on the processing of personal data with regard to the management of conflicts of interest in EU institutions and bodies, according to which 'the balancing of interests might be in favour of publication of … decisions [including on Article 16(3) of the Staff Regulations] … for example regarding former senior staff members who take positions in the private sector'.[74]

With a view to further strengthening public scrutiny and the enforcement of imposed lobbying and advocacy bans, the Ombudsman suggested in 2017 that the

[71] See n 21, para 71. See also the Ombudsman's 2017 inquiry where the EO O'Reilly noted that 'the EU institutions must always assess "revolving doors" cases from the perspective of the public interest and from their institutional knowledge of what information and access the public servant might potentially give to the new employer', in n 31, para 5.

[72] ibid (n 21).

[73] See n 29.

[74] Report of the European Ombudsman on the publication of information on former senior staff so as to enforce the one-year lobbying and advocacy ban: SI/2/2017/NF, www.ombudsman.europa.eu/en/doc/inspection-report/en/110521.

Commission publishes information on former senior staff members' lobbying bans directly on the Transparency Register.[75] This would give the public a better picture of the hiring practices of lobbyists in the EU. Complementing external openness with internal transparency, she also suggested that the Commission should consider actively informing the colleagues of a former senior staff member of the fact that s/he has been placed under a lobbying and advocacy ban for a certain period of time.[76] Despite these and other appeals, EU institutions and agencies, including the Commission, are unwilling to publish the information. This institutional behaviour is not unexpected, considering the institutions' hesitance in many other transparency-related design disputes. Any advancements in this particular aspect of institutional design will likely occur concurrently with other improvements related to transparency, underlining the importance of the EO's role as an institutional designer beyond any specific policy problems.

The second example where the EO's institutional design role is apparent pertains to hiring practices and more generally the EU's role as a public sector employer. I noted in the introduction how revolving doors are increasingly viewed as a means to bring more expertise and competent staff to the public sector employers. The revolving doors mobility emphasises the significance of the EU as an employer, and it is intriguing how limited attention there has been on the Commission's role as an appointing authority. As pointed out by Peterson in his 1971 published article, its 'unique independence among international bodies and its ability to develop effective and acceptable solutions to Community problems depend upon the skills of these administrators and the efficiency with which their skills are organized in an administrative structure'.[77] In particular, the procedures for recruitment and promotion of administrators on the staff of the Commission are 'of potential importance to the Commission's independence and its ability to carry out its role actively'.[78] However, Peterson also acknowledges the unique nature of the Commission as a civil service organisation, for the Commission cannot rely on a purely merit career structure but it 'continues to need large numbers of specialists who, in many cases, can best be provided by lateral entry'.[79]

Four decades later, governments, including EU institutions, bodies and agencies, justify revolving door transitions by asserting that they need a large number of experts and individuals making such moves effectively bring valuable expertise to organisations that might otherwise operate in isolation. This implies that governments' understanding is that while the public sector loses competent employees they will also gain new experienced officials.[80] They may also reason that by letting

[75] See n 31.

[76] ibid, para 54.

[77] RL Peterson, 'Personnel Decisions and the Independence of the Commission of the European Communities' (1971) 10 *Journal of Common Market Studies* 117–37, 117.

[78] ibid.

[79] ibid, 119.

[80] Economist Elise S Brezis has argued that the political elite does not want to restrict the possibility of the revolving door, because it would mean difficulties recruiting competent bureaucrats, which would consequently mean lowering the quality of the bureaucrats in the economy and lower economic growth, see ES Brezis, 'Legal Conflicts of Interest of the Revolving Door' (2017) 52 *Journal of Macroeconomics* 175–88.

employees take up positions in the private sector would encourage them one day to return to the ranks of public service.

The EO, while seeking optimal solutions to ensure that EU institutions and agencies can benefit from a pool of experienced experts, has emphasised that her main concern with revolving door transitions is that they will, in most cases, enhance the expertise of the new employer. When hiring 'revolvers', the employer benefits from insights gained from 'the other side' – an employee who understands public policies, rules, processes, backgrounds and the overall system, including potential legal remedies. The mobility through revolving doors creates a bridge between the public and private sectors, facilitating the transfer of expertise to the private sector.

Expertise convinces and sells, with the EO describing how

> many Brussels-based law firms and public affairs companies place a high premium on the recruitment and advertising of staff with experience in the EU institutions … The clear message from such firms is that 'we have insiders', thereby suggesting a potential competitive advantage for their clients.[81]

Companies eager to ensure expertise and regulatory experience often hire directly from EU agencies and specific Commission Directorates-General, such as the Competition DG.[82]

This perspective, which sees revolving door transitions as a circulation of expertise between employers, helps elucidate why the EO has, in the role of umpire, increasingly identified instances of maladministration, particularly concerning EU agencies. As regulators, agencies often function in highly technical and specialised domains, rendering them more vulnerable to the adverse effects of revolving door transitions for two reasons. First, the revolving doors within EU agencies may negatively impact an agency by diminishing its expertise. Second, hiring an official from the agency results in the transfer of expertise in the form of information and access to the new employer, often law or commercial lobbying firms or companies intensely affected by EU regulations.[83]

In the role of institutional designer, the EO's recommendations entail guidance to EU administration to more effectively monitor cases where staff members move within the same area of expertise as their role within the EU administration. EU agencies or specific Commission Directorates-General, such as the Competition DG, should also be more inclined to impose restrictions on departing officials.

[81] See n 31, para 5 (emphasis in the original). This is also in focus in Case SI/5/2024KR, see n 57.

[82] For instance, the EO's 2021 inquiry specifically focused on the DG Competition which has over the years seen officials take up jobs in law firms, see P. Lombardi, 'EU Watchdog Puts Spotlight on Exodus of Competition Officials', Politico EU, 19 October 2021, www.politico.eu/article/eu-watchdog-puts-spotlight-on-exodus-revolving-door-competition-officials/. Studies show that ministers who have served in a contractor or regulator portfolio have higher chances of being hired by corporations, see S Claveria and T Verge, 'Post-ministerial Occupation in Advanced Industrial Democracies: Ambition, Individual Resources and Institutional Opportunity Structures' (2015) 54 *European Journal of Political Research* 819–35.

[83] Brezis explains the dynamics using the notion 'bureaucratic capital': a revolver 'is offered a position such as joining a firm's board of directors, thereby enabling her to cash in on the *bureaucratic capital* she accumulated. In return, this bureaucratic capital under the business elite's control enables increasing the firm's revenue', see in n 80, 178 (emphasis in the original). She continues that 'while this bureaucratic capital is valuable to the firm, it is in fact a social waste'.

In contrast to cases involving suggestions for improvement in agency or institution specific rules, when the EO identifies opportunities for a broader design overhaul, institutions and agencies are less eager to adhere to the EO's advice. The commitment of the Commission to enforce strict criteria when evaluating requests from staff members on leave of absence for engaging in external activities, especially in law firms or public affairs consultancies within the same expertise area as their role within EU administration, shows however the Commission's acknowledgment of the concern raised by the Ombudsman.[84]

While the majority of destinations for former officials are in the corporate sector, there are moves to non-corporate private sector positions such as NGOs. It will be interesting to see whether the EO assesses the move and associated transfer of expertise differently in a case where former EU officials move to an NGO.[85]

C. The Role of Trendsetter

The third and final role pertains to the EO as a trendsetter. This role differs from the second one in that here, the EO could be perceived as thinking outside the box of formal competences as an ombudsman institution. A good example of this is the importance attached to the role of the private sector in the revolving doors mobility.[86]

The Ombudsman can investigate an EU institution on the grounds of maladministration, but her powers do not extend to investigating private actors, such as corporations.[87] Given the growing significance of private actors in rule-making and other areas, the EO has increasingly made references to the private sector while staying within her mandate to investigate complaints concerning EU administration.

The EO has frequently emphasised the institutions' need to consider the new employer when approving a revolving door move.[88] The Commission's implementing rules, adopted in 2018, mention the new employer as a factor it should take into account when assessing risks of conflicts of interest in the revolving doors mobility.[89] While the Commission must pay attention to a relation between the occupational activity and the work carried out by the former staff member during the last three

[84] See n 52, para 26.

[85] See n 55.

[86] Another example would be the EO O'Reilly's idea of seeing revolving doors as part of 'the human rights playbook', see www.ombudsman.europa.eu/en/speech/en/98393. The right to good administration in the EU is usually perceived as an individual's right in a specific scenario, ensuring their matters are managed by public officials in alignment with the principle of diligence.

[87] Art 1 of Regulation (EU, Euratom) 2021/1163 of the European Parliament of 24 June 2021 laying down the regulations and general conditions governing the performance of the Ombudsman's duties (Statute of the European Ombudsman): 'No action by any other authority or person may be the subject of a complaint to the Ombudsman'.

[88] Starting from the EO's 2017 inquiry in n 31.

[89] Commission Decision of 29.6.2018 on outside activities and assignments and on occupational activities after leaving the Service, C(2018) 4048 final, http://ec.europa.eu/transparency/regdoc/rep/3/2018/EN/C-2018-4048-F1-EN-MAIN-PART-1.PDF.

years of service and whether the occupational activity would involve working on specific files for which the former staff member was responsible during the last three years of service, it should also consider the 'quality of a future employer (for example whether it is a public authority or a private/commercial company or the situation of self-employment)'.[90] There is no available information on which to base an assessment of whether the Commission engages in this practice and to what extent.

In her 2021 inquiry, the EO took additional steps. She suggested that the Commission could conditionally approve a new job, contingent on the staff member securing a commitment from the new employer to publicly disclose the restrictions imposed by the Commission on the new employer's website.[91] This condition is deemed particularly necessary when it is known or anticipated that the transition of a former senior official will prominently feature on the new employer's website, commonly referred to as the 'shop window'. For the Ombudsman, it is crucial that any restrictions are clearly visible on the new employer's website, potentially alongside the former staff member's profile.[92] At the very least, the Commission should mandate the staff member to provide evidence that the imposed restrictions were communicated to the new employer.

The EO made the similar suggestion in the case concerning the ECB, decided a year later.[93] The ECB should ask staff members to submit a formal description of their tasks with their prospective employer in their requests to take up an external activity while on unpaid leave or as a post-employment activity. Furthermore, the authorisation of occupational activities of staff on leave or former staff should be made conditional on the new employer making public the conditions imposed by the ECB. At a minimum, former staff members, and those on leave, should be required to notify their new employer of the mitigation measures in the authorisation imposed by the ECB, as well as their continuing duty not to disclose information that is subject to professional secrecy.[94]

While the Commission asks former staff members to inform their new employer about the restrictions, it does not require this. The Commission considers that it 'is not in a position to interfere in the relationship between former staff members and their new employer. Therefore, it does not ask for evidence that the restrictions imposed are shared with the new employer'.[95] The Commission said that compliance with restrictions is ensured in the same manner as for post-service occupational activities. The Commission '*trusts* that staff members authorised to carry out an

[90] ibid, para 41. Other factors relate to the reputation of the Commission, the question of whether or not the new activity involves lobbying vis-à-vis the institution and whether the new activity is renumerated.

[91] See n 52, para 43.

[92] ibid. The EP in its resolution has also called 'for the EU institutions to make sure that restrictions imposed on former senior staff members or staff members on leave for personal grounds are effectively shared with and enforced by the new employer', www.europarl.europa.eu/doceo/document/LIBE-AD-737243_EN.pdf.

[93] See n 15.

[94] ibid.

[95] See n 52, para 18.

outside activity during leave on personal grounds will inform their new employers about the restrictions imposed on them and that they will comply with the restrictions'.[96] There is no information on how the ECB has reacted to the EO's proposal.

There is no obligation for the Commission to rely solely on trust, nor are there legal provisions preventing it from requiring former staff members to disclose imposed restrictions to a new employer and furnish evidence of such disclosure. The Independent Ethical Committee, responsible for evaluating the new activities of former Commissioners, has, in a few opinions, directed former Commissioners to share the restrictions with their new employers and provide evidence of proper notification. As a result, the Commission has integrated the notification duty into its final decision.[97]

The above EO recommendations concerning the Commission and the ECB prompt broader considerations regarding the potential social responsibility role of the private sector when recruiting from public administration. Companies have actively participated in Corporate Social Responsibility (CSR) initiatives and developed their own codes that entail rules on lobbying and revolving doors.[98] For example, the Columbia Center on Sustainable Investment has developed a handbook to assist companies in aligning with the Sustainable Development Goals (SDGs) through four distinct pillars of action: Beneficial Products, Sustainable Operations, Sustainable Value Chains and Good Corporate Citizenship.[99] In terms of the fourth pillar (Good Corporate Citizenship), there are various commitments related to lobbying and, more broadly, participation in the political process. SDG aligned companies should, inter alia,

> refrain 'from or ceasing all lobbying that seeks influence, legislation, regulation, trade agreements or negotiations in ways that undermine the 2030 Agenda'.[100]
>
> address 'risks associated with the revolving door phenomenon, which requires top leadership, government relations, and lobbying staff to sign "non-complete-type" [sic] clauses that stipulate they may not undertake roles in lobbying, drafting, or enforcing legislation or regulations related to the industry within three years after employment with an SDG-aligned company. *This three-year cooling-off period also applies to hiring people directly from government positions*'.[101]

[96] ibid, para 29 (emphasis added).

[97] See, eg, Decision of the European Commission on Former Commissioner Miguel Arias Cañete's post term of office professional activities with Beka Finance and Balam Agriculture. Strasbourg 6.7.2021, https://commission.europa.eu/system/files/2021-07/commission-decision-arias-canete_en.pdf.

[98] Y Wei, N Jia and J-P Bonardi, 'Corporate Political Connections: A Multidisciplinary Review' (2022) 49(6) *Journal of Management* 1870–910; A Favotto and K Kollman, 'Mixing Business with Politics: Does Corporate Social Responsibility End Where Lobbying Transparency Begins?' (2021) 15 *Regulation & Governance* 262–79; J Steen Knudsen and J Moon, 'Corporate Social Responsibility and Government: The Role of Discretion for Engagement with Public Policy' (2021) *Business Ethics Quarterly* 1–29.

[99] CCSI Report, https://ccsi.columbia.edu/sites/default/files/content/docs/19%20CCSI%20Four%20pillars%20full%20report%20rhr.pdf. See also OECD, *Lobbying in the 21st Century. Transparency, Integrity and Access*, https://doi.org/10.1787/c6d8eff8-en.

[100] ibid (CCSI report), 223.

[101] ibid, emphasis added.

Regarding cooling-off periods, which were above described as non-compete clauses, they are commonly included in relevant legislation on revolving doors in many jurisdictions. What is noteworthy about the SDG pledge is the introduction of a hiring freeze, wherein companies commit not to directly hire individuals from government positions.[102]

The EO's trendsetter recommendations, situated in the context of broader trends involving corporate social codes, lead to two conclusions, indicating potential paths for future action. First, reliance on individual ethics alone cannot be the basis for compliance with revolving doors rules. Instead, there is a collective responsibility on the part of employers, both those from which a person departs and those to which the person arrives, to ensure that officials seeking positions outside of the EU institutions – whether after their service or during personal leave – adhere to the established rules. Second, the integrity of the Commission, and of the EU institutions and agencies more broadly, should be regarded as a matter of common concern. Similar to companies motivated to adhere to rules in their lobbying interactions with EU agencies to maintain the expert reputation of these agencies, private sector employers should ensure that their actions, such as hiring former EU staff, do not tarnish the reputation of public regulators and contribute to the loss of their regulatory standing.[103]

In essence, ensuring that its staff undergoes a scrutinised transition, preventing the unchecked departure with valuable connections and knowledge, is, as the EO has emphasised, 'sound business sense' for the EU administration.[104] It should also be considered 'sound business sense' for the private sector to ethically recruit and for their part contribute to the legitimacy and integrity of the EU administration.

IV. CONCLUSION

This chapter delineates how revolving doors have emerged as one of the key concerns during the EO O'Reilly's two consecutive mandates. Her office has consistently urged EU institutions, especially the Commission, to acknowledge the detrimental impacts of revolving doors on the legitimacy of EU administration and to take all necessary actions to mitigate any negative effects. The specific case of revolving doors illustrates how the EO's role can be applied in a versatile manner to support and inspire EU administration's efforts in addressing the revolving doors phenomenon.

The umpire role involves the EO investigating revolving doors cases, both on an individual basis and systematically in terms of institutional practice, using the

[102] Art 5 of the Code of Conduct of the Society of European Affairs Professionals (SEAP) require that when employing former staff, officials or members of the EU institutions, European affairs professionals 'take all the necessary measures to comply with the rules and regulations laid down by the EU institutions in that respect, in particular with regard to confidentiality', see www.seap.nu/code.php#:~:text=SEAP%20members%20agree%20not%20to,a%20verbal%20warning%20to%20expulsion.

[103] R Joosen, 'Persuading the Independent: Understanding Why Interest Groups Engage with EU Agencies' (2021) 10 *Interest Groups & Advocacy* 19–46.

[104] See n 52.

conflict of interest framework. However, the framework's ambiguity weakens the EO's findings of maladministration in revolving doors cases and their impact on the addressees. The institutional designer role sees the EO scrutinising the rules that EU institutions and agencies have implemented and their monitoring. In this role, the EO addresses issues that extend beyond a specific institution, such as transparency and recruiting practices in an era where public sector employers prioritise expertise and experience. Finally, the trendsetter role positions the EO as emphasising the role of private sector employers. Although the EO's formal mandate confines her findings to apply to EU administration, her recommendations increasingly align with broader corporate social responsibility themes, emphasising ethical conduct on the part of private sector employers.

In the conclusion of her first inquiry in 2012, O'Reilly soberly noted that

> perhaps no set of rules can ever fully protect against the negative consequences associated with the 'revolving doors' phenomenon and it is therefore incumbent on EU institutions to ensure, to the greatest extent possible, that the spirit of its rules in this area is respected.[105]

A decade later, after completing two full mandates, the case law of the EO O'Reilly demonstrates that her observations were accurate, and the negative impacts of the revolving doors remain challenging to mitigate. Consequently, it is even more essential for the EU administration, as well as for the employers of (former) EU officials – this being one of the most important parts of her legacy in this domain – to do their utmost to respect and be seen respecting the rules on revolving doors.

[105] The conclusions of the inquiry in n 25.

7

The Role of the European Ombudsman in Fostering Transparency and Accountability of EU Agencies: Zooming-in on Europol and Frontex

SARAH TAS

I. INTRODUCTION

IN ONE OF the first speeches by the first European Ombudsman (EO) in 1996, Jacob Söderman stated that the 'institution was meant to deal with instances of maladministration and to represent an effective means of redress for European citizens who do not get proper administrative treatment by Community institutions or bodies'.[1] The EO was to act as a bridge between citizens and the EU administration, including the EU institutions and other bodies, such as EU agencies. Since then, several inquiries were conducted on the EU agencies' functioning. A first stepping stone took place, for example, with the visiting program to EU agencies launched in 2011.[2] Within it, the EO visited six EU Agencies at programme's inception,[3] as well as eight the following year,[4] aiming at promoting good administration and share best practices. In the past years, the EO has dealt with significant cases involving EU agencies. Following the Covid-19 crisis, an inquiry was opened by the EO to examine the work of the European Centre for Disease Prevention and Control during the crisis,

[1] European Ombudsman Jacob Söderman, 'Speech of the European Ombudsman – The Ombudsman concept and types of control of maladministration in Greece and Europe', hold on 11 November 1996.

[2] European Ombudsman, *Annual Report 2014* [2015], 16.

[3] The European Environmental Agency, the European Monitoring Centre for Drugs and Drug Addiction, the European Maritime Safety Agency, the European Banking Authority, the European Medicines Agency and the European Police College.

[4] The European Centre for the Development of Vocational Training, the European Foundation for the Improvement of Living and Working Conditions, the EU's Judicial Cooperation Unit, the European Police Office, the European Systemic Risk Board, ENISA, the European Chemicals Agency and Frontex.

particularly with regards transparency.[5] More recently, the EO also opened an own-initiative inquiry, after the tragic Adriana shipwreck, on the role of Frontex in search and rescue activities.[6] These are only some examples of the increasing work the EO conducts over EU agencies.

This chapter intends to offer a comprehensive analysis of the work of the EO over EU agencies and, more specifically, to explore the extent to which the EO can foster institutional legitimacy of EU institutions. Institutional legitimacy encompasses, as noted in the introductory chapter of this edited book, institutional transparency and accountability.[7] Transparency and accountability are core values of good governance.[8] The EO can foster institutional legitimacy of decentralised EU agencies, particularly by further enhancing the transparency of the Agency's functioning and operations, as well as (intrinsically connected) by strengthening its accountability. Increasing transparency and accountability of Agencies in turn strengthen public trust in Frontex. As the Ombudsman noted in an inquiry into Frontex, 'it is a matter of public trust for EU citizens to be able to question and hold EU bodies to account'.[9] As will be demonstrated in this chapter, the EO may trigger these changes through its decisions on individual complaints, or through launching own-initiative inquiries to tackle more systemic problems within an Agency.

Focusing on every EU Agency, however, would be impossible. This chapter, instead, focuses specifically on two Justice and Home Affairs EU Agencies – Frontex and Europol. Both the Europol and the Frontex Regulation establish that the activities of the Agencies will be subject to inquiries by the EO.[10] In addition, both Agencies work in a sensitive field, namely border management and security, are surrounded by a certain opacity and secrecy, and their powers are continuously expanding.[11] Yet, as this chapter will show, there is a notable difference in the role

[5] Case OI/3/2020/TE, Decision in strategic inquiry OI/3/2020/TE on how the ECDC gathered and communicated information during the COVID-19 crisis, decided on 5 February 2021.

[6] Case OI/3/2023/MHZ, Decision on how Frontex complies with its fundamental rights obligations with regard to search and rescue in the context of its maritime surveillance activities, in particular the Adriana shipwreck, decided on 26 February 2024.

[7] Deirdre Curtin, Tanja Ehnert, Anna Morandini and Sarah Tas, 'Introduction: The European Ombudsman Beyond Old Battles and Navigating New Challenges', in this volume.

[8] Merijn Chamon, 'Transparency and Accountability of EU Decentralised Agencies and Agencification in Light of the Common Approach on EU Decentralised Agencies' in Sacha Garben, Inge Govaere and Paul Nemitz (eds), *Critical Reflections on Constitutional Democracy in the European Union* (Oxford, Hart, 2019).

[9] Case 1062/2021/ABZ, Decision on Frontex's refusal to give public access to documents concerning the 'European Border and Coast Guard Day', decided on 7 December 2021.

[10] Art 69 of Regulation (EU) 2016/794 of the European Parliament and of the Council of 11 May 2016 on the European Union Agency for Law Enforcement Cooperation (Europol) and replacing and repealing Council Decisions 2009/371/JHA, 2009/934/JHA, 2009/935/JHA, 2009/936/JHA and 2009/968/JHA, OJ L 135/53; and Art 119 of Regulation (EU) 2019/1896.

[11] Europol's Regulation has been amended in 2022, Regulation (EU) 2022/991 of the European Parliament and of the Council of 8 June 2022 amending Regulation (EU) 2016/1794, as regards Europol's cooperation with private parties, the processing of personal data by Europol in support of criminal investigations, and Europol's role in research and innovation, OJ L 169/1; see also Statewatch, 'New Europol rules massively expand police powers and reduce rights protections' (10 November 2022) www.statewatch.org/news/2022/

the EO undertook over these two Agencies, despite their common characteristics. While the Ombudsman adopts a strong proactive role over Frontex, its role over Europol remains rather shy. The chapter will try to discuss why these differences emerge and see whether the EO can extrapolate its success over Frontex to Europol, as well as other EU agencies, thereby determining as well the EO's potential to further institutional legitimacy.

II. A TIMID (AND LIMITED) ROLE OVER EUROPOL

A. A Quantitative Analysis of Decisions on Europol

The EO has been in place for almost 30 years to deal with instances of maladministration in the activities of EU institutions, bodies, offices or *agencies* (except the Court of Justice in its judicial function).[12] As has been analysed throughout this book, the Ombudsman essentially deals with complaints, and can open own-initiative investigations.[13] This section intends to delve into the decisions the EO has taken on Europol since its establishment.

According to the Ombudsman's website, 40 decisions have been adopted on Europol since the establishment of the EO. Among the 40 decisions, the essential part arose from individual complaints and only three decisions are the product of own-initiative inquiries.[14] In addition, some decisions may have not been taken directly against Europol but may have still concerned the agency.[15] The figure below gathers the decisions taken against Europol differentiating between decisions adopted after a complaint by an individual, and own-initiative inquiries by the EO. It shows a progressive increase over the mandates of the three different EO's.

november/new-europol-rules-massively-expand-police-powers-and-reduce-rights-protections/; Frontex's Regulation has been amended in 2019, Regulation (EU) 2019/1896 of the European Parliament and of the Council of 13 November 2019 on the European Border and Coast Guard and repealing Regulations (EU) No 1052/2013 and (EU) 2016/1624, OJ L 295/1.

[12] Art 228 of the Consolidated version of the Treaty on the Functioning of the European Union (TFEU) [2012] OJ C 326/125.

[13] European Ombudsman, *Annual Report 2014* [2015], 5, 7 and 8; European Ombudsman, 'All strategic inquiries', www.ombudsman.europa.eu/en/strategic-issues/strategic-inquiries/all-strategic-inquiries.

[14] Case OI/1/99/IJH, Decision of the European Ombudsman closing own-initiative inquiry OI/1/99/IJH as regards Europol, decided on 24 September 1999; Case OI/4/2013/CK, Decision of the European Ombudsman closing the own-initiative inquiry OI/4/2013/CK into the EU Agencies practices regarding disclosure of the names of Selection Board members, decided on 16 May 2014; Case OI/9/2012/OV, Conclusions of the European Ombudsman's visit to the European Police Office (Europol): decision closing own-initiative inquiry OI/9/2012/OV, decided on 11 June 2014.

[15] See for example, Case 201/12201/OV, Decision of the European Ombudsman on complaint 201/2001/OV against the Council, decided on the 4 February 2002 on the Council's refusal to give access to Europol's Work Programme for 2001.

Figure 1 Decisions taken by the European Ombudsman on Europol between 1999–2024

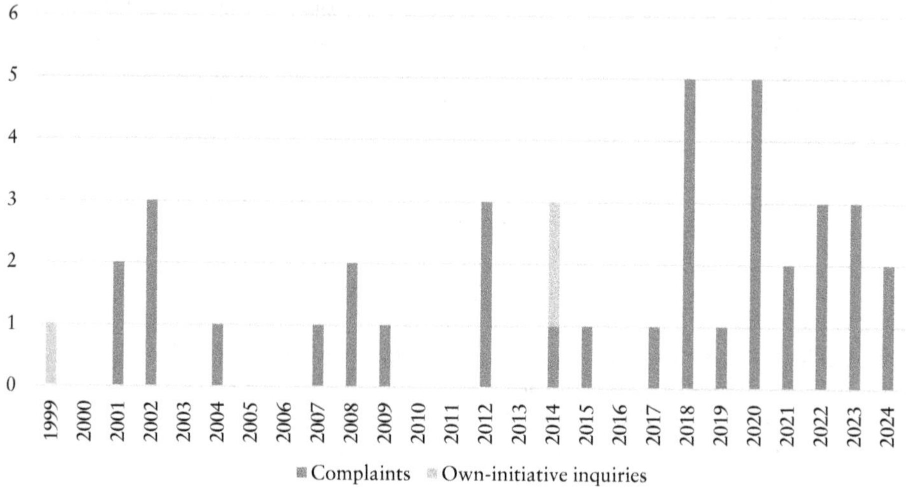

The first EO, Jacob Söderman held the position of Ombudsman from 1995 to 2003. During his mandate, encompassing the period between Europol's creation (1995)[16] and the beginning of its operations (1999), six decisions were taken on Europol regarding employment matters,[17] and access to documents.[18] It was also the first time an own-initiative inquiry was opened on public access to documents of EU bodies, including Europol.[19]

The second Ombudsman, Nikiforos Diamandouros was elected in 2003 and held the position for 10 years. Under his mandate, eight more decisions were adopted on Europol, on similar matters as before, namely access to documents and recruitment. In addition, in May 2011, he launched a programme of visits to EU Agencies, including Europol, on topics of transparency, dialogue and accountability to better understand their rules on access to documents.[20] The own-initiative investigation was concluded afterwards under Emily O'Reilly's Office, with several suggestions ranging from more transparency, dialogue, accountability to better rules on selection and recruitment.

[16] Convention based on Article K.3 of the Treaty on European Union, on the establishment of a European Police Office (Europol Convention) OJ C 316.

[17] See, Case 721/2001/GG, Decision of the European Ombudsman on complaint 721/2001/GG against Europol, decided on 19 November 2001; and Case 1788/2001/OV, Decision of the European Ombudsman on complaint 1788/2001/OV against Europol, decided on 12 June 2002.

[18] See, Case 202/2001/OV, Decision of the European Ombudsman on complaint 202/2001/OV against Europol, decided on 24 October 2001; and Case 785/2002/OV, Decision of the European Ombudsman on complaint 785/2002/OV against Europol, decided on 17 December 2002.

[19] Case OI/1/99/IJH, Decision of the European Ombudsman closing own-initiative inquiry OI/1/99/IJH as regards Europol, decided on 24 September 1999.

[20] See Case 2166/2012/BEH, Decision of the European Ombudsman closing his inquiries into complaints 2166/2012/BEH, 2167/2167/2012/BEH and 2168/2012/BEH, decided on 10 December 2012, referring to the own-initiative inquiry on Europol (OI/9/2012/OV).

Emily O'Reilly has been the third EO, and, under her mandate, 26 decisions were adopted on Europol, including at the time of the writing of this chapter two of which are still pending. She concluded two own-initiative inquiries under her mandate. On the one hand, the own investigation opened under Nikiforos Diamandouros, within the visiting programme to EU Agencies.[21] On the other hand, an own-initiative inquiry into EU Agencies policies regarding disclosure of the names of Selection Board members, and their compliance with data protection requirements.[22] All the other decisions are the result of complaints brought to the Office. It is, however, undeniable that there has been a strong increase in decisions taken, linked to an increase in complaints brought to the Ombudsman. This can be connected, in turn, to Europol's expansion of competences and to the efforts put towards making the Agency more visible. Similarly to before, the complaints brought under her mandate essentially deal with access to documents, and recruitment and employment matters. The question now is to what extent the EO increased the institutional legitimacy of Europol.

B. A Shy Push Towards More Transparency

As noted in the introduction, the EO can foster institutional legitimacy by increasing transparency, and thereby also accountability. Nevertheless, it is unclear, for several reasons, whether this objective is achieved as regards Europol.

On the surface, the analysis of all the EO's decisions regarding Europol shows that most cases end with no evidence of maladministration or, otherwise, with a concerted solution between the EO and the Agency. In these remaining instances, Europol is granted the possibility to re-assess its decision and, thereby, either confirm or modify it according to the Ombudsman's suggestions. Either situation, however highlights that the EO's progress in furthering Europol's transparency remains quite limited. If one delves deeper into the minority of cases that end in agreement, it can be noted that the EO's impact is still reduced. The Ombudsman may increase transparency through inquiries related to individual complaints, but also through own-initiative investigations.

When it comes to individual complaints, a distinction must be made between complaints that further transparency in a specific situation, and complaints that triggers changes beyond the given case. An example of the former can be seen in the case 1849/2019/DL in which a complaint was brought on public access to documents related to Europol's tasks in combatting illegal migrant smuggling.[23] The EO

[21] Case OI/9/2012/OV, Conclusions of the European Ombudsman's visit to the European Police Office (Europol): decision closing own-initiative inquiry OI/9/2012/OV, decided on 11 June 2014.

[22] Case OI/4/2013/CK, Decision of the European Ombudsman closing the own-initiative inquiry OI/4/2013/CK into the EU Agencies practices regarding disclosure of the names of Selection Board members, decided on 16 May 2014.

[23] Case 1849/2019/DL, Decision in case 1849/2019/DL on the European Union Agency for Law Enforcement Cooperation's refusal to grant public access to documents relating to its operational tasks in combating illegal migrant smuggling, decided on 10 October 2019.

argued for granting partial access to the documents, and Europol complied with it to an extent – adding more redaction than the EO proposed – expanding thereby the access to document for the complainant. Evidence of the latter can be seen in the case 111/2008/TS: a journalist complained about Europol's refusal to grant him access to *The Strategy for Europol* and the procedural handling of the request.[24] After the Ombudsman opened the investigation, Europol granted access to the documents to the journalist, and ensured that it was 'committed to rectifying, without delay, the administrative shortcomings identified'. In fact, Europol subsequently modified its procedure for handling requests for access to documents, having thus an impact not only on this specific case, but all the forthcoming ones. Another example relates to a complaint dealing more generally with Europol's public register of documents and its compliance with EU rules on public access to documents.[25] The decision of the EO triggered changes within the Agency, which improved and updated its public register system to transform it into a more useful tool for the public. While both these cases strengthen the procedure to render Europol more transparent (through access to document requests), it does not expressly increase the Agency's transparency and accountability.

Turning to the own-initiative inquiries, as mentioned above three were launched on Europol. They respectively improved the rules concerning public access to documents,[26] Europol's practices regarding disclosure of the names of Selection board members[27] and pushed Europol to set up a public register of documents as well as update the procurement section of its website to include further information on the possibility to complain to the Ombudsman.[28] Interestingly, in the latter inquiry, the Ombudsman noted that 'she encourages Europol to follow the example of Frontex' when it comes to deadlines for requests for access. Yet the fact remains that only three instances exist so far in which the EO has in fact triggered some broader institutional changes, relates essentially to *reactive* transparency. This concept will be further clarified in the following sub-section, however, in sum it means that Europol is asked to react to requests for transparency but is not pushed to become transparent on its own initiative (*proactive* transparency).[29]

With these considerations, the EO can push Europol to improve its institutional legitimacy, notably by increasing its transparency. However, in practice the changes

[24] Case 111/2008/TS, Decision of the European Ombudsman closing his inquiry into complaint 111/2008/TS against Europol, decided on 21 November 2008.

[25] Case 2272/2019/MIG, Decision in case 2272/2019/MIG on the European Union Agency for Law Enforcement Cooperation's (Europol) public register of documents, decided on 4 February 2021.

[26] Case OI/1/99/IJH, Decision of the European Ombudsman closing own-initiative inquiry OI/1/99/IJH as regards Europol, decided on 24 September 1999.

[27] Case OI/4/2013/CK, Decision of the European Ombudsman closing the own-initiative inquiry OI/4/2013/CK into the EU Agencies practices regarding disclosure of the names of Selection Board members, decided on 16 May 2014.

[28] Case OI/9/2012/OV, Conclusions of the European Ombudsman's visit to the European Police Office (Europol): decision closing own-initiative inquiry OI/9/2012/OV, decided on 11 June 2014.

[29] Also developed in chapter 13 of Dirk Detken and Laura Weemering, 'Transparency That is Fit for Purpose: EFSA's Experience with the European Ombudsman and Proactive Transparency', in this volume.

remain marginal, and the Ombudsman often finds no maladministration by Europol, which can still use several means to ensure its secrecy. Among others, it still asserts that disclosure may undermine its investigations and operational activities,[30] or that there is a need to protect the public interest, public security and the decision-making processes.[31]

Furthermore, in an exceptional case, the EO was limited in its inspection. The case concerned a refusal of Europol to give access to a document on the implementation of the EU-US Terrorist Finance Tracking Program Agreement.[32] In cases on access to documents, the Ombudsman must inspect the document in question, however here, this required the consent of the US authorities, who refused vetoed the Ombudsman access to relevant information. The EO saw their hands tied by international law, which may happen in some cases involving Europol or Frontex.

III. A MORE PROACTIVE ROLE OVER FRONTEX

A. A Quantitative Analysis of Decisions on Frontex

Section III starts by quantifying the decisions the EO took over Europol since the establishment of Frontex in 2004.[33] According to the EO website, 62 decisions have been adopted against Frontex, with already four cases expecting a decision in the following year.[34] In addition, there are also some decisions which indirectly deal with Frontex, particularly in cases brought against the European Commission,[35] or strategic initiatives on how EU institutions, bodies, offices and agencies deal with a specific matter.[36] Figure 2 gathers the decisions taken against Frontex by the Ombudsman, distinguishing between decisions adopted after a complaint by an individual, and own-initiative inquiries by the Ombudsman.

[30] See case 1270/2017/EIS, Decision in case 1270/2017/EIS on the European Police Office's refusal to grant full access to documents regarding Joint Investigation Teams and operational plans at EU border 'hotspots', decided on 10 May 2019.

[31] See case 1167/2023/PB, Letter from the European Ombudsman to Europol Executive Director on how the EU Agency for Law Enforcement Cooperation handled a request for public access to documents related to online child sexual abuse, sent on 13 July 2023.

[32] Case 1148/2013/TN, Decision of the European Ombudsman closing the inquiry into compliant 1148/2013/TN against the European Police Office, decided on 2 September 2014.

[33] Council Regulation (EC) No 2007/2004 of 26 October 2004 establishing a European Agency for the Management of Operational Cooperation at the External Borders of the Member States of the European Union (Frontex) OJ L349/1.

[34] Case 1885/2023/ACB; Case 344/2023/PVV; Case 1845/2023/AV; Case 219/2024/TM opened on the 7 February 2024.

[35] See for example Case 2496/2023/NH opened on 8 January 2024 against the Commission but on the Joint Operation Terra coordinated by Frontex, in Bulgaria.

[36] See for example case SI/4/2021/MIG, Strategic initiative on how EU institutions, bodies, offices, and agencies record text and instant messages sent/received by staff members in their professional capacity, decided on 13 July 2022.

Figure 2 Decision adopted against Frontex by the Ombudsman between 2004–2024

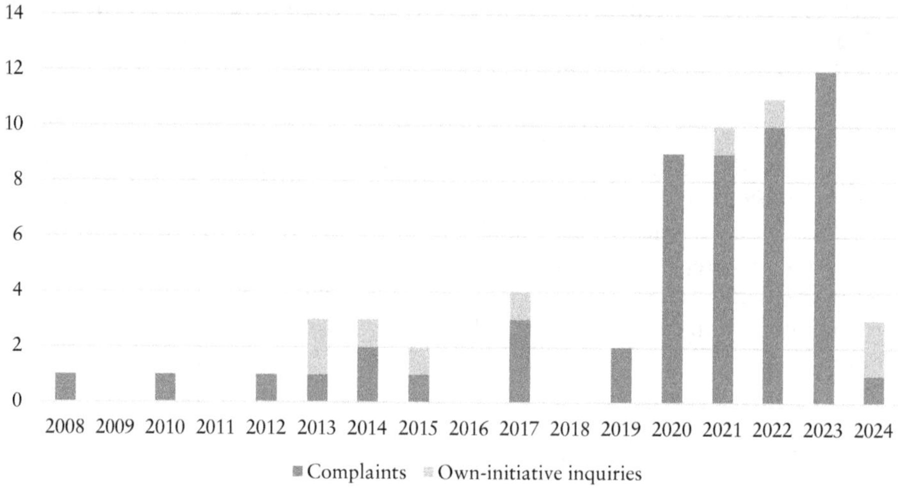

Figure 2 shows an increase in decisions adopted on Frontex in the past years, with nine decisions adopted in 2020, 10 in 2021, 11 in 2022 and a peak of 12 decisions adopted in 2023. This may be linked to the strong pressure put by politicians, journalists, NGOs and other accountability forums on Frontex in the past years,[37] which further put Frontex on the forefront of criticism and the object of complaints and own-initiative inquiries by the EO. All this pressure led to the resignation of the former Executive Director of Frontex, Fabrice Leggeri on 28 April 2022.[38] However, already before that the EO was active *vis-à-vis* Frontex, with in total nine own-initiative inquiries conducted over the Agency's actions on various field, which will be further analysed in the subsequent sub-section. In particular, they concern various topics ranging from recruitment matters, to access to document requests, and Frontex's compliance with fundamental rights in the course of its operations.

In quantitative terms, it is thus clear that the EO has adopted more decisions over Frontex, than over Europol – 40 decisions on Europol (including three own-initiative inquiries) compared to 62 decisions on Frontex (including nine own-initiative inquiries). In the following sub-section, the various decisions over Frontex will be explored to demonstrate that qualitatively as well, more has been achieved over Frontex.

[37] Ilaria Aversa and Mariana Gkliati, 'Frontex investigations: what changes in the EU border agency's accountability?' (*Statewatch*, 30 March 2021) www.statewatch.org/analyses/2021/frontex-investigations-what-changes-in-the-eu-border-agency-s-accountability/; particularly OLAF Report, *Final Report on Frontex Case No OC/2021/0451/A1* OLAF.03(2021)21088, https://fragdenstaat.de/dokumente/233972-olaf-final-report-on-frontex/.

[38] European Commission, 'Commission statement on the resignation of Fabrice Leggeri' (29 April 2022), https://ec-europa-eu.eui.idm.oclc.org/commission/presscorner/detail/%20en/statement_22_2751.

B. A Strong Proactive Role of the Ombudsman in Fostering the Agency's Institutional Legitimacy

The Ombudsman work both from own-initiative investigations and complaints can thus be divided into (i) its proactivity towards the Agency's transparency, and (ii) its proactivity towards Frontex's accountability. Both are very closely interlinked, and thus some decisions might fall under both categories.

i. The EO's Active Role in Fostering Transparency

Starting with the own-initiative inquiries, it is worth mentioning four inquiries that either improved the procedure to access documents or directly pushed for stronger transparency of the Agency's operations.

On the one hand, two inquiries specifically focused on Frontex's practices when it comes to public access to documents. The first own-initiative inquiry was part of the broader program visits to various agencies initiated in 2011 by former Ombudsman Nikiforos Diamandouros.[39] The Ombudsman made several suggestions meant to foster the accessibility and transparency of the Agency: making information on Frontex's functions available in all EU languages, publishing codes of good administrative behaviour and related documents on the website, as well as offering more clarity on requests for access to document.[40] While many of the suggestions were implemented after the inquiry further developing the transparency of Frontex, the Agency did not include a list of sensitive documents in the register. The second inquiry analysed in this sub-section was adopted under Emily O'Reilly and focused specifically on Frontex's practices on requests for access to documents.[41] It concerned the Agency's practice to suspend the statutory time-limit to process requests, or not apply it when the requests for public access to documents were considered too complex (concerning large number of documents) or imprecise. The EO found maladministration by Frontex and asked it to cease these practices, as they were not in line with EU legislation on public access to documents and may be interpreted as Frontex attempting to avoid timely public scrutiny.[42] The EO took a strong stance in favour of transparency. Even though Frontex did not implement the proposals, the EO took a strong stance in favour of transparency.

On the other hand, it is noteworthy to mention two cases that triggered proactive transparency of the Agency's operation. Starting chronologically, one of the cases relates to an inquiry concluded in 2015, on Frontex's coordinating role in Joint Return Operations (JRO) and its compliance with fundamental rights.[43] While most of the

[39] Case OI/13/2012/MHZ, Decision of the European Ombudsman closing own-initiative inquiry OI/13/2012/MHZ (Visit to Frontex), decided on 26 September 2013.

[40] ibid.

[41] Case OI/4/2022/PB, Decision in the case OI/4/2022 on practices Frontex has in place for dealing with requests for access to documents, decided on 13 March 2024.

[42] Case OI/4/2002/PB, Recommendation on practices Frontex has in place for dealing with requests for access to documents, adopted on 30 May 2023.

[43] Case OI/9/2014/MHZ concerning Frontex, decided on 4 May 2015.

inquiry will be discussed below when analysing EO's work on accountability, it also addresses the transparency of the JRO. In the decision adopted following this inquiry, the EO suggested Frontex to publish among others the JRO Evaluation Reports, specific sections of the JRO implementation plan, as well as best practices for JROs. As the EO noted, this would allow for a better right to an effective remedy for returnees in the event of fundamental rights violation, thus improving judicial accountability.[44] Since then, some Evaluation Reports have been published in the public register of documents,[45] following a request for access to documents. However, this seems to be more of a reactive transparency than proactive, namely Frontex publishing the documents directly on the website.

The ultimate own-initiative inquiry to be explored has been decided in January 2022. The EO looked into the Agency's transparency with regards its operational plans, and its fundamental rights compliance related to the suspension, termination or refusal to launch an activity.[46] The inquiry concluded with several recommendations for improvements, centring notably around Frontex's need to ensure more proactive transparency.[47] The EO noted, for example, that the prompt publication of comprehensive summaries of operational plans and fundamental rights analysis would facilitate scrutiny and provide further legitimacy of Frontex's operations. This follows the fact that operational plans are the footprint of an operation coordinated by Frontex, since they contain all the operational elements of an operation. Nowadays, some Operational Plans have been disclosed on the public register of documents.[48] Once again, it seems to be more of a reactive rather than proactive transparency. However, it still increases the transparency of Frontex's operations.

Turning now to the main activities of the EO over Frontex – the complaints – several points can be mentioned. While there are cases where the EO fully agreed with Frontex's refusal,[49] in others the EO rather triggered more transparency about the specific individual complaint.[50] Moreover, in some cases, and more frequently

[44] ibid.

[45] See notably Frontex Evaluation Report : Returns in the 1st Half of 2023, https://prd.frontex.europa.eu/wp-content/themes/template/templates/cards/1/dialog.php?card-post-id=2722&document-post-id=12421; and Frontex Evaluation Report: Returns in the 2nd Half of 2022, https://prd.frontex.europa.eu/wp-content/themes/template/templates/cards/1/dialog.php?card-post-id=2722&document-post-id=11639.

[46] Case OI/4/2021/MHZ, Decision in OI/4/2021/MHZ on how Frontex complies with its fundamental rights obligations and ensures accountability in relation to its enhanced responsibilities, decided on 17 January 2022.

[47] On this, see also chapter 13 by Dirk Detken and Laura Weemering, 'Transparency That is Fit for Purpose: EFSA's Experience with the European Ombudsman and Proactive Transparency', in this volume.

[48] For example Operation Plans: Triton and Themis (2014-2020) disclosed on 21 June 2023, https://prd.frontex.europa.eu/document/operational-plans-triton-and-themis-2014-2020/.

[49] See for example case 1328/2017/EIS, Decision in case 1328/2017/EIS on the refusal by Frontex to grant access to a document concerning the vessels used in the Poseidon and Triton border control operations, decided on 23 November 2017; or case 1087/2022/SF, Decision on how Frontex dealt with a request for data concerning the resources deployed in two joint operations, decided on 27 March 2023.

[50] See for example case 1610/2021/MIG, Decision on the refusal by Frontex to give public access to documents concerning search and rescue operation, decided on 31 January 2022; case 1877/2022/NH, Decision on Frontex refusal to give public access to a document containing information on return operations in a machine-readable format, decided on 16 March 2023; and case 652/2023/VB, Decision on Frontex refusal to give public access to a report by its Fundamental Rights Officer concerning a Frontex operation in Albania, decided on 7 November 2023.

than for Europol, the EO adopts more general requirements of transparency going beyond the specific individual complaint. To name a few, general recommendations were for example made for Frontex to better explain the redaction or refusal to access to documents, for which there should be reasonably foreseeable risks.[51] Suggestions were also made for Frontex to publish the number of sensitive documents it holds in the register,[52] for Frontex to improve communications with applicants for access to documents[53] and for Frontex in compliance with good administration to provide lists of documents identified under an access to document request.[54] Thus, even in decisions adopted on the basis of individual complaints, recommendations may have a broader impact on the overarching transparency of the Agency, particularly when it comes to rules on access to documents. No broader recommendation resulted in enhanced transparency of Frontex's concrete operations.

ii. The EO's Proactivity to Strengthen Frontex's Accountability

Accountability refers to the idea of giving reasons or explanations for one's action ex post,[55] with an actor having to justify their conduct (in this case Frontex).[56] The EO, in this sense, has contributed to strengthening the accountability of Frontex operations through various investigations, many of which concern fundamental rights protection.[57]

Following a similar approach as in the previous sub-section, the EO opened several own-initiative inquiries on the matter, and five of them particularly deal with the Agency's accountability. First, the own-initiative inquiry OI/5/2012/BEH-MHZ launched in 2012 to check the implementation of the former Frontex Regulation of 2011,[58] for example as regards the Fundamental Rights strategy, the Fundamental Rights Officer (FRO), the effective monitoring mechanism, as well as the termination of joint operations and pilot projects.[59] Frontex followed some of the recommendations contained in the decision. Nonetheless, it dismissed the EO's

[51] Case 1616/2016/MDC, Decision in case 1616/2016/MDC on the alleged failure by Frontex to make public Serious Incident Reports concerning Frontex or joint operations in Bulgaria, decided on 17 November 2017.

[52] Case 2273/2019/MIG on Frontex public register of documents, decided on 3 February 2021.

[53] Case 1939/2020/ABZ, Decision on how Frontex dealt with a request for public access to correspondence with journalists, decided on 14 July 2021; and Joined cases 1261/2020/PB and 1361/2020/PB, Decision on issues related to how Frontex communicates with citizens in relation to its access to documents portal, decided 15 December 2022.

[54] Case 1129/2023/OAM, Recommendation on the refusal by Frontex to provide lists of documents it identifies as falling within the scope of requests for public access to documents, adopted on 15 February 2024.

[55] Carol Harlow, *Accountability in the European Union* (Oxford, OUP, 2002) 10.

[56] Mark Bovens, 'Analysing and Assessing Accountability: A Conceptual Framework' (2007) 13(4) *European Law Journal* 447, 450.

[57] European Ombudsman, 'European Ombudsman Annual Report 2017' [2018] 3.

[58] Regulation (EU) No 1168/2011 of the European Parliament and of the Council of 25 October 2011 amending Council Regulation (EC) No 2007/2004 establishing a European Agency for the Management of Operational Cooperation at the External Borders of the Member States of the European, OJ L 304/1.

[59] Case OI/5/2012/BEH-MHZ, Decision of the EO closing own-initiative inquiry OI/5/2012/BEH-MHZ concerning Frontex, decided 12 November 2013.

advice to set up an internal complaints mechanism to deal directly with complaints from affected individuals.[60] Frontex rejected this on the grounds that Member States shall be the sole responsible for fundamental rights infringements. As a response, the EO used her power to submit a special report to the Parliament for further institutional support on the matter.[61] The change here was not triggered directly, however, a few years later, in 2016, the internal complaints mechanism became a legal requirement.[62]

Following this, the EO opened a new own-initiative inquiry in 2020 to assess the overall effectiveness of the (newly) adopted complaints mechanism and the role of the FRO.[63] The EO identified several potential shortcomings and made numerous suggestions to improve the accessibility of the mechanism (eg, awareness of the mechanism, handling of complaints and follow-up on them). Frontex noted that it would work on further enhancing the accessibility and visibility of the complaint's mechanism,[64] to strengthen Frontex's accountability.

The third own-initiative investigation related to accountability was already mentioned above, on Frontex's role as coordinator of JROs.[65] Aside the points on transparency addressed previously, the EO pointed out that the Agency 'must do all in its powers to promote independent and effective monitoring of JROs'.[66] This means involving independent monitors physically present on return flights, and more comprehensive and transparent monitoring, as well as enhanced cooperation among the monitoring bodies. Changes were implemented at a later stage in the legislative amendments of 2016, with increasing European supervision.[67] However, 'the dilemma of how to ensure accountability for multi-layered operations involving Frontex and national staff was not satisfactorily resolved'.[68]

The fourth inquiry (mentioned in the sub-section on transparency) dealt with Frontex's compliance with fundamental rights in joint operations, the monitoring of returns and the Agency's role in screening procedures.[69] Besides a call for proactive transparency, the EO also made several recommendations to improve Frontex's accountability. Among them, she underscored the need for Frontex to

[60] ibid.

[61] Case OI/5/2012/BEH-MHZ, Special Report of the EO in own-initiative inquiry OI/5/2012/BEH-MHZ concerning Frontex, adopted on 7 November 2013.

[62] Regulation (EU) 2016/1624 of the European Parliament and of the Council of 14 September 2016 on the European Border and Coast Guard and amending Regulation (EU) 2016/399 of the European Parliament and of the Council and repealing Regulation (EC) No 863/2007 of the European Parliament and of the Council, OJ L 251/1, Art 72.

[63] Case OI/5/2020/MHZ, Decision in OI/5/2020/MHZ on the functioning of Frontex complaints mechanism for alleged breaches of fundamental rights and the role of the Fundamental Rights Officer, decided on 15 June 2021.

[64] European Ombudsman, 'European Ombudsman Annual Report 2021' [2022] 14.

[65] Case OI/9/2014/MHZ concerning Frontex, decided on 4 May 2015.

[66] ibid.

[67] Regulation (EU) 2016/1624.

[68] Emily O'Reilly, Transparency and accountability in the management of European borders, speech of 23 April 2021.

[69] Case OI/4/2021/MHZ, Decision in OI/4/2021/MHZ on how Frontex complies with its fundamental rights obligations and ensures accountability in relation to its enhanced responsibilities, decided on 17 January 2022.

issue specific instructions to screening teams and strengthen the monitoring of forced returns.

Finally, the EO concluded, earlier this year, an own-initiative inquiry in search and rescue operations, following the Adriana shipwreck – a fishing vessel that capsized and sank in international waters off the Greek coast, causing the death of over 600 migrants.[70] As a result, the EO concluded that Frontex followed the applicable rule, but identified several shortcomings in Frontex's reaction in maritime emergency. The EO noted, in particular, that further guidance and clarity is needed for Frontex units to respond to potential emergency situations, as well as on the role and responsibility Frontex plays in these cases. Furthermore, the EO suggested Fundamental Rights monitors to be involved in the decision-making processes occurring in surveillance operations. This own-initiative inquiry shows that the EO is very proactive in monitoring Frontex's activities. In fact, search and rescue operations are under the primary responsibility of Member States, yet the EO found it important to clearly delineate the Agency's role in it.[71] This is striking, since the EO is a small office,[72] and has a lot of cases to deal with. However, they took it as a mission to continuously scrutinise Frontex, even if its role is more subsidiary in the operation.

When it comes to decisions on individual complaints, two cases decided in 2023 dealt with the accountability of the Agency. First, there was a decision on how Frontex ensures compliance with fundamental rights during debriefing interviews of migrants.[73] While the EO concluded that there was no maladministration by Frontex, it suggested Frontex do more to ensures the respect of migrant's fundamental rights, particularly the right to human dignity (eg, access to interpretation, consent recorded, legal representation or confidentiality). Second, a decision adopted on Frontex's Human Rights Impact assessment before providing assistance to third countries.[74] The EO found that there was a sufficient procedure to assess whether to assist a third country or not, but found that the latter could be improved, for example by basing the assessment on the Due Diligence Procedure, and for setting up a prior advice procedure for ad hoc activities of the Agency in third countries. It is unclear whether the suggestions proposed by the EO in these two cases were followed. However, as they have in any case been shared with the Agency, it may happen that, in the future or in the practice, they trigger some tangible change.

All in all, this qualitative assessment of the EO's inquiries and decisions shows very clearly that the Ombudsman is very proactive on Frontex, be it through

[70] Case OI/3/2023/MHZ, Decision on how Frontex complies with its fundamental rights obligations with regard to search and rescue in the context of its maritime surveillance activities, in particular the Adriana shipwreck, decided on 26 February 2024.

[71] European Ombudsman, Exchange of views on Adriana shipwreck at the European Parliament's LIBE Committee – Speech by Emily O'Reilly, held on 14 February 2024.

[72] European Ombudsman, 'European Ombudsman Annual Report 2022' [2023] 28, in 2022, there were 73 posts in the Ombudsman's establishment plan.

[73] Case 1452/2022/MHZ, Decision on how Frontex ensures respect of the rights of migrants in 'debriefing' interviews, decided on 3 July 2023.

[74] Case 1473/2022/MHZ, Decision on how Frontex assessed the human rights impact before providing assistance to non-EU countries for developing surveillance capabilities, decided on 8 December 2023.

own-initiative investigation but also following individual complaints. The EO continuously provides suggestions for Frontex to improve its transparency and accountability, and even went as far as submitting a Special Report to the European Parliament. This ended up in a success, with the internal complaints mechanism finally seeing light in the 2016 Frontex Regulation.[75] This shows that the EO has the potential to play an influencing role in fostering the institutional legitimacy of Agencies, as it is the case here with Frontex. This role of the EO will be dissected further in the following section.

IV. THE EO'S POTENTIAL IN FOSTERING INSTITUTIONAL LEGITIMACY OF EU AGENCIES?

This section still deals particularly with Frontex and Europol, but its findings may ultimately also apply to other EU agencies, such as the European Union Asylum Agency (EUAA). The EO noted in her speech on the Adriana shipwreck:

> I have inquired into Frontex many times and this scrutiny will continue and expand, not only for Frontex, but for many EU institutions as the EU increasingly assumes the role of a hands-executive body on everything from the processing of asylum claims and the procurement of vaccines to the delivery of armaments – all issues that have a substantial impact on individuals fundamental rights.[76]

The EO emphasises here not only that scrutiny will continue over Frontex, but also other EU agencies that may significantly impact fundamental rights. She underscored the need of a direct correlation between the strengthening of the role of EU agencies, and a strengthening of their monitoring, notably by the EO. In fact, as the European Data Protection Supervisor (EDPS) also pointed out after the latest amendment to Europol's Regulation,[77] 'with a stronger mandate [of Europol] should always come a stronger oversight'.[78]

This section intends to discuss how the EO fosters the institutional legitimacy of EU agencies, as evidenced by the EO's role over Frontex, and explore the potential lessons that may be learned for EO's actions over Europol. The notable differences between the two Agencies will be laid down, explaining a potential reluctance or difficulty for the Ombudsman to show the same proactiveness towards Europol.

A. The Success Story of Frontex: A Strong Interaction with Various Actors

Section III of this chapter showed that the EO has been very active in strengthening the transparency and accountability of Frontex throughout the years. This is

[75] Regulation (EU) 2016/1624, Art 72.

[76] European Ombudsman, Exchange of views on Adriana shipwreck at the European Parliament's LIBE Committee – Speech by Emily O'Reilly, held on 14 February 2024.

[77] Regulation (EU) 2022/991.

[78] European Data Protection Supervision, Opinion 4/2021 EDPS Opinion on the Proposal for the Amendment of the Europol Regulation [2021] 4.

undoubtedly linked to the impact Frontex has on fundamental rights, and to the spotlight that was brought on Frontex's operations through NGOs, investigative journalists and other monitoring bodies.[79] However, another aspect that has increased the efficiency of the EO's work on Frontex is its collaboration with other actors, particularly national ombudsmen. In fact, EU agencies have been considered to be 'in-betweeners', meaning bodies between the EU institutions and Member States.[80] Agencies, like Frontex, closely collaborate with national authorities in their operations, a common characteristic of the EU integrated administration. This requires a rethinking of how to monitor EU agencies.[81]

In some investigations, the EO included the national ombudsmen part of the European Network of Ombudsmen (ENO). The latter was launched in 1996 and is an informal forum set up to share information and best practices between various ombudsmen.[82] National ombudsmen have been consulted on three instances in a matter concerning Frontex. The first case was during an own-initiative inquiry launched in 2012 on the implementation of the 2011 Regulation,[83] particularly with regards the effective monitoring mechanism, as well as the termination of joint operations and pilot projects.[84] The EO informed the members of the ENO of the inquiry and consulted the Greek national ombudsman on the matter. The latter pointed out complaints it received both from individuals and NGOs about the Agency's operations in Greece (eg, screening procedure and registration) and notes a need to set up a monitoring mechanism for fundamental rights breaches at the EU level.[85] This aligns with what the EO ultimately suggested in its assessment of the case.

The second instance is in the case OI/9/2014/MHZ on Frontex's role in joint return operations (JROs).[86] National ombudsmen were invited to share their experience, since they play a key role in either monitoring JROs or dealing with complaints resulting from JROs. 20 national ombudsmen and one regional ombudsman submitted observations on the feasibility and desirability of greater

[79] See for example Statewatch, 'Frontex: the ongoing failure to implement human rights safeguards' (2022) www.statewatch.org/analyses/2022/frontex-the-ongoing-failure-to-implement-human-rights-safeguards/; Human Rights Watch, 'Frontex Failing to Protect People at EU Borders: Stronger Safeguards Vital as Border Agency Expands' (2023) www.hrw.org/news/2021/06/23/frontex-failing-protect-people-eu-borders; Lighthouse reports, 'Investigating Frontex: How a reporting team put an EU super-agency in the spotlight' www.lighthousereports.com/investigating-frontex-how-a-reporting-team-put-an-eu-super-agency-in-the-spotlight/; Sarah Tas, 'Fundamental Rights Violations in the Hotspots: Who is Watching over Them?' (2022) 7(1) European Papers 215.

[80] Ellen Vos, 'EU Agencies, Common Approach and Parliamentary Scrutiny – European Implementation Assessment' (2018) European Parliamentary Research Service Study 23.

[81] ibid 53.

[82] European Ombudsman, 'About the European Network of Ombudsmen' www.ombudsman.europa.eu/en/european-network-of-ombudsmen/about/en.

[83] Regulation (EU) No 1168/2011.

[84] Case OI/5/2012/BEH-MHZ, Decision of the EO closing own-initiative inquiry OI/5/2012/BEH-MHZ concerning Frontex, decided 12 November 2013.

[85] Case OI/5/2012/BEH-MHZ, Observations concerning the own-initiative inquiry into the implementation by Frontex of its fundamental rights obligations received from the Greek Ombudsman, sent on 2 October 2012.

[86] Case OI/9/2014/MHZ concerning Frontex, decided on 4 May 2015.

cooperation amongst monitoring bodies.[87] The observations were taken into account by the EO to adopt its own recommendations for Frontex, notably to further promote independent and effective monitoring of the JROs.

Finally, a parallel investigation was launched in 2022 – where both the EO and members of the ENO look into the same issue – on Frontex's complaints mechanism and how the Agency dealt with fundamental rights breaches.[88] Since national ombudsmen may be responsible for the follow-up of complaints brought to the complaints mechanisms, the EO decided to consult them. The consultation covered their role in the complaint's mechanism, namely whether they forwarded any complaints, and how they responded to complaints against national authorities. Out of the 38 members of the ENO, 12 ombudsmen replied, and the Greek ombudsman noted for example that it is hard for national authorities to reply to complaints in a 'comprehensive, transparent and timely manner'.[89] The contribution by national ombudsmen allowed the EO to note for instance that complaints submitted directly to national ombudsmen about fundamental rights violations in operations coordinated by Frontex are rare.

In these three instances, the EO reached out to national ombudsmen to unravel potential issues. Conversely, ENO members may also submit queries to the EO about issues that arose during their own investigations. This allows them to obtain expert opinions by other EU institutions through the EO. A query was submitted by the Spanish Ombudsman in 2018 about Frontex's complaints mechanism.[90] More specifically, the national Ombudsman observed deficiencies in the accessibility of the mechanisms in its monitoring of Joint Return Operations. It thus agreed with the EO to ask questions to Frontex on the process of the complaints mechanisms (eg, accessibility and language of the complaint form, and the possibility to submit complaints orally). The EO played the role of middleman between the Spanish Ombudsman and Frontex, which allowed it to confirm, following the query, that improvements were made as regards the inclusivity of the complaints mechanism, notably by translating the complainant form into Spanish, Russian, Serbian and Albanian. Once again this shows that the cooperation between the national Ombudsman and the EO triggered some positive change for Frontex, and particularly to render Frontex accountable for its potential fundamental rights violations. The cooperation in both ways shows that the EO has grasped the complexity of the EU integrated administration and has taken advantage of cooperation between the national and European level. In fact, Emily O'Reilly noted when talking about Frontex that the 'multi-level structure makes it difficult to ensure accountability'.[91]

[87] National Ombudsmen from Belgium, Bulgaria, Croatia, Cyprus, the Czech Republic, Denmark, Estonia, Finland, Germany, Hungary, Ireland, Latvia, Lithuania, Malta, the Netherlands, Poland, Slovakia, Sweden, Slovenia, Spain and the Regional Ombudsman of the German Land Schleswig-Holstein.

[88] Case OI/5/2020/MHZ, Decision in OI/5/2020/MHZ on the functioning of Frontex complaints mechanism for alleged breaches of fundamental rights and the role of the Fundamental Rights Officer, decided on 15 June 2021.

[89] ibid.

[90] Query Q3/2017/MDC, Query from the Spanish Ombudsman concerning Frontex's obligation to make information about the complaints mechanism readily available, decided on 23 March 2018.

[91] Emily O'Reilly, Transparency and accountability in the management of European borders, speech of 23 April 2021.

It is thus one of their priorities to increase strategic cooperation between the members of the ENO.[92]

Alongside the involvement of national ombudsmen, the EO also frequently consults other organisations active in the protection of fundamental rights, such as international organisations, NGOs, private persons such as academics, as well as the Fundamental Rights Agency.[93] It also may exchange views with members of the European Parliament, through the LIBE Committee.[94] This strong involvement of other actors has significantly contributed to the success of the EO's investigations into Frontex. As will be demonstrated in the subsequent section, this may offer opportunities to strengthen the EO's role over Europol.

B. Towards More Proactiveness on Europol? Opportunities and Limits

In all the EO cases analysed on Europol, none of them was followed by the consultation of the ENO or other relevant parties. This may be related to the fact that the Ombudsman only opened three own-initiative inquiries against Europol on (1) public access to documents;[95] (2) the disclosure of the names of Selection board members;[96] and (3) the Agency's best practices (eg, rules on transparency, accountability, recruitment, conflicts of interest).[97] These do not concern Europol's concrete operations, nor compliance with fundamental rights, and thus did not trigger the involvement of national ombudsmen. In the same manner, no queries were made by members of the ENO to the EO.

Europol is essentially a *keyboard* Agency, in the sense that staff of the Agencies are only rarely deployed in the field.[98] Thus, it is harder for national ombudsmen and individuals to grasp Europol's impact on fundamental rights. Europol is less in the spotlight than Frontex, that is the object of every controversy in the past

[92] As mentioned already in 2015, Press Release No 7/2015, Ombudsman: How Frontex can ensure respect for migrants' fundamental rights during 'forced returns', published on 6 May 2015.

[93] In the case OI/5/2020/MHZ, the EO received observations from the Fundamental Rights Agency, from academics, from NGOs (eg, Amnesty International, Caritas Europa, Jesuits Refugee Service Europe, Human Rights Watch), and from international organisations (eg, the Committee on Migration, Refugees and Displaced Persons of the Parliamentary Assembly of the Council of Europe).

[94] For example, in the case OI/3/2023/MHZ, Exchange of views on Adriana shipwreck at the European Parliament's LIBE Committee, 14 February 2024.

[95] Case OI/1/99/IJH, Decision of the European Ombudsman closing own-initiative inquiry OI/1/99/IJH as regards Europol, decided on 24 September 1999.

[96] Case OI/4/2013/CK, Decision of the European Ombudsman closing the own-initiative inquiry OI/4/2013/CK into the EU Agencies practices regarding disclosure of the names of Selection Board members, decided on 16 May 2014.

[97] Case OI/9/2012/OV, Conclusions of the European Ombudsman's visit to the European Police Office (Europol): decision closing own-initiative inquiry OI/9/2012/OV, decided on 11 June 2014.

[98] Europol, 'Europol setting up team of 200 investigators to deploy to migration hotspots' (2016) www-europol-europa-eu.eui.idm.oclc.org/media-press/newsroom/news/europol-setting-team-of-200-investigators-to-deploy-to-migration-hotspots#:~:text=Europol%20setting%20up%20team%20of%20200%20investigators%20to%20deploy%20to%20migration%20hotspots,-news&text=Europol's%20Management%20Board%20today%20approved,in%20Greece%20and%20other%20countries; David Fernández Rojo, 'An Enforcement Role for Europol in the Aftermath of the "Refugee Crisis"?' (*EU Law Enforcement*, 31 May 2018) https://eulawenforcement.com/?p=740.

years. The only instance where Europol was put in the forefront was in the 'Big Data' saga.[99] In sum, it came to the ears of the EDPS that Europol continuously received and processed vast amounts of data from Member States, including individuals who had no clear link with any criminal activity. Nevertheless, the opacity of Europol's operation makes it hard for individuals to complain. Thus, it is harder for national ombudsmen and individuals to grasp Europol's impact on fundamental rights.

The power of the EO to open own-initiative investigations presents itself as an opportunity to monitor the Agency and further strengthen its transparency and accountability. In this way, the role of Europol would become clearer for EU citizens, which may in turn trigger further complaints sent to the EO, and more inquiries opened into Europol. This would also allow for the participation of national ombudsmen. Since Europol collects and processes data it receives from Member States, the involvement of national ombudsmen would prove itself highly relevant to monitor Europol. This is an approach that the EDPS has tried to adopt recently in a *joint* investigation on the processing of minors by Europol.[100] The EDPS is the central external supervisor of Europol, tasked with ensuring Europol's (as well as Frontex's)[101] compliance with data protection.[102] In this *joint* investigation, the EDPS asked national data protection authorities to verify the lawfulness of the data about minors transmitted to Europol.[103] It is key to have some joint supervision for EU agencies, and the EO may offer this through its ENO. Since Europol's power continuously grows, and affects fundamental rights, it is important to strengthen the EO's role over it.

However, there is one aspect intrinsically linked to the specific nature of Europol's power, which is closely related to the protection of personal data, that limit the EO's role over it and favour the involvement of the EDPS. In fact, both the EDPS and EO have competences over the Europol. To avoid potential overlaps, they adopted a Memorandum of Understanding in 2007 for constructive cooperation.[104] According to the latter, data protection cases must in principle be lodged with the EDPS, and broader issues of maladministration remain in the realm of the Ombudsman. Accordingly, the Ombudsman informs complainants of the special expertise of the EDPS in data protection matters. Vice versa, the EDPS informs complainants of the competence of the Ombudsman over maladministration. In both cases, the bodies do not take a view on the merits of the case, but simply advise the complainant to contact the other specialised authority. They follow a hands-off approach, and mutually trust each other and respect each other's autonomy, for efficiency reasons. Nevertheless, this could ultimately limit the possibility

[99] Sarah Tas, 'Europol's 'Big Data Challenge'' (*Digi-Con*, 10 February 2022) https://digi-con.org/europols-big-data-challenge-a-neutralisation-of-the-european-watchdog/.

[100] EDPS, Audit report on Europol Case number 2022-0382, published on 16 December 2022.

[101] See for example EDPS, EDPS Decision concerning the investigation into Frontex's move to the Cloud (Case 2020-0584), done on 1 April 2022.

[102] Article 43 of Regulation (EU) 2022/991.

[103] EDPS, Audit report on Europol Case number 2022-0382, published on 16 December 2022, 3.

[104] Memorandum of Understanding between the European Ombudsman and the European Data Protection Supervisor (2007/C 27/07) 2007.

of the EO to open own-initiative inquiries into matters of data protection, which are the majority of cases over Europol.

However, the EO may still through its investigation further strengthen the transparency of the Agency, which falls under its competences, and not the ones of the EDPS. Alternatively, stronger cooperation could be set up between the EDPS and the Ombudsman. This has not yet occurred; however, they have shared expertise on the topic of Artificial Intelligence and EU administration during a meeting held in March 2022.[105] Similar exchanges could be envisaged on Europol and the EDPS may point out issues it noticed over Europol and suggest for the EO to open an inquiry into it.

Thus, even though both Frontex and Europol have divergent competences, it remains possible for the EO to be more proactive over Europol, for the Agency to become more transparent and accountable. To this end, it is key to have some joint supervision for EU agencies, and the EO may offer this through its ENO and cooperation with other institutional and public actors. Since Europol's power continuously grows, and affects fundamental rights, it is important to strengthen the EO's role over it.

V. CONCLUDING REMARKS

This chapter delved into the potential for the EO to foster institutional legitimacy of EU agencies, particularly of Frontex and Europol. It used a quantitative and qualitative methodology to offer a comprehensive in-depth assessment and analysis of the work of the EO's over these two EU Agencies. This assessment showed a timid role of the EO over Europol, not only in terms of numbers with a total of 40 decisions adopted on Europol since the establishment of the EO (from which three are own-initiative inquiries), but also in light of the topics covered. The Ombudsman essentially strengthens the transparency of the EU Agency, albeit in a limited way, but did not (yet) deal with substantive fundamental rights compliance issues related to Europol. When it comes the EO's role over Frontex, a different strategy was adopted, that of strong proactiveness by the Ombudsman since the setting up of the Agency. The EO 'inquired into Frontex many times and this scrutiny will continue and expand'.[106] At the time of the writing of this chapter, the EO adopted more than 60 decisions on Frontex, and concluded nine own-initiatives inquiries, covering various themes including the transparency and accountability of the Agency. As a result, the EO further strengthened the transparency and accountability of Frontex. The best example is the introduction of the internal complaints mechanism within Frontex, which was triggered by the EO

[105] European Ombudsman, 'Report on the Meeting between European Ombudsman Representatives and European Data Protection Supervisor Representatives' (*European Ombudsman*, 4 April 2022) www.ombudsman.europa.eu/en/doc/inspection-report/en/154290.

[106] European Ombudsman, Exchange of views on Adriana shipwreck at the European Parliament's LIBE Committee – Speech by Emily O'Reilly, held on 14 February 2024.

recommendations.[107] Underlying this success was the EO's strategic approach the complex functioning of EU agencies, which leveraged integrated mechanism of monitoring such as the ENO.

It is undeniable that Europol – as other EU agencies – has different powers and tasks. However, it is also clear that more could be done by the EO to further shed light on the Agency's work. As explained in the previous section, a clear road ahead in monitoring EU agencies would be to extrapolate and further leverage the use of parallel inquiries within the ENO's framework. In the end, this approach is well suited for the in-between characteristic of EU agencies and the integrated administration. Likewise, it allows for a more efficient and impactful work. While the chapter focused on Europol and Frontex, the EO clearly stated in her speech in February 2024, the EO's inquiries shall continue for all EU institutions and bodies that are becoming more 'hands-on executive body' (eg, by processing asylum claims or procuring vaccines).[108] For now, not many decisions were for example adopted against the EUAA (previously the European Union Asylum Support Office). The recommendations used above for Europol for more proactiveness by the EO, may equally apply to the EUAA, and to other EU Agencies. Yet, due to the fact that the EO remains a small office with limited resources, this can only be done within reasonable limits.

[107] Case OI/5/2012/BEH-MHZ, Special Report of the EO in own-initiative inquiry OI/5/2012/BEH-MHZ concerning Frontex, adopted on 7 November 2013.

[108] European Ombudsman, Exchange of views on Adriana shipwreck at the European Parliament's LIBE Committee – Speech by Emily O'Reilly, held on 14 February 2024.

8

Barriers to Obtaining Information to Protect the Environment: The Role of the European Ombudsman

ANNE FRIEL AND ONNO BROUWER

I. INTRODUCTION

THIS CONTRIBUTION DEALS with the continuous challenges faced by members of the public and environmental non-profit organisations (eNPO) to access environmental information held by the EU institutions and bodies. In the first section, we identify the legal framework relating to environmental information that binds the European Union and the objectives it seeks to attain. The second section looks at a selection of the case law of the Court of Justice of the European Union and European Ombudsman cases to identify some indicative examples of the environmental information sought by the public and eNPOs, and the direct link to environmental protection. The third and final section discusses the role that the European Ombudsman can play in addressing barriers in obtaining environmental information, through the specific powers and competences attributed to that office, and concludes there is still much to be done to implement both the letter and spirit of the Aarhus Convention at the level of the EU institutions.

II. THE LEGAL FRAMEWORK REGULATING PUBLIC ACCESS TO ENVIRONMENTAL INFORMATION

The general EU transparency framework, comprised of Article 1 TEU, Article 15 TFEU and Regulation 1049/2001[1] also applies to environmental information held by the EU institutions and bodies. However, specific obligations apply when environmental information is at stake. These are enshrined in the United Nations Economic Commission for Europe Aarhus Convention on access to information, public

[1] Regulation (EC) No 1049/2001 of the European Parliament and of the Council of 30 May 2001 regarding public access to European Parliament, Council and Commission documents [2001] OJ L 145.

participation in decision-making and access to justice in environmental matters. In addition to each of its Member States, the EU itself signed the Convention in 1999 and ratified it in 2005,[2] ensuring that its provisions form an integral part of the EU legal order[3] and apply to the EU institutions themselves. These obligations have been transposed through Regulation 1367/2006 on the application of the provisions of the Aarhus Convention on Access to Information, Public Participation in Decision-making and Access to Justice in Environmental Matters to Union institutions and bodies,[4] which modifies the general EU transparency framework when environmental information is concerned.

Unlike most other international environmental agreements, 'the Aarhus Convention is primarily concerned with the obligations that Parties have towards the public, rather than simply those between Parties', marking it out as being both a living human rights treaty, as well as an environmental one.[5] The rights granted to the public cover three pillars of environmental democracy: access to environmental information; public participation in environmental decision-making; and access to justice in environmental matters. When it comes to accessing environmental information, the Aarhus Convention places both reactive and active disclosure obligations on the EU institutions. Article 4 of the Convention provides the right for the public to request and receive environmental information from the institutions, unless one of the strictly interpreted exceptions applies, while Article 5 contains several obligations regarding the organisation and dissemination of environmental information.

The preamble to the Convention and its operative provisions establish the premise that there is a direct link between the procedural rights it enshrines and positive environmental outcomes. In other words, active and engaged members of the public who participate in the complexities of environmental decision-making and wish to ensure compliance with environmental rules are essential to long-term environmental protection and the realisation of the right to a healthy environment.[6] The right to access environmental information is therefore a fundamental right that empowers individuals, and the organisations they form (eNPOs), to pursue effective environmental protection, by allowing them inter alia to participate in environmental decision-making, to legally challenge environmental wrongdoing, make informed political and consumer choices and organise and protest against

[2] Decision 2005/370/EC: Council Decision of 17 February 2005 on the conclusion, on behalf of the European Community, of the Convention on access to information, public participation in decision-making and access to justice in environmental matters [2005] OJ L 124.

[3] Case C-279/12 *Fish Legal and Shirley*, ECLI:EU:C:2013:853, [2013], para 35.

[4] Regulation (EC) No 1367/2006 of the European Parliament and of the Council of 6 September 2006 on the application of the provisions of the Aarhus Convention on Access to Information, Public Participation in Decision-making and Access to Justice in Environmental Matters to Community institutions and bodies [2006] OJ L 264.

[5] E Barritt, *The Foundations of the Aarhus Convention: Environmental Democracy, Rights and Stewardship* (Oxford, Hart Publishing, 2020) 5.

[6] In particular, the Convention's objective is expressed in its Art 1 in the following terms: 'In order to contribute to the protection of the right of every person of present and future generations to live in an environment adequate to his or her health and well-being, each Party shall guarantee the rights of access to information, public participation in decision-making, and access to justice in environmental matters in accordance with the provisions of this Convention.'

environmentally harmful conduct. This is perhaps why Kofi Annan described the Aarhus Convention as 'the most ambitious endeavor in the area of environmental democracy so far undertaken under the auspices of the United Nations'.[7]

This is the context in which the EU legislation implementing the Convention must be applied and interpreted by EU institutions and bodies.[8] While the European Ombudsman has demonstrated that this office has a pivotal role to play in ensuring adequate protection of this fundamental right, there is still a lot to be done at EU level to ensure that citizens, eNPOs and other members of the public can access the information they need.

III. WHAT INFORMATION AND WHY? SOME INDICATIVE EXAMPLES

It is impossible to underestimate the impact that decisions taken at EU level have on the environment and the protection of related fundamental rights, like the right to life[9] and the right to respect for privacy and private life.[10] Therefore, for members of the public and eNPOs to perform their role as environmental defenders, they need access to the environmental information collected and held by EU institutions.

In our work as practitioners, we are often questioned about why we want access to a specific piece of information and what difference it will make to environmental protection. While the public is not obliged to provide reasons for why it needs or wants access to environmental information,[11] cases before the Courts of Justice of the EU and the European Ombudsman provide insights into the kind of environmental information sought by the public and the reasons why. Three pertinent examples include: information on Member State positions in legislative and comitology processes; information on Member State implementation of and compliance with EU environmental law; and information on the scientific basis for EU decisions.

A. Access to Member State Positions in EU Decision-Making

Member States play a central role in both EU legislative and comitology processes, deciding the laws and regulations that shape the environment we live in. Despite

[7] Implementation Guide, 1st edition, Foreword. Note that this statement predates the adoption of the Regional Agreement on Access to Information, Public Participation and Justice in Environmental Matters in Latin America and the Caribbean (the Escazu Agreement).

[8] Regulation (EC) No 1049/2001 of the European Parliament and of the Council of 30 May 2001 regarding public access to European Parliament, Council and Commission documents [2001] OJ L 145; Regulation (EC) No 1367/2006 of the European Parliament and of the Council of 6 September 2006 on the application of the provisions of the Aarhus Convention on Access to Information, Public Participation in Decision-making and Access to Justice in Environmental Matters to Community institutions and bodies [2006] OJ L 264.

[9] Art 2 of the European Convention of Human Rights and Art 2 of the European Charter of Fundamental Rights.

[10] Art 8 of the European Convention of Human Rights and Art 7 of the Charter of Fundamental Rights.

[11] Aarhus Convention, Art 4(1)(a); Regulation 1049/2001, Art 6(1).

this, the positions they defend and amendments they put forward are not always published and delays (lawful and unlawful) in treating access requests mean that this information, once obtained, can often not be used anymore for the purpose for which it was requested. Without timely access to Member State positions, public participation in decision-making is practically impossible, because the public and eNPOs cannot identify and engage with Member States that advocate unsustainable positions. The lack of publicly available information also prevents national governments from being held accountable for the positions they defend at EU level, which in turn affects the legitimacy of EU decision-making and, arguably, the European project itself.[12] Several CJEU judgments[13] and European Ombudsman cases[14] have decided that greater public access to Member State positions in legislative processes is needed[15] but progress is slow-moving, incomplete and inconsistent. Unfortunately, it is our experience that there has been no progress on accessing Member State positions in comitology processes and other decision-making that are not based on the ordinary legislative process, again despite explicit decisions from the European Ombudsman and the General Court of the EU.[16]

B. Information on Member State Compliance with EU Environmental Law

Several cases before the Court of Justice[17] also testify to the need for the public and eNPOs to access information on how Member States implement and comply with their European law obligations, particularly those impacting the environment. From an environmental protection point of view, the reason for this is clear and compelling. While the European Commission is meant to be the 'guardian' of the EU Treaties, it does not have the resources nor the political capital to follow-up on every EU law breach it detects. It is widely recognised that this effort needs to be supplemented by members of the public and eNPOs acting in the public interest, and this necessitates

[12] See European Ombudsman, 'Ombudsman calls for "blame Brussels" culture to end', press release 1/2019, 17 January 2019.

[13] Cases C-280/11 *P Council v Access Info Europe* ECLI:EU:C:2013:671, [2013] and T-163/21 *De Capitani v Council* ECLI:EU:T:2023:15, [2023].

[14] Decision in Strategic Inquiry OI/2/2017/TE on the Transparency of the Council legislative process, 15 May 2018.

[15] See, for example, European Ombudsman, 'Ombudsman welcomes steps to make EU law making more accessible to the public' press release 2/2020, 16 July 2020.

[16] Regarding legislative documents related to the Council's competence under Art 43(3) TFEU, see Reply from the Council of the European Union to the European Ombudsman's recommendation concerning the case 640/2019/TE on Council's lack of transparency in the decision-making process leading to the adoption of regulations setting fishing quotas (total allowable catches), 30 January 2020; regarding comitology documents, see case C-726/22 P *Commission v Pollinis France*, currently pending, in which the Commission has appealed against the General Court's finding that Member State positions in a comitology process should have been disclosed to eNPO, Pollinis.

[17] For example, see Cases C-514/11 P and C-605/11 P *LPN and Finland v Commission* ECLI:EU:C:2013:738 [2013]; C-612/13 P *ClientEarth v Commission* ECLI:EU:C:2015:486 [2015]; T-727/15 *Justice & Environment v Commission* ECLI:EU:T:2017:18, [2017]; case C-249/23 P *ClientEarth v Commission* ECLI:EU:C:2024:691 [2024] and 'EU failing to enforce illegal fishing rules, say campaigners' *The Guardian* (6 September 2024) www.theguardian.com/environment/article/2024/sep/06/eu-failing-to-enforce-fishing-rules-say-campaigners.

access to the information collected and held by EU institutions, giving the public the possibility to take these issues up with their elected representatives and governments, and organise locally to avoid or minimise the resulting irreversible environmental degradation. This is not a luxury, the cost of not implementing environmental laws is alarming.[18] Access to this type of information is also crucial when specific environmental laws are reviewed and revised by the EU legislature.[19] Unfortunately, almost all information held by the European Commission relating to Member States' EU law compliance is covered by a general presumption of confidentiality and, as a result, largely inaccessible to the public.[20] This needs to be revisited as a blanket and general presumption of non-disclosure of this information (in particular environmental information) – 'to defend a relationship of trust' between the Commission and Member States – is outdated with today's pressing environmental concerns and in a union based on citizenship and fundamental rights.

C. Scientific Basis for Environmental Decision-Making

A point of particular importance is also that there is a discernible need for members of the public and eNPOs to have better access to the scientific basis for EU decision-making,[21] in order to verify its accuracy and whether it was given adequate weight in the final decision taken. When it comes to authorisation procedures,[22] toxicity studies[23] or carcinogenicity studies,[24] disclosure of this information is often refused by EU institutions on the basis of commercial interests and intellectual property. And while the Court of Justice has ruled that legislative impact assessments should be disclosed before the final legislative proposal is adopted, this ruling has not been observed by the Commission in a number of cases where requests have been made[25]

[18] The Commission's 2019 Environmental Implementation Review put the costs of poor implementation of EU environmental legislation at 55 billion euros per year, COM(2019) 149 final.

[19] C-249/23 P *ClientEarth v Commission* ECLI:EU:C:2024:691 [2024].

[20] Cases C-514/11 P and C-605/11 P *LPN and Finland v Commission* ECLI:EU:C:2013:738 [2013]; C-249/23 P *ClientEarth v Commission* ECLI:EU:C:2024:691 [2024]). See also the European Ombudsman's Decision in case 452/2018/AMF on the European Commission's failure to disclose information on the existence of EU Pilot dialogues and to publish proactively Member State reports on the implementation of the Fisheries Control Regulation, 16 December 2019. Despite a finding of maladministration, the European Commission maintained its refusal to grant access to basic information on pre-infringement proceedings, so-called EU Pilot cases. It should be noted that the Court's case law makes it clear that the EU institutions are never obliged to apply general presumptions of confidentiality, and are entitled to carry out a concrete examination of the requested documents. To this effect, see case C-178/18 P MSD Animal Health Innovation and Intervet International v EMA, ECLI:EU:2020:24 [2020], paragraph 57.

[21] For example, Case C-60/15 P *Saint Gobain Glass Deutschland v Commission* ECLI:EU:C:2017:540, [2017].

[22] Case C-673/13 P *Commission v Stichting Greenpeace Nederland and PAN Europe* ECLI:EU:C:2016:889, [2016].

[23] Case T-716/14 *Tweedale v EFSA* ECLI:EU:T:2019:141, [2019].

[24] Case T-329/17 *Hautala and Others v EFSA* ECLI:EU:T:2019:142, [2019].

[25] See orders in cases T-661/21 *ClientEarth v Commission* ECLI:EU:T:2022:286, [2022]; T-792/21 *ClientEarth v Commission*, and the European Ombudsman's recent Recommendation in case 1053/2023/MIK on how the European Commission handled two requests for public access to the impact assessments and opinions of the Regulatory Scrutiny Board regarding the envisaged revision of REACH and the Mercury Regulation, 25 September 2023.

and we continue to see a general unwillingness to publish these documents until the proposal is adopted.

IV. OPPORTUNITIES AND CHALLENGES FOR THE EUROPEAN OMBUDSMAN

As practitioners working with and on behalf of environmental defenders, academics and other environmental actors, we encounter structural, legal and practical barriers to accessing environmental information from EU institutions and bodies. It is the authors' opinion that these barriers are symptomatic of an EU which has not yet embedded the specific environmental information obligations and the spirit of the Aarhus Convention within its administrative procedures and the mindsets of its officials. In this final section, we will look at the opportunities available to the European Ombudsman for removing barriers to accessing environmental information, taking into account the particular powers available to that office, as well as the limits.

The Ombudsman is an important and reliable forum for complaining of maladministration when the EU institutions fail to provide timely access to environmental information. Our practical experience of submitting complaints is positive: inquiry officers are professional and experienced, and show dedication to making the EU a better place for its citizens by acting as an objective interlocutor between complainants and EU institutions. Although the Ombudsman risks political capital when her findings of maladministration and recommendations are rejected and ignored by EU institutions, we firmly believe that taking a robust and uncompromising approach to addressing the EU institutions' failure to comply with the spirit and letter of the Aarhus Convention is much more likely to lead to systemic change. Notably, her finding of maladministration in response to the Commission's refusal to disclose comitology documents related to the risk assessment of pesticides on bees (the 'Bee Guidance' case)[26] was a significant step forward for transparent EU environmental decision-making, that was eventually followed by the General Court.[27] We are also very supportive of the Ombudsman's efforts to address the delays with which EU institutions deal with access requests,[28] and her clear stance that 'access delayed is access denied'.[29]

In terms of the specific barriers faced by environmental actors, we appreciate that there are limits to what the Ombudsman's role can achieve. For example,

[26] Recommendation of the European Ombudsman in case 2142/2018/TE on the European Commission's refusal to grant access to Member State positions on a guidance document concerning the risk assessment of pesticides on bees, 10 May 2019.

[27] Decision of the European Ombudsman in case 2142/2018/EWM on the European Commission's refusal to grant access to Member State positions on a guidance document concerning the risk assessment of pesticides on bees, 3 December 2019.

[28] See European Ombudsman, 'Ombudsman asks Parliament to act on Commission delays in dealing with access to documents requests', press release 3/2023, 21 September 2023.

[29] Recommendation in Strategic Inquiry OI/2/2022/OAM on the time the European Commission takes to deal with requests for public access to documents, 24 March 2023.

we observe that the practice of applying general presumptions of confidentiality to cover several,[30] ever-expanding[31] categories of documents, is contrary to the Aarhus Convention as it runs counter to the requirement in Article 4(4) to carry out a concrete examination of the documents in question and actively balance the interests at play in the specific circumstances of the request.[32] Yet, because this practice has been sanctioned by the Court of Justice of the EU, the Ombudsman is prevented from coming to a contrary conclusion. This is because the CJEU is the only institution competent to give an authoritative interpretation of EU law, as reflected in Article 1(5) of the Ombudsman's statute, which states: 'In the performance of his or her duties, the Ombudsman may not question the soundness of a court's ruling or a court's competence to issue a ruling.'

Nevertheless, there remain several aspects of the EU's implementation of the Aarhus Convention which could be tackled by the Ombudsman, either because they do not respect the CJEU's case law or because they are a matter of practice rather than law, and may be due in part to inadequate resources and/or expertise in EU administrations.

The EU's approach to publishing environmental information in line with Article 5 of the Aarhus Convention and Article 4 of Regulation 1367/2006 is one example. The purpose of these obligations is to ensure that certain environmental information becomes available to the public as a matter of urgency,[33] without having to submit a request. It also ensures that environmental information is organised and listed on public registers, even if it is not disseminated directly, to allow the public to know of its existence and submit access requests if necessary. The lack of a structured and consistent approach to implementing Article 5 of the Aarhus Convention ultimately leads to a greater number of requests for access to environmental information, causing delays and inefficient use of public resources. It can also obstruct the public's right to challenge decisions which breach EU environmental law before national and EU courts, for example through the internal review mechanism in the Regulation 1367/2006, since deadlines for legal challenge are often shorter than the length of time that EU institutions take to deal with information requests.[34]

This phenomenon regretfully extends further than only environmental information. It is for instance painful to see that not even legislative documents are consistently published or even listed on public registers, despite the case law of the EU Courts having consistently held that the EU legislative process must be open (Article 15(2) TFEU and Article 12 of Regulation 1049/2001). The result is that

[30] See Case 57/16 P *ClientEarth v Commission* ECLI:EU:C:2018:660, [2018] para 81.

[31] See, for example, the expansion of the general presumption of confidentiality covering infringement proceedings to EU Pilot proceedings in case C-562/14 P *Sweden v Commission* ECLI:EU:C:2017:356, [2017] para 45.

[32] See the Aarhus Convention Compliance Committee's findings in Communication ACCC/C/2007/21, para 30(c).

[33] Aarhus Convention Implementation Guide, 2nd edition, 2014, p 95.

[34] For example, ClientEarth submitted a request for environmental information related to the EIB financing decision at issue in joined cases C-212/21 P and 223/21 *EIB and Commission v ClientEarth* ECLI:EU:C:2023:546, [2023], which was answered long after the deadline for internal review expired.

crucially important information is being withheld from citizens and eNPOs that would allow for participation in important EU legislative decision-making, a democratic right laid down in Article 10 TEU.

When it comes to legislative documents, the Ombudsman fortunately intervened to address this breach. In one complaint filed by ClientEarth regarding the Council's failure to publish Member State positions on the Regulation fixing the Total Allowable Catches (TACs) in the Northeast Atlantic, the Ombudsman found maladministration and issued a recommendation to 'proactively make public documents related to the adoption of the TAC Regulation at the time they are circulated to Member States or as soon as possible thereafter'.[35]

Unfortunately, this approach has not been followed with regard to environmental information that is not related to a legislative process, and we note with regret that the Ombudsman's approach in this context has been at times formalistic and hesitant, showing a reluctance to state that Article 4 of Regulation 1367/2006 places clear obligations on EU institutions.[36] To date, failures to actively disseminate environmental information have been met with *suggestions* for active dissemination, rather than findings of maladministration and recommendations.[37] This is particularly disappointing when it comes to repeat offenders, like the European Investment Bank and its failure to publish environmental information on the projects it funds in a timely manner.[38]

The Ombudsman could also take effective action to secure a more consistent approach to how the EU institutions apply certain aspects of the Aarhus framework to information requests. First, the concept of 'environmental information' is often disputed. While Article 2(3) of the Aarhus Convention defines the concept of 'environmental information' in broad terms, and has been transposed faithfully into Article 2(1)(d) of the Regulation 1367/2006, a recurrent theme in our interactions with EU institutions is their reluctance to qualify certain information as having an environmental quality at all, with the consequence that the Aarhus framework is not applied to the case at hand. Second, the components of the legal test to ascertain whether there is an overriding public interest in disclosure of environmental information[39]

[35] Recommendation of the European Ombudsman in case 640/2019/FP on the transparency of the Council of the EU's decision-making process leading to the adoption of annual regulations setting fishing quotas (total allowable catches), 25 October 2019.

[36] Decision in case 367/2017/CEC on the European Commission's alleged wrongful refusal to grant public access to conformity checking studies in the field of EU environmental law, 10 September 2018, para 48.

[37] Recommendation of the European Ombudsman in case 452/2018/AMF on the European Commission's failure to disclose information on the existence of EU Pilot dialogues and to publish proactively Member State reports on the implementation of the Fisheries Control Regulation, 16 December 2019, para 24.

[38] See, for example, Decision in case 2252/2022/OAM on how the European Investment Bank discloses environmental and social information on projects prior to decisions on funding, 20 November 2023; and Decision in case 1065/2020/PB on how the European Investment Bank discloses environmental information in relation to projects that it finances directly, 21 April 2022.

[39] Art 4 of the Aarhus Convention and Art 4 of Regulation 1049/2001, read in conjunction with Art 6 of Regulation 1367/2006, require that where an exception to disclosure applies to a request for environmental information, the institution must nevertheless disclose the information when there is an overriding public interest in doing so.

give too much discretion to the institution, with the result that very little information is disclosed on this basis.[40]

V. CONCLUSION

The public consultation opened by the European Ombudsman regarding transparency and participation in EU decision-making related to the environment[41] gives us cause for optimism. This has provided a much-needed opportunity for civil society to feed back their experiences to the Ombudsman, and the timing could not be more important. As we approach the 2024 European elections with the European Green Deal as yet incomplete, the Ombudsman is well placed to play its part to ensure that the EU delivers on the environmental commitments it promised to citizens, and in a way that complies fully with the rights enshrined in the Aarhus Convention.

As we wait for the Ombudsman to announce the next steps in this initiative, we would suggest that she continue to take the same unequivocal approach to upholding the spirit and letter of the Aarhus Convention as she did in the Bee Guidance case. For example, an own-initiative inquiry into how the EU institutions discharge their duty to weigh the public interest in the context of environmental information would help the public to understand the nature of the overriding public interest test, and ensure that the institutions approach their obligations in a consistent and citizen-friendly manner. We also suggest that she continue to reference the findings of the Aarhus Convention Compliance Committee in her decisions and recommendations,[42] and continue the recently established contact with the Compliance Committee which can offer advice and counsel on the application of the Aarhus Convention.[43] Having at times experienced the reluctance of EU officials in other institutions and even the Court to recognise the authority of the Committee's findings, we find this to be a particularly important development that should enhance the EU's implementation of the Convention.

We also note that there is significant legal expertise within the European Ombudsman's office which, combined with in-depth knowledge of the systemic barriers the public faces in accessing environmental information, could usefully be put before the CJEU through third-party interventions in strategic cases brought by members of the public.[44]

[40] See D Wyatt, 'The Anaemic Existence of the Overriding Public Interest in Disclosure in the EU's Access to Documents Regime' (2020) 21 *German Law Journal* 686.

[41] European Ombudsman, 'Public consultation – Transparency and participation in EU decision making related to the environment', SI/5/2022/KR, 7 September 2022, www.ombudsman.europa.eu/en/public-consultation/en/160313.

[42] Decision on the European Commission's refusal to give full public access to documents concerning a Horizon 2020 mineral exploration research project (cases 1132/2022/OAM and 1374/2022/OAM), 17 April 2023, para 33.

[43] Decision on how the European Investment Bank discloses environmental information in relation to projects that it finances directly (case 1065/2020/PB), 21 April 2022.

[44] Art 40 of the Statute of the Court of Justice of the European Union.

In addition to the complaints received on a regular basis, the recent consultation now gives the Ombudsman an opportunity to identify systemic issues to be pursued on her own-initiative through well-targeted inquiries, reports to the European Parliament and strategic third-party court interventions. We are looking forward to seeing what next steps will be announced.

9

The Role of the European Ombudsman in Curtailing Undue Corporate Lobbying Influence

OLIVIER HOEDEMAN

DURING MORE THAN 25 years, Corporate Europe Observatory (CEO) has helped expose a wide range of examples of corporate lobbying influence that undermine the independence and legitimacy of the EU institutions. The risk of excessive and undue corporate influence is obvious considering that corporations invest enormous amounts in EU lobbying and that there are many thousands of well-resourced corporate lobbyists working to influence EU decision-making on a daily basis.[1] The European Ombudsman has played in crucial role in promoting strong, well-enforced lobby regulations to tackle these problems.

Until 15 years ago, rules to secure the transparency, accountability and independence of the EU institutions were very limited. The turning point came in 2005 when newly arrived European Commissioner Siim Kallas took the Brussels establishment by surprise by announcing that he would set up a lobby transparency register.[2] The idea instantly faced a heavy backlash both from corporate lobbyists and from within the Commission, whereas non-governmental organisations (NGOs) formed the Alliance for Lobbying Transparency and Ethics Regulation (ALTER-EU) in support of Kallas' initiative.[3] Before the Transparency Register was created, the secrecy around lobbying in Brussels was shocking. If you were to ask one of the

[1] The Economist in 2021 wrote that there are '25,000 lobbyists with a combined annual budget conservatively estimated at more than €3bn ($3.6bn) seek to influence EU policy', see The Economist, 'The power of lobbyists is growing in Brussels and Berlin', 15 May 2021, htw.economist.com/business/2021/05/15/the-power-of-lobbyists-is-growing-in-brussels-and-berlin.

Transparency International has estimated that 'at least 48,000 individuals work in this European capital in organisations seeking to influence the EU institutions and decisions, with 7,500 of these possessing an accredited lobby badge to the European Parliament. The nearly 12,000 organisations on the current voluntary EU lobby register declare a combined annual lobby budget of 1.8 billion euros', htnsparency.eu/priority/eu-money-politics/lobbying/.

[2] Siim Kallas, 'The need for a European transparency initiative', Speech delivered at The European Foundation for Management, Nottingham Business School, Nottingham, 3 March 2005, SPEECH/05/130.

[3] Further information about the initiative is available at: www.alter-eu.org/about/coalition.

many large lobby consultancy firms in the EU quarter for which multinational companies they were lobbying, as CEO did,[4] they simply refused to answer, arguing they had promised their clients confidentiality and that they had no obligation to be transparent. Significant progress in lobbying transparency and ethics rules has been made since then, but genuine transparency is still far from achieved, let alone adequate regulation to prevent undue influence and the capture of decision-making by narrow economic interests.

This chapter provides an account of the successes achieved through the work of civil society organisations and the European Ombudsman – and of the many ongoing battles. Its examples mainly focus on the work of the European Commission: the Transatlantic Business Dialogue, lobbying of the tobacco and Big Tech industries, reforms of transparency registers and the capture of advisory positions by the finance and oil industry. The conclusion points to the European Parliament as a crucial actor in the way forward.

I. PROMOTING COMMISSION TRANSPARENCY AND ETHICS

The European Ombudsman has played a crucial role in advancing the transparency, accountability and independence of the EU institutions during the last decades. CEO submitted its first complaint to the Ombudsman in 2002, against the European Commission's secrecy around the Transatlantic Business Dialogue (TABD).[5] The TABD was a mechanism, co-created by the Commission, that enabled EU and US corporate executives to highlight 'regulatory barriers' to transatlantic trade and investment, barriers which the EU and the US would then attempt to remove.[6] In practice, such perceived 'barriers' were often entirely legitimate environment and public health regulations that corporations disliked. The European Ombudsman at the time, Jacob Söderman, agreed with CEO's complaint and found that the Commission's secrecy around the TABD was maladministration.[7]

Since then, CEO has submitted complaints to the Ombudsman on more than a dozen different problem areas, all related to conflicts of interest and undue influence in EU decision making. In numerous cases, this led to high-impact decisions of the

[4] CEO had written to 35 Brussels-based public affairs companies, asking for 'an overview of the clients for which your firm in the last 12 months has provided PA/PR services on REACH, the relevant budget and towards which EU institutions the efforts were directed', see Corporate Europe Observatory, 'Bulldozing REACH – the industry offensive to crush EU chemicals regulation', March 2005, htchive.corporateeurope.org/docs/lobbycracy/BulldozingREACH.pdf.

[5] Corporate Europe Observatory, 'Ombudsman Clams Commission Over TABD Secrecy', CEObserver, Issue 12, archive.corporateeurope.org/observer12/ombudsman.html.

[6] The TABD used its privileged access to decision-making to delay and weaken a wide range of existing and proposed regulations aimed to protect the environment, consumers and workers. An example was a planned EU ban on marketing of animal-tested cosmetic products, which the TABD brought into the EU-US 'Early Warning' system, claiming that a ban would violate WTO rules. The TABD at the time also successfully pressurised the Commission into watering down a draft directive on Electrical and Electronic Equipment. Corporate Europe Observatory, 'TABD in Troubled Water', CEO issue briefing, October 2001, archive.corporateeurope.org/tabd/troubled.pdf.

[7] Decision of the European Ombudsman on complaint 1128/2001/IJH against the European Commission, 9 December 2002.

Ombudsman that sparked significant improvements in (the implementation of) EU transparency and ethics rules.[8] This progress came both from Ombudsman inquiries into specific complaints and from broader and deeper own-initiative investigations into systemic problems that had surfaced via complaints. These own-initiative investigations into systemic problems, a strong feature of the current Ombudsman's years in office, have made a particularly strong contribution to progress in lobbying regulation, for instance on the issue of revolving door moves between the European Commission and the corporate lobbying world.[9]

The Commission's approach to transparency and ethics regulation is mainly a reaction to scandals, when they occur.[10] The Commission's typical pattern of reaction to the many lobbying scandals that have emerged over the years has often been first denial and dismissal of concerns and then, in some cases, half-hearted reforms that do not effectively solve the problems. There is still a lack of a pro-active and determined effort by the Commission to properly tackle the problems: civil society groups continue to document and expose new examples of unsolved problems and demand action, but in itself this is often not enough to force the Commission to act. That is another reason why the Ombudsman's strategic inquiries, such as the 2021 in-depth investigation into revolving doors, are so important.[11] The Ombudsman has the mandate and resources for going deep into the problems, carrying out inspections, delivering facts and demanding improvements to the Commission's enforcement of its own rules.

An example of the key role of the Ombudsman in promoting lobbying transparency and accountability is the issue of tobacco industry lobbying, where the European Commission continues to resist an adequate implementation of UN rules for protecting decision-making against tobacco industry influence.[12] Back in 2016, the European Ombudsman had investigated and eventually concluded that the Commission's weak implementation of these UN rules is maladministration.[13] The inquiry found that only the Commission's health department properly implemented Article 5.3 of the UN tobacco convention, which requires governments to limit contacts with the tobacco industry to a minimum and ensure pro-active transparency

[8] Examples include: Decision closing the inquiry based on complaints 2077/2012/TN and 1853/2013/TN concerning the European Commission's handling of the 'revolving doors' phenomenon, 9 September 2016; Decision concerning the European Commission's compliance with the Tobacco Control Convention (852/2014/LP), 6 December 2016; Decision in joint cases 85/2021/MIG and 86/2021/MIG on the European Commission's refusal to give public access to documents concerning the purchase of vaccines against COVID-19, 12 May 2021.

[9] For example the own initiative inquiries on revolving doors with the Commission: Decision of the European Ombudsman in her strategic inquiry OI/3/2017/NF on how the European Commission manages 'revolving doors' situations of its staff members, 28 February 2019; Decision on how the European Commission manages 'revolving door' moves of its staff members (OI/1/2021/KR), 16 May 2022.

[10] Examples include the 2012 'Dalligate' tobacco lobbying scandal, former Commission President Barroso's revolving door move to Goldman Sachs in 2016, the Qatargate scandal in 2022, etc.

[11] Decision on how the European Commission manages 'revolving door' moves of its staff members (OI/1/2021/KR), 16 May 2022.

[12] World Health Organization Framework Convention on Tobacco Control, fctc.who.int/publications/i/item/9241591013.

[13] Decision concerning the European Commission's compliance with the Tobacco Control Convention (852/2014/LP), 6 December 2016.

about all such contacts. All other Commission departments failed in this respect and some even appeared to have an open-door policy for the tobacco industry.[14] Together with other civil society groups, CEO has regularly reminded the Commission of the need to implement Article 5.3 across all Commission departments.[15] So far, however, the Commission stubbornly refuses change.[16] It is therefore extremely important that the Ombudsman recently took the initiative to examine the Commission's meetings with tobacco lobbyists during the last two years, with an inspection that concluded that the problems remained.[17] In April 2023, the Ombudsman wrote a letter to the European Commission, criticising its approach and asking for improvements. It is this type of pressure that is needed to avoid that the von der Leyen Commission's five-year term ends without any progress on these issues, just like the Barroso and Juncker Commissions did. If the Commission cannot get it right when it comes to preventing tobacco lobbying interference (an industry producing a deadly product, with a proven record of manipulating science and regulatory processes,[18] and with a UN convention obliging governments to act), then that does not bode well for its general capacity to protect the public interest.

CEO's investigations show that also other corporations with a controversial business model frequently use lobbying tactics developed by the tobacco industry.[19] During the decision-making process on the EU's Digital Services and the Digital Markets laws, some Big Tech giants made use of front group strategies to give the impression that their lobbying demands were supported by small and medium-sized firms.[20] The EU Transparency Register remains far too weak and poorly enforced to prevent the use of deceptive lobbying strategies of this kind. CEO submitted complaints to the EU's Transparency Register secretariat about these front groups, which led to minor adjustments of the information in the register. The register lacks the kind of investigative powers and sanctions needed to discourage deceptive industry lobbying tactics. Members of the European Parliament (MEPs) reacted forcefully and called on the Parliament's president to sanction the Big Tech corporations using these tactics.[21] In the absence of a properly functioning EU transparency system, civil society initiatives are needed to tackle deceptive lobbying by Big Tech

[14] Corporate Europe Observatory, 'Smoke and mirrors – Weak EU transparency rules allow tobacco industry lobbyists to dodge scrutiny', 2 July 2020, corporateeurope.org/en/2020/07/smoke-and-mirrors.

[15] European Public Health Alliance, 'Dear EC Vice-President Jourová, please protect EU policy and law-making from vested tobacco industry interests', Statement, 2 July 2020, epha.org/dear-ec-vice-president-jourova-please-protect-eu-policy-and-law-making-from-vested-tobacco-industry-interests/.

[16] Previous Commission Presidents Barroso and Juncker refused to act, repeating the flawed argument that its existing general rules in the field of transparency and ethics were sufficient.

[17] Preliminary findings in OI/6/2021/KR on the European Commission's interactions with tobacco interest representatives, 14 April 2023.

[18] STOP. A Global Tobacco Industry Watchdog, 'Decades of Lies Show Tobacco Companies Can't Be Trusted', Blog, 14 March 2023, exposetobacco.org/news/tobacco-industry-lies/.

[19] Corporate Europe Observatory, 'How corporate lobbying undermined the EU's push to ban surveillance ads', 18 January 2022, corporateeurope.org/en/2022/01/how-corporate-lobbying-undermined-eus-push-ban-surveillance-ads.

[20] Corporate Europe Observatory, 'Lobby watchdogs file complaint against Apple front group', 3 July 2023, corporateeurope.org/en/2023/07/lobby-watchdogs-file-complaint-against-apple-front-group.

[21] Clothilde Goujard, 'Big Tech accused of shady lobbying in EU Parliament', Politico, 14 October 2022, www.politico.eu/article/big-tech-companies-face-potential-eu-lobbying-ban/.

corporations. In early 2023, CEO launched the LobbyLeaks.eu website, jointly with LobbyControl and supported by a cross-party group of MEPs. LobbyLeaks.eu is a hotline that enables the confidential sharing of examples of Big Tech lobbying in an opaque and misleading manner.

Another monumental failure of the Transparency Register is its inability to ensure that the lobbying on behalf of repressive regimes is disclosed. CEO has for many years published in-depth reports about covert repressive regime interference in EU decision-making (lobbying that is most often facilitated by lobby consultancy firms, PR firms, law firms, and think-tanks), and made concrete proposals to tackle the problem.[22] In the most recent reform of the Transparency Register, it was clarified that those lobbying on behalf of non-EU governments had to disclose it in the register. But in practice these activities remain invisible: repressive regime lobbyists easily bypass the EU register because it is weak, voluntary and poorly enforced. After the Qatargate scandal,[23] the European Commission has launched a legislative proposal for a directive on 'Transparency of Interest Representation on behalf of Third Countries' (part of the 'Defence of Democracy package').[24] It includes a proposal for 'foreign influence' registers, focusing on funding from outside of the EU. Remarkably, the most obvious, long overdue step is missing in the Commission's plans: to finally make the EU Transparency Register legally binding and ensure that it can be properly enforced, in order to secure full transparency of lobbying, including influencing by repressive regimes. Instead, the Commission embarked on a poorly prepared initiative that sparked a backlash from civil society groups that pointed out that measures 'intended to help counter covert foreign interference … risk having a serious negative impact on civil society organisations and on civic space' and insisted on an impact assessment to be undertaken.[25]

II. CHANGING POLITICAL CULTURE: A LONG WAY TO GO

Oftentimes the battle for transparency, accountability and independence of the EU institutions feels like a Sisyphean task. Take the example of the European Commission's industry-dominated advisory groups, the so-called expert groups. In the years before the financial crisis, the advisory groups that helped prepare EU banking regulation were captured by banking lobbyists, predictably resulting in the all too soft regulations that enabled the financial bubble that sparked the

[22] Corporate Europe Observatory, 'European PR firms whitewashing brutal regimes', Report, 20 January 2015, corporateeurope.org/en/pressreleases/2015/01/european-pr-firms-whitewashing-brutal-regimes-report.

[23] Corporate Europe Observatory, 'Qatargate: Time to close the door on repressive regime lobbying', Press Release, 12 December 2022, corporateeurope.org/en/2022/12/qatargate-time-close-door-repressive-regime-lobbying-0.

[24] European Commission, 'Defence of Democracy: Questions & Answers', 12 December 2023, ec.europa.eu/commission/presscorner/detail/en/qanda_23_6454.

[25] Sarah Wheaton and Clothilde Goujard, 'Under pressure, Commission delays foreign funding disclosure plan', Politico, 1 June 2023, www.politico.eu/article/european-union-election-foreign-interference-vera-jourova/.

2008 crisis.[26] The Ombudsman did crucial work on this during the previous Commission terms, in fruitful cooperation with MEPs, and contributed to new better rules for the composition of and transparency around such groups.[27] But old habits are hard to change, as shown in the Ombudsman's recent inquiry into the high-level forum on the EU capital markets union, in which rules on actual and potential conflicts of interest of its members were not enforced.[28] Despite the introduction of new rules in 2016,[29] the Commission regularly sets up advisory groups that are imbalanced or even fully captured by commercial interests. An example is the EU Energy Platform Industry Advisory Group (EPIAG, launched in autumn 2022),[30] which is an industry-only advisory group and includes oil and gas giants such as BP, TotalEnergies, Eni, E.ON and Repsol. This group was first proposed by the CEOs of these oil and gas companies in spring 2022, in one of many meetings that Commission President von der Leyen had with the European Roundtable of Industrialists (ERT) in the aftermath of the Russian invasion of Ukraine. The privileged access which these corporations enjoy via the EPIAG creates unacceptable conflicts of interest as energy companies get the exclusive opportunity to shape EU policy – as well as regulatory and financial decisions – in ways that serve their narrow commercial interests. These interests, moreover, are obviously at odds with the public interest in a rapid phase-out of fossil fuels, a stated objective of the EU's European Green Deal. In February 2023, CEO wrote to the Commission to point out that the industry-only EPIAG violates the Commission's horizontal rules on expert groups, in which the Commission committed to strive for a balanced composition of these groups.[31] Several months later, the Commission responded with a letter dismissing the concerns and announcing a one-off meeting with civil society to take place in July 2023, eight months after the industry-only EPIAG had started its work. While this was a form of acknowledgement that the Commission had failed to follow its own rules for a balanced composition of advisory groups, the NGO meeting was clearly too little and came too late. Following a complaint by CEO, the Ombudsman opened an inquiry into the EPIAG in November 2023.[32]

[26] The Alliance for Lobbying Transparency and Ethics Regulation in the EU (ALTER-EU), 'Securing balanced representation in expert groups dealing with financial issues', Open Letter to Michel Barnier, European Commissioner for Internal Market and Services, Brussels, 2 November 2010, www.alter-eu.org/sites/default/files/documents/alter-eu_letter_to_commissioner_barnier_november_2010.pdf.

[27] Decision of the European Ombudsman in her strategic inquiry OI/6/2014/NF concerning the composition and transparency of European Commission expert groups, 14 November 2017.

[28] Decision on how the European Commission handled concerns about the composition of the High Level Forum on Capital Markets Union and alleged conflicts of interest of some of its members (case 1777/2020/KR), 27 October 2021. www.ombudsman.europa.eu/en/recommendation/en/141318.

[29] Commission Decision establishing horizontal rules on the creation and operation of Commission expert groups, C(2016)3301, 30 May 2016.

[30] Corporate Europe Observatory, 'A "gastastrophic" mistake – New expert group invites fossil fuel giants to steer Europe's energy', 26 October 2022, www.corporateeurope.org/en/AGastastrophicMistake.

[31] Corporate Europe Observatory, 'Corporate Europe Observatory complaint on EU Industry Advisory Group', Complaint to the European Ombudsman, November 2023, corporateeurope.org/sites/default/files/2023-11/CEO%20IAG%20complaint.pdf.

[32] Corporate Europe Observatory, 'European ombudsman opens case into fossil-fueled EU advisory group', 9 November 2023, corporateeurope.org/en/2023/11/european-ombudsman-opens-case-fossil-fueled-eu-advisory-group.

Sometimes, the apparent blindness to conflicts of interest can only be explained by a problematic political culture and ideological bias within (parts of) the Commission's apparatus, including at the top level. Excessively close contacts and cooperation with big business lobbyists are considered unproblematic. An example of this is the awarding of consultancy contracts for policy development roles to corporations with fundamental conflicts of interest, as happened when giant investment firm BlackRock was tasked to help define EU criteria for sustainable investment. With the ChangeFinance coalition, CEO challenged the European Commission's absurd decision to hand investment giant BlackRock a consultancy contract to advise it on sustainable finance.[33] BlackRock makes massive unsustainable investments itself, and has a track record of lobbying against strong environmental, social and governance (ESG) rules.[34] Based on findings of the European Ombudsman,[35] MEPs asked the European Commission to change its financial rules around policy-related consultancy contracts to prevent such conflicts of interest from arising in the future. The Commission indicated it was open to this.[36]

Earlier this year, however, it became clear that the European Commission has not amended its internal procedures. CEO's research found that the European Commission had hired consultants working for Google and other Big Tech corporations to evaluate its merger enforcement policies.[37] In this context, it emerged that the European Commission had barely explored if there was a conflict of interest in such an appointment, ignoring the European Ombudsman's suggestions. The consultancy firm in question – RBB Economics – works for some of the largest corporations in the world to push through mergers and acquisitions. The company was involved in many of the most controversial high-profile mergers in recent history. Also, this consultancy firm has for years lobbied in favour of weak enforcement of the EU's merger rules, and against key provisions of the Digital Markets Act, which aims to rein in Big Tech's monopoly power. There was clearly a serious risk that the final recommendations in the report that RBB will produce for the Commission will feed into the hands of the very corporations RBB Economics works for. As a result of the Ombudsman opening an inquiry into these matters, the Commission announced that it will terminate the contract with RBB Economics.[38]

[33] Corporate Europe Observatory, 'Time to block BlackRock', 9 July 2020, corporateeurope.org/en/2020/07/time-block-blackrock.

[34] Reclaim Finance, 'BlackRock's lobbying machine vs EU green finance rules', 30 June 2021, reclaimfinance.org/site/en/2021/06/30/blackrocks-lobbying-machine-vs-eu-green-finance-rules/.

[35] Decision of the European Ombudsman in joint inquiry 853/2020/KR on the European Commission's decision to award a contract to BlackRock Investment Management to carry out a study on integrating environmental, social and governance (ESG) objectives into EU banking rules, 23 November 2020.

[36] Reply of the European Commission to the Decision of the European Ombudsman in case 853/2020/KR, 12 April 2021.

[37] Corporate Europe Observatory, 'How the Commission outsourced its merger policy to Google's best friend', 26 April 2023, corporateeurope.org/en/2023/04/how-commission-outsourced-its-merger-policy-googles-best-friend.

[38] Decision on how the European Commission dealt with concerns about conflicts of interest relating to a contract for a study on EU policy on mergers (cases 972/2023/KR & 1292/2023/KR), 13 November 2023.

Finally, there is the little known but powerful Regulatory Scrutiny Board (RSB), which the Commission set up as part of its 'Better Regulation' agenda.[39] With the 'Better Regulation' agenda, the Commission has introduced a range of mechanisms that are used to weaken or abolish current rules, while significantly hampering or even stopping the introduction of new ones. The RSB, for instance, scrutinises all draft laws, and intervenes in a very large number of cases, demanding changes to these laws. The RSB in effect is more of a 'de-regulatory board' whose mandate includes checking if proposed EU legislation will damage business 'competitiveness' or become too 'burdensome' for industry. The RSB de facto acts as a conservative force, weakening the level of social and environmental ambitions. With its neoliberal orientation, the RSB becomes yet another channel of corporate influence in EU decision-making. This became very clear in 2022, when the RSB gave a second 'red card' to draft Commission proposals for global corporate accountability rules for EU corporations.[40] In addition, there are major problems with transparency and accountability of the RSB: the RSB meets in secret and minutes of its meetings are not published. An investigation by CEO showed that while the RSB – according to its own rules[41] – should not discuss individual legislative proposals in meetings with lobbyists, this did not prevent corporate lobbyists from deliberately targeting it as part of its campaign against strong corporate accountability rules.[42] The European Commission dismissed CEO's criticism and CEO submitted a complaint to the Ombudsman who opened an inquiry in spring 2023.[43]

The examples discussed in this chapter mainly focus on the European Commission, but issues relating to lacking transparency, accountability and independence are no less severe in other EU institutions. CEO's 2019 report 'Captured states'[44] – as well as later reports like 'Tainted love'[45] – exposed how EU governments frequently channel industry lobbying demands into EU decision-making, and how a lack of transparency and accountability in the decision-making of the Council of the EU makes it easier for Member States to side with corporate lobbies. CEO's campaigning on these issues, jointly with other civil society groups and online petitions supported by tens of thousands of EU citizens, contributed to the German Government's public avowal in 2020 to not take any sponsorship

[39] Corporate Europe Observatory, '"Better Regulation": corporate-friendly deregulation in disguise', 18 February 2020, corporateeurope.org/en/better-regulation-corporate-friendly-deregulation-disguise.

[40] See RSB opinion here: https://eur-lex.europa.eu/legal-content/EN/TXT/PDF/?uri=PI_COM:SEC(2022)95&from=EN.

[41] See RSB rules of procedure: https://commission.europa.eu/system/files/2023-02/2%20RSB%20Rules%20of%20procedure-%20revision%202023%20signed.pdf.

[42] Corporate Europe Observatory, 'Inside job – How business lobbyists used the Commission's scrutiny procedures to weaken human rights and environmental legislation', 8 June 2022, corporateeurope.org/en/inside-job.

[43] Corporate Europe Observatory, 'European Ombudsman announces new inquiry into Regulatory Scrutiny Board', 5 April 2023, corporateeurope.org/en/2023/03/european-ombudsman-RSB.

[44] Corporate Europe Observatory, 'Captured states – When EU governments are a channel for corporate interests', 6 February 2019, corporateeurope.org/en/2019/02/captured-states.

[45] Corporate Europe Observatory, 'Tainted love – Corporate lobbying and the upcoming German EU Presidency', 23 June 2020, corporateeurope.org/en/Taintedlove.

for its EU Presidency,[46] and to proactively publish the lobby meetings of their Permanent Representation in Brussels. It is now established practice that Member States' Permanent Representations publish their lobby meetings 12 months before and during their Presidency of the Council of the EU. But governments have been hesitant about wider transparency and ethics reforms, for instance around the corporate sponsorship of the rotating EU Presidencies. Coca-Cola, BMW, and other big corporations have been sponsoring the EU Council Presidency for years and this shoddy practice continues until today.[47] Other sponsorship deals in recent years have been with fossil fuel companies, car manufacturers, and Big Tech. In one of several crucial interventions to promote the accountability of the Council of the EU, the European Ombudsman concluded that these deals with companies were a reputational risk to the EU and that guidelines should be put in place.[48] In summer 2021, new guidelines were thus agreed by the Council but unfortunately they do not go far enough to ensure that future presidencies will be free from sponsorship. Member States have been unable to disassociate themselves from corporate interests and implement a ban. They instead believe that transparency is enough. However, transparency is not enough to avoid conflicts of interest.

III. WAYS FORWARD

Reflecting on the many battles against undue influence over the last decades, the European Ombudsman emerges as a crucial factor. Very few improvements in transparency, accountability and independence of the EU institutions have been achieved without the Ombudsman – directly or indirectly – playing a role in this.

Progress has been made in the form of new rules for a wide range of problematic areas. Often, however, new rules have soon proved to be inadequate. There is still no genuine lobbying transparency nor adequate protection against conflicts of interest. Undue influence and capture of decision-making by vested economic interests continues to be a significant problem. The European Commission and other EU institutions have yet to learn the key message: half-hearted measures do not work. Broader and deeper proactive transparency is needed, making it easier for citizens to scrutinise EU decision-making. This is both crucial for public trust and for enabling public involvement in EU decision-making.

One crucial factor in strengthening the impact of the excellent work of the European Ombudsman is the cooperation with MEPs. There are some very good examples of such cooperation during the current parliamentary term, but there also

[46] Rafael Cereceda and Carolin Kuter, 'Germany's EU Presidency rules out private sponsors in the name of "independence" and "integrity"', euronews, 9 July 2020, www.euronews.com/2020/07/09/germany-s-eu-presidency-rules-out-private-sponsors-in-the-name-of-independence-and-integri.

[47] Emma Beswick, 'Coca-Cola, BMW, and Microsoft – is there an issue with corporate sponsorship of the EU presidency?', 24 July 2019, www.euronews.com/2019/07/24/coca-cola-bmw-and-microsoft-is-there-an-issue-with-corporate-sponsorship-of-the-eu-preside.

[48] Decision of the European Ombudsman in case 1069/2019/MIG on sponsorship of the Presidency of the Council of the European Union, 29 June 2020.

seems to be unused potential for further impact.[49] In previous parliamentary terms, the Parliament's budget control committee very actively used its budget control powers to pressure the Commission and EU agencies to improve transparency, accountability, and independence. This seems to happen less in recent years, as a result of the composition of the committee. It is crucial that the new European Parliament, elected in June 2024, makes full use of its parliamentary powers to promote accountability of the EU institutions.

[49] Such as around the BlackRock case mentioned in this chapter.

10

The European Ombudsman's Role in Fostering Institutional Legitimacy

TANJA EHNERT AND KOEN ROOVERS[1]

THIS CONTRIBUTION EXPLORES the unique role of the European Ombudsman (EO) in fostering institutional legitimacy in the EU context. Taking two core areas of the EO's work – transparency and ethical issues related to post-service employment of EU staff (what is referred to as 'revolving doors') – this contribution analyses how the EO investigates the administration's conduct and how it can stimulate systemic change. It outlines some major challenges faced by the EO in both areas.

I. FOSTERING TRANSPARENCY

Transparency is an essential prerequisite for the public to participate in the EU's decision-making process and to hold those involved in that process to account. It is a cornerstone of the legitimacy of the EU administration. A large part of the EO's work is therefore dedicated to making the EU administration – and the influences on it – more transparent. In 2023, about one third of all EO inquiries concerned issues relating to the transparency, including the transparency of the EU legislative process and public access to documents,[2] which will be the focus of this section.

A. Legislative Transparency

The transparency of the EU legislative process has been a particular priority for the current EO since the start of her first mandate in 2013. Determined to shed light into the 'black box' of the Council's legislative process and, in particular, the role of national governments therein, the EO launched an inquiry on her own initiative

[1] Tanja Ehnert authored the part of the contribution that focuses on the EO's role in fostering transparency. Koen Roovers authored the part of the contribution that focuses on 'revolving doors'.

[2] European Ombudsman, Annual Report 2023, 10 March 2024, 21.

in 2017.[3] While Council preparatory bodies, comprised of national civil servants, have a decisive influence on EU legislation, they do not meet in public. The public can thus follow legislative discussions only by accessing records of their meetings.

Within the scope of the inquiry, the EO inspected all documents relating to three sample legislative files. The EO also launched a public consultation to gather feedback on any issues the public is facing when seeking to access documents from Council preparatory bodies.[4] Based on her inquiry, the EO identified issues ranging from inconsistencies with the documentation and the recording of the positions of Member States, to the systematic unavailability of documents related to ongoing legislative procedures. The inquiry was concluded with a finding of maladministration and corresponding recommendations. The EO also brought the issue to the attention of the European Parliament, through the means of a 'special report',[5] which endorsed her findings in a parliamentary resolution.[6]

While there was no immediate reaction from the Council, gradual improvements can be observed over time. A few months after the EO had closed her inquiry, the General Secretariat of the Council circulated a draft policy paper on legislative transparency[7] to Member State delegations, which suggested that certain legislative documents associated with defined 'milestones' could be made directly accessible to the public. One year later, the Finnish Presidency launched a pilot initiative on 'Openness and Transparency',[8] which listed several documents that could be made public. This pilot project was finally endorsed by Member States in 2020.[9]

The EO's inquiry has also been invoked by civil society,[10] journalists[11] and national parliaments,[12] as they call for more transparency at the Council. Furthermore, the own-initiative inquiry triggered complaints, mostly from civil society organisations and journalists, who failed to get public access to Council documents in ongoing legislative procedures. These complaints have allowed the EO to revisit the matter and remind the Council of her findings in concrete cases related to negotiations

[3] Strategic inquiry OI/2/2017/TE into the transparency of the Council legislative process, opened on 10 March 2017.

[4] European Ombudsman, Public consultation on the transparency of legislative work within Council preparatory bodies in case OI/2/2017/TE, www.ombudsman.europa.eu/en/public-consultation/en/84270.

[5] Special Report in strategic inquiry OI/2/2017/TE on the transparency of the Council legislative process, 16 May 2018.

[6] European Parliament resolution of 17 January 2019 on the Ombudsman's strategic inquiry OI/2/2017 on the transparency of legislative discussions in the preparatory bodies of the Council of the EU, 2018/2096(INI).

[7] General Secretariat of the Council, 'Draft policy paper on legislative transparency', Brussels, 13 July 2018, 11099/18.

[8] Council of the European Union, 'Openness and Transparency – Finland's Presidency of the Council of the European Union', Brussels, 6 September 2019, 11999/19.

[9] Council of the European Union, 'Strengthening legislative transparency', Brussels, 9 July 2020, 9493/20.

[10] For example, Corporate Europe Observatory, 'Reform of Council transparency in stalemate', October 2019, corporateeurope.org/en/2019/10/reform-council-transparency-stalemate.

[11] For example, Investigate Europe, 'Secrets of the Council', November 2020, www.investigate-europe.eu/en/2020/secrets-of-the-council/.

[12] 'Opening up closed doors: making the EU more transparent for its citizens', Paper from the Dutch COSAC delegation on EU transparency, Tallinn, 26–28 November 2017, www.tweedekamer.nl/kamerstukken/detail?id=2017D32584&did=2017D32584.

on fishing quotas, motor vehicle emissions, the regulation of online platforms and minimum wages.[13] Recently, the Ombudsman decided to follow-up on her earlier work, by looking into how the Council, as well as the European Parliament and the European Commission, deal with requests for public access to legislative documents from a more systemic point of view.[14]

B. Public Access to Documents

Public access to documents is a closely linked yet broader aspect of the EO's transparency work. Next to the EU courts, the EO is a redress mechanism for those who are seeking access to documents held by the EU institutions.[15] In such cases, the EO inquiry team inspects the requested documents to assess whether the institution's decision to refuse access was justified. The requested documents often relate to issues of public interest or to decision-making that is politically sensitive. Recent examples include EO inquiries into refused public access to documents related to negotiations on the purchase of Covid-19 vaccines,[16] national recovery and resilience plans,[17] sanctions against Russia[18] and the Commission's proposal for a regulation on preventing child sexual abuse online.[19]

Members of the public turn to the EO in public access cases as an alternative to court proceedings, because they may expect the EO to be more accessible, flexible and faster. And indeed, the EO is accessible to any citizen of the EU or any natural or legal person residing or having its registered office in an EU Member State.[20] Complaining to the EO does not entail any financial cost. Furthermore, the EO's introduction of a 'Fast-Track' procedure for public access cases has enabled the EO to process such complaints within significantly shorter time frames.[21] The EO can moreover propose flexible solutions, for example indicating that specific parts of a document should be disclosed or that, instead, the institution should consider providing the complainant with relevant information contained in the documents.[22]

[13] Case 640/2019/TE, closed on 29 April 2020; Case 360/2021/TE, closed on 11 October 2021; Case 1499/2021/SF, closed on 27 June 2021; Case 1834/2022/NH, closed on 25 September 2023.

[14] Strategic inquiry into how the European Parliament, the Council of the EU and the European Commission deal with requests for public access to legislative documents (OI/4/2023/MIK), opened on 2 October 2023.

[15] Under Regulation (EC) No 1049/2001 of the European Parliament and of the Council of 30 May 2001 regarding public access to European Parliament, Council and Commission documents [2001] OJ L 145.

[16] Decision in joint cases 85/2021/MIG and 86/2021/MIG on the European Commission's refusal to give public access to documents concerning the purchase of vaccines against Covid-19, 12 May 2021.

[17] Eg, case 925/2022/LDS, closed on 29 November 2022.

[18] Case 1288/2022/SF, closed on 11 July 2023.

[19] Eg, case 1791/2023/FA, opened on 20 September 2023.

[20] Art 228(1) TFEU.

[21] An internal review of the EO's Fast-Track procedure concluded that 'the average time for handling public access complaints is now one third what it was before the procedure was introduced'. Overall, for Fast-Track inquiries, the average time to reach an outcome was 67 working days, Review of the Ombudsman's Fast-Track procedure, 24 February 2021, www.ombudsman.europa.eu/en/document/en/138509.

[22] Eg, in case 795/2022/OAM, closed on 28 July 2023; case 74/2023/MIK, closed on 2 October 2023; case 53/2023/NK, closed on 22 June 2023.

Rather than exclusively assessing compliance with the applicable law, the EO's inquiries thus take a wider look drawing on the principles of good administration: What could be the most citizen-friendly and reasonable way to resolve a particular complaint?

Through information-gathering exercises, the EO has also been able to compare and assess institutional practices when implementing the EU legislation on public access to documents (Regulation 1049/2001). While Regulation 1049/2001 was adopted more than 20 years ago, public access to documents has been constantly evolving, not least in view of technological advances and an increased public demand for transparency. The EO has tried to fill this gap by guiding EU institutions on what policies and practices they should have in place to fully implement their obligations to give effect to the fundamental right of public access to documents,[23] including when it comes to requests for documents that could cover modern communication tools such as text and instant messages[24] and the use of online access to documents portals.[25]

Yet, independent of how timely or convincing the EO's guidance, suggestions and recommendations may be, the EU institutions must also be willing to follow them, despite their non-binding nature. This has proven to be a challenge, especially for larger EU institutions, after they have adopted final decisions refusing access in lengthy internal procedures.[26] Another major challenge to the effective exercise of the fundamental right of public access to documents[27] is the delayed processing of access requests. As the EO has found on numerous occasions, 'access delayed is access denied'.[28] The often-cited reason by EU institutions, in particular the Commission, for delays is the significant increase in the number and complexity of access requests they receive, as well as staffing limitations in a context of substantial additional tasks received by the EU administration over the past years (in areas such as the energy crisis, the war of aggression against Ukraine and humanitarian crises).[29] Since 2020, the EO has thus witnessed a sharp increase in complaints that concern delays.[30]

[23] European Ombudsman, 'A short guide for the EU administration on policies and practices to give effect to the right of public access to documents', SI/7/2021/DL, 27 October 2021.

[24] European Ombudsman, 'The recording of text and instant messages sent/received by staff members in their professional capacity – Practical recommendations for the EU administration', SI/4/2021/MIG, 13 July 2022.

[25] Decision on issues related to how Frontex communicates with citizens in relation to its access to documents portal (Joined Cases 1261/2020 and 1361/2020), 15 December 2022.

[26] See, eg, the institutions' replies in cases 2142/2018/EWM, 1527/2020/DL, 1316/2021/MIG, 717/2021/SF, 790/2021/MIG.

[27] Art 42 of the Charter of Fundamental Rights of the EU.

[28] Recommendation on the time the European Commission takes to deal with requests for public access to documents (strategic inquiry OI/2/2022/OAM), 24 March 2023, para 35.

[29] See, eg, European Commission's opinion on the Ombudsman recommendation in strategic inquiry OI/2/2022/OAM on the time the European Commission takes to deal with requests for public access to documents, 25 August 2023.

[30] In 2020, the Ombudsman opened 13 such inquiries; in 2023, the Ombudsman had opened 54 such inquiries until 15 September 2023. See Decision on the time the European Commission takes to deal with requests for public access to documents (strategic inquiry OI/2/2022/OAM), 18 September 2023, para 19.

To address these challenges, the EO has recently drawn the public and the European Parliament's attention to the delays, following an own-initiative inquiry into the matter.[31] Furthermore, the EO has sought to inspect the requested documents in 'delay cases' based on an implicit refusal of the institution concerned and has conducted preliminary assessments that it shared with the institution concerned on that basis.[32] Finally, the EO has proposed flexible solutions, such as encouraging the institution concerned to release relevant information rather than the requested document itself, thus avoiding the need for the institution to reconsider its final decision on an access request.[33]

At the same time, smaller EU bodies, in particular EU agencies, very often appreciate the EO's recommendations, proposals or suggestions in public access cases, as the contribution from Dirk Detken and Laura Weemering of the European Food Safety Authority emphasises. Recent encouraging examples include the European Insurance and Occupational Pensions Authority, which accepted to publish the voting records of its Board on draft Regulatory Technical Standards,[34] the European Data Protection Board, which granted access to draft versions of authoritative guidance on the GDPR[35] and the European Food Safety Authority, which agreed to follow the EO's recommendations in a case that concerned significant delays in its handling of a public access request.[36] Following inquiries, EU institutions have also informed the EO of wider efforts to revisit their processing of access requests, such as by increasing proactive transparency[37] or by developing technological solutions that are expected to support a swifter processing of access requests.[38]

II. LOBBYING TRANSPARENCY AND THE ISSUE OF 'REVOLVING DOORS'

Brussels is said to be one of the biggest lobbying centres of the world,[39] which could be explained by the global impact, directly or indirectly, that EU regulation can have.[40]

[31] Special Report of the European Ombudsman in her strategic inquiry concerning the time the European Commission takes to deal with requests for public access to documents (OI/2/2022/OAM), 20 September 2023.

[32] For example, Decision on how the European Commission dealt with a request for public access to documents concerning sanctions against Russia (case 1288/2022/SF), 11 July 2023.

[33] E.g., Decision on the European Commission's refusal to give full public access to declarations of interests by the members of its Regulatory Scrutiny Board (case 74/2023/MIK), 2 October 2023.

[34] Case 1564/2020/TE, closed on 18 May 2021.

[35] Case 386/2021/AMF, closed on 7 September 2021.

[36] Case 2124/2021/MIG, closed on 14 November 2022.

[37] Decision on how the European Medicines Agency (EMA) deals with requests for public access to documents (case 2243/2022/SF), 13 December 2023, para 34.

[38] Report on the meeting of the European Ombudsman inquiry team with representatives of the European Food Safety Authority (presentation of IT tool), 2124/2021/MIG, 22 March 2023.

[39] The Brussels Commissioner for Europe and International Organisations estimates that there are between 10,000 and 14,000 lobbying jobs in Brussels. See Brussels Commissioner for Europe and International Organisations, 'Annual report 2022', 5 July 2023, www.commissioner.brussels/en/component/fleximedia/624-annualreport-ceoi2022-web?Itemid=304. By comparison, based on Senate Office of Public Records data, in 2022 there were 12669 lobbyists in Washington DC. See Open Secrets, 'Lobbying Data Summary', www.opensecrets.org/federal-lobbying.

[40] Anu Bradford, *The Brussels Effect: How the European Union Rules the World*, Faculty Books 232 (Oxford, Oxford University Press, 2020).

Therefore, the question who is wielding influence within the EU administration is a prominent theme in much of the work of the EO. Whose voices are being listened to? What impact for good or for bad do those voices have? And who is defending the public interest? The interaction of the private sector with the EU administration is a key aspect of many EO inquiries.

As the EU is increasingly entrusted with responsibilities in areas ranging from defence to healthcare,[41] public trust in the administration is essential. Any perception that public servants pursue private interests that conflict with, or are seen to conflict with, their public work is therefore highly damaging. The 'revolving door' describes the phenomenon whereby EU civil servants leave the EU institutions to take up jobs in the private sector. The EO has long identified this as an issue that can give rise to risks of conflicts of interest and damage public trust if not adequately managed, as Emilia Korkea-aho also argued in her chapter in this volume. Even a small number of high-profile moves can generate significant public disquiet and cause reputational damage.[42]

The EO has conducted several high-profile inquiries, following complaints, into how the EU administration handles revolving door situations involving (former) staff members.[43] The EO has also conducted systemic own-initiative inquiries related to this issue involving the European Central Bank and the Commission.[44] This section explores the latter inquiry and its impact.

The EO's inquiry into revolving doors in the Commission[45] involved the inspection of a sample of 100 decisions taken by the Commission in the period between 2019 and 2021, across 14 Directorates-General, all Commissioner cabinets, the Commission's Legal Service, and the Secretariat-General. Of these 100 decisions, the Commission prohibited only two activities.

The inquiry found genuine improvements since the EO had last examined the issue,[46] including guidance on how to conduct more rigorous examinations of each move. However, in some instances, the Commission approved requests from

[41] See, eg, the work that the European Commission has done in relation to securing Covid-19 vaccinations: commission.europa.eu/strategy-and-policy/coronavirus-response/safe-covid-19-vaccines-europeans_en, as well as the Commission's work on Defence: commission.europa.eu/about-european-commission/departments-and-executive-agencies/defence-industry-and-space_en.

[42] See, eg, the public petitions covered by euronews, 'Barroso "Goldman Sachs" petition handed to EU officials', 12 October 2016, www.euronews.com/my-europe/2016/10/12/barroso-goldman-sachs-petition-handed-to-eu-officials, and WeMoveEurope, 'Barroso, don't sell our public interest to Goldman Sachs', act.wemove.eu/campaigns/eu-revolving-doors. The work of the European Ombudsman in this area has also been widely covered, for example, Huw Jones, 'EU ombudsman probes "revolving door" at banking watchdog', Reuters, www.reuters.com/article/us-eu-banks-regulator/eu-ombudsman-probes-revolving-door-at-banking-watchdog-idUSKBN1ZK17P?il=0.

[43] The Ombudsman's Decisions on the European Banking Authority's decision to approve the request from its Executive Director to become CEO of a financial lobby group (2168/2019/KR), 18 November 2020, and on how the European Investment Bank (EIB) handled the move of a former Vice-President to an energy utility company that had received EIB loans (1016/2021/KR), 27 July 2022, for example.

[44] Decision on how the European Central Bank (ECB) deals with 'revolving door' cases (OI/1/2022/KR), 26 October 2022.

[45] Decision on how the European Commission manages 'revolving door' moves of its staff members (OI/1/2021/KR), 16 May 2022.

[46] Decision on how the European Commission manages 'revolving doors' situations of its staff (OI/3/2017/NF), 28 February 2019.

former senior staff members to take up activities, despite reservations as to whether the conditions imposed on the moves would mitigate the potential risks (such as conflicts of interest and access to knowledge or contacts within the administration). The EO is of the view that such moves should be authorised only where the activity can be made subject to restrictions that adequately mitigate the risks and which can be credibly monitored and enforced. Where such restrictions and enforcement are not possible, the Commission should temporarily block the former staff members from taking up the intended jobs. Not doing so risks undermining public confidence in the EU institutions.

When approving an activity with mitigating measures, the EO found that the Commission should explore the full range of measures available. For instance, the Commission could make its approval of a new job conditional upon the staff member obtaining a commitment from the new employer that the restrictions imposed by the Commission are made public on the new employer's website. As a minimum, the EO proposed that the Commission should require the (former) staff member to submit evidence that the restrictions imposed were shared with the new employer.

The difficulties encountered by the Commission in monitoring compliance led the EO to reiterate her suggestion that the Commission makes public in a more timely way information on all post-service activities of former senior staff members that it assesses. This would improve public scrutiny of these decisions, which could reinforce the Commission's monitoring of compliance.

In reply to the EO's proposals, the Commission said that, particularly in cases concerning former senior staff members, it imposes more severe restrictions in terms of duration, or new types of restrictions (for example a prohibition to take as clients, stakeholders of the former department).[47] The Commission also said it forbids envisaged activities fully where requests concern positions involving the lobbying of the EU institutions on matters for which former senior officials were responsible in the last three years of service, or activities related to a specific file or project (for instance a grant or a tender) on which the former staff member worked while at the Commission.

The Commission further adopted a more restrictive approach to activities of staff on unpaid leave after the EO inquiry was opened. For example, it no longer approves applications to take up jobs that include representing private interests before the Commission (for example in law firms, consultancies or public affairs departments of organisations). More specifically, this concerns activities related to matters the staff members works on at the Commission or where the Commission acts as an enforcer (for example in the area of competition policy) or has a regulatory role.

The Commission is following up on the EO's suggestion to enhance the accountability of former staff members as regards their compliance with restrictions, by imposing a condition of periodical reporting on the compliance with restrictions, in cases where its reputation is exposed.

[47] Follow up of the European Commission to the decision of the European Ombudsman in OI/1/2021/KR on how it manages 'revolving doors' moves of its staff members, 31 October 2022.

In order to enhance the transparency of its revolving door decisions, the Commission committed to making public its annual report on post-service jobs of former senior officials in the first part of the year (instead of at the end) to enable at least some public scrutiny. The Commission is reflecting on whether to disclose the conditions attached to individual authorisations of post-service activities of former senior staff members, for example to show adequate protection of the general interest after questions on specific individual cases are raised publicly.

The EO has undoubtedly raised awareness of the risks to which revolving door moves by EU staff can give rise, and contributed to what is arguably a significant shift in the way the EU administration handles revolving doors situations involving its (former) staff members.

Other initiatives that the EO has taken to improve the way in which the EU administration deals with lobbying include issuing practical recommendations for EU civil servants interacting with lobbyists,[48] suggestions to improve the Transparency Register[49] and recommendations on the EU's compliance with the UN Framework Convention on Tobacco Control.[50]

III. CONCLUSION

Inquiries related to legislative transparency and the EU administration's approach to public access to documents as well as to the revolving door have been important pillars of the EO's work since 2013. In numerous instances, including in a number of inquiries referred to in this chapter, this work resulted in tangible administrative improvement. This contribution has also shown that, even if EO inquiries do not result in immediate change, they may still contribute to administrative reform in the longer term, especially if likeminded actors within and outside the EU administration echo the need for change.

The EU administration, in particular the Commission, is increasingly working on sensitive issues. In recent years, this has included trade negotiations, the purchase of vaccine, the regulation of digital services, the purchase of gas, the screening of foreign investments and sanctions against third countries. In this context, it is likely that assessing the application of EU transparency law and ethics regulation will remain hallmarks of the EO's work in the years to come.

To remain relevant, the EO needs to follow developments within the EU administration, such as the use of artificial intelligence. Only by being responsive to shifting institutional and societal realities will the EO be able to sustain its relevance and impact on making the EU administration more transparent and ethical.

[48] European Ombudsman, 'Practical recommendations for public officials' interaction with interest representatives', SI/7/2016/KR, 24 May 2017.

[49] Efforts to improve the EU Transparency Register (SI/7/2016/KR), 26 May 2016.

[50] Decision on the European Commission's interactions with interest representatives of the tobacco industry (OI/6/2021/KR), 19 December 2023.

Part III

The European Ombudsman as an Influencer of Future Change

11

The European Ombudsman as a Good Administration 'Influencer': Revisiting Concepts, Methodological Challenges, and Promises Ahead

MARIOLINA ELIANTONIO AND DANAI PETROPOULOU IONESCU

I. INTRODUCTION

THE EUROPEAN OMBUDSMAN (EO) is not a Court. It cannot issue binding decisions. Its powers are 'soft' in nature. In order to achieve the office's objectives to promote good administration, the Ombudsman must therefore act in effect as an 'influencer' in Brussels. Much like a lifestyle influencer, the EO must produce compelling decisions which, while not binding, are sufficient to convince and encourage the EU administration to engage with its recommendations and suggestions or other soft tools.[1] There are many ways in which this is realised, for example through constructing compelling arguments, using less or more assertive language, or through constructive interactions between the EO and officials from other EU institutions.[2] As Krajewski recently put it, 'in the lack of binding powers may lie her greatest strength'.[3] While this statement may well be true, the EO's successes are also difficult to assess in terms of success and are rather difficult to systematically study. How can we know whether the EO's office is a successful influencer in the EU administrative space? And what can that tell us about the role of the Ombudsman as maladministration 'watchdog'?

Largely, the main source of information about the work of the EO's office, in terms of handling complaints and issuing recommendations for EU institutions,

[1] Michał Krajewski, *Relative Authority of Judicial and Extra-judicial Review: EU Courts, Boards of Appeal, Ombudsman* (Oxford, Hart, 2021); Alexandros Tsadiras, 'The European Ombudsman's Remedial Powers: An Empirical Analysis in Context' (2013) 38 *European Law Journal* 52.

[2] Madalina Busuioc, *European Agencies: Law and Practices of Accountability* (Oxford, Oxford University Press, 2013); Nikos Vogiatzis, *The European Ombudsman and Good Administration in the European Union* (Basingstoke, Palgrave Macmillan, 2018); Herwig Hofmann and Jacques Ziller, *Accountability in the EU: the role of the European Ombudsman* (Cheltenham, Edward Elgar Publishing, 2017).

[3] Krajewski (n 1) 139.

comes from the Office's own *Annual Reports* and *Putting it Right?* reports.[4] While these reports are informative, they do not set a particularly sound foundation for research. How can we then find out more about the Ombudsman's role as an 'influencer' in practice? Is there a way of determining whether the EO's recommendations are, in fact, an agent of positive change in the EU administration? We find that there are several conceptual and methodological hurdles in this endeavour. These relate, for instance, to how we can conceptualise success of the EO's work. Can we really talk about 'compliance' with the recommendations of the office when those are not binding? Is success simply a binary concept that can be achieved through compliance with the EO's recommendations? We argue that the idea of 'compliance' requires some relative broadening when it comes to the work of the Ombudsman and her soft powers in the EU administration. More specifically, it must make space for gradation and account for different avenues of achieving change in the behaviour of EU institutions. Other challenges relate to how we can, robustly, assess this success as researchers when faced with issues ranging from incomplete or unreliable data to the general impenetrability of administrative processes inside the EU institutions.

This chapter suggests a roadmap to overcome these hurdles. First, the chapter explores the soft powers of the EO and the strategies that the office uses in order to fulfil its role as an agent of good administration in EU institutions. We then revisit the concept of 'compliance' and attempt to position it against the soft character of the European Ombudsman in order to broaden how we can understand and study the way in which institutions and bodies as the EO carry out their influence-based role. Subsequently, we explore the methodological challenges linked to evaluating the EO's success as an 'influencer'. On this basis, the chapter will propose a number of methodological avenues to carry out sound academic research on how to measure the success of the EO's work, through compliance with the EO's formal and informal recommendations and beyond. In particular, the chapter will suggest that to accommodate the particularities of the EO's work, research strategies need to be in-depth, flexible and adaptive, mainly taking the form of in-depth case studies.

II. THE ABCs OF THE EO: THE POWERS, THE ROLE, THE CHALLENGES

Executive power in the European Union, both from a national or EU-level perspective, is significantly dispersed over several actors – such as, among others, the European Commission, national governments, EU agencies, the Council or the European Central Bank acting on their own capacity or in cooperation with each other. In simple terms, EU administration is complicated, and the exact locus of executive power is far from straightforward. Still – no matter how complex – where there is power, there is also need for control. Such control, which is commonly operationalised in the Union as mechanisms of accountability and supervision, can take several forms and is

[4] These reports are published annually on the website of the European Ombudsman's office. Respectively see for instance, European Ombudsman, 'Annual Report 2022' available at www.ombudsman.europa.eu/en/doc/annual-report/en/167855; European Ombudsman, 'Putting it Right?- How the EU institutions responded to the Ombudsman in 2019' available at www.ombudsman.europa.eu/en/doc/follow-up/en/135909.

entrusted to different bodies. In the EU sphere, legal accountability falls under the responsibility of the Court of Justice of the European Union, political accountability under the work of the European Parliament and the Council, and administrative accountability to the European Ombudsman, the European Court of Auditors and the European Anti-Fraud Office.[5]

These administrative accountability mechanisms, including that offered by the European Ombudsman, have attracted comparatively little academic attention,[6] despite the well-known pitfalls of the system of judicial review in the EU (in particular linked to the limited access to court, fluctuating and often limited intensity of control especially in cases requiring expert knowledge).[7] While not being a court, and not being able to issue binding decisions, the EO has, nevertheless, in common with the Court the mandate to control the EU administration and frame its discretionary powers, although through a different avenue. Namely, that of maladministration. This mandate became especially important in light of the 'mushrooming' of EU agencies in the first two decades of the 2000s, as well as the 2004 EU enlargement.[8]

These circumstances enabled the EO to fulfil its intended role as an oversight body charged with the task of combating issues falling under the umbrella term of 'maladministration', a term which has been considered as encompassing more than only illegality by the former EO Diamandouros himself.[9] In his view, good administration should also be regarded as including other principles of 'service' towards the citizens. Thus, moving to a 'life beyond legality',[10] where public administration – for example, states, civil servants, administrative authorities – does not only refrain from breaking the law, but actively pursues fairness, proportionality and attention to ethical principles and values when taking decisions that affect citizens. In short, the vision of the EO in this regard, as captured in the European Code of Good Administrative Behaviour,[11] is to place the citizen as the main beneficiary of good administration, with the ultimate aim to build trust and enhance the necessary social capital for the maintenance of a fair society.[12]

Though it is true that there is, to date, no comprehensive legal definition of the term 'maladministration' in primary or secondary law, including in the EO's own statute,[13] we can conceptually place it as the opposite of 'good administration' – referring to, inter alia, respecting procedural and substantive rights, protecting

[5] For a more in-depth discussion of the overall accountability framework in the Union, see Anchrit Wille, 'The Evolving EU Accountability Landscape: Moving to an Ever Denser Union' (2016) 82 *International Review of Administrative Sciences* 694.

[6] See, however, the comprehensive analyses by Vogiatzis (n 2) and the contributions in Hofmann and Ziller (n 2).

[7] Krajewski (n 1) 5–7.

[8] Nikiforos Diamandouros, 'From Maladministration to good administration: retrospective reflections on a ten-year journey' in Hofmann and Ziller (n 2), 225.

[9] Ibid, 227.

[10] Ibid, 227.

[11] European Ombudsman, 'The European Code of Good Administrative Behaviour' (2015) available at www.ombudsman.europa.eu/en/publication/en/3510.

[12] ibid, Introduction section, 4–11.

[13] Regulation (EU, Euratom) 2021/1163 of the European Parliament of 24 June 2021 laying down the regulations and general conditions governing the performance of the Ombudsman's duties (Statute of the European Ombudsman) and repealing Decision 94/262/ECSC, EC, Euratom (2021) OJ L253/1, hereafter 'the Statute'.

fundamental rights or complying with the rule of law but also, for example, timely response to citizens' requests, courtesy transparency of decision-making or issues of ethics.[14] In fact, this broad definition is endorsed by the official summary of the EO's statute where maladministration is described as the 'failure to act according to the law or principles of good administration or violation of human rights'.[15] Per the former EO's words, when thinking of good administration, stripped to its core elements, it speaks to the respect for the rule of law and the pursuit of fair and equitable solutions on the basis of the minimum requirements prescribed by law *and beyond*.[16] To this end, the EO's inquiries may be carried out – 'reactively' – in response to complaints, or – 'proactively' – on the Ombudsman's own initiative. The potential to act in this parallel manner, also sets out a sort of a double mandate for the EO as an actor in the Union's administrative space. Not only as a watch-dog combating maladministration and safeguarding the rights of individual citizens, but also as a promotor and systematic pursuer of good administration by seeking to modify the administrative practices of EU institutions.[17]

III. #GOODADMINISTRATION: THE INFLUENCER ROLE OF THE EUROPEAN OMBUDSMAN BETWEEN CORRELATION, CAUSATION AND SLIPPERY SEMANTICS

How does the EO make an impact in EU institutions as an agent of good administration? Given its soft power, how does the Ombudsman's office realise its mission of holding EU institutions to account and promoting good administration in the Union? We argue that in order to achieve these objectives, the EO must act as an influencer in Brussels in order to promote good administration and motivate action from the side of the institutions to adjust to new norms or establish new procedures that conform with the office's overall objectives. That being said, how this influencer function takes place in reality may greatly vary and is highly dependent on the type of action taken – that is, an informal initiative might bear different fruits than an official inquiry. This section explores the potential strategies that the office employs to achieve its objectives by tracing the office's work throughout its history and revisiting examples from its practice.

The flexibility of the EO is reflected in the office's statute which entrusts the EO with the responsibility of helping to uncover maladministration in the activities of the Union's institutions,[18] as well as the power to make recommendations, proposals

[14] See also the European Ombudsman, 'The European Code of Good Administrative Behaviour' (2015) available at www.ombudsman.europa.eu/en/publication/en/3510.

[15] Regulation (EU, Euratom) 2021/1163 of the European Parliament of 24 June 2021 laying down the regulations and general conditions governing the performance of the Ombudsman's duties (Statute of the European Ombudsman) and repealing Decision 94/262/ECSC, EC, Euratom (2021) OJ L253/1, hereafter 'the Statute'. Available at https://eur-lex.europa.eu/EN/legal-content/summary/the-european-ombudsman.html.

[16] Diamandouros (n 7) 226.

[17] Petia Kostadinova, 'Improving the Transparency and Accountability of EU Institutions: The Impact of the Office of the European Ombudsman' (2015) 53 *Journal of Common Market Studies* 1077, 1080.

[18] Regulation 2021/1163, Art 1(3).

or suggestions for improvement where appropriate.[19] This leaves a wide room for manoeuvre for the EO to act. And indeed, the EOs have understood their role and 'powers' rather differently throughout the years. The first two EOs sought to play a more 'dispute-settlement' role and tried to find equitable solutions without being overly confrontational, with a sparing use made of own-initiative inquiry powers.[20] On the other hand, the current EO sees her role in the EU system of governance as more 'political'. This is shown through a more intense use of own-initiative enquiry powers and in the prioritisation of 'systemic' issues of the EU administration, such as the lack of transparency,[21] recently exemplified by the EO's inquiry into transparency in the interactions of the European Commission with lobby groups.[22]

The flexibility embedded in the relevant provisions, however, also makes it difficult to establish the extent to which the EO does successfully play an influencer role. As noted by Krajewski, the procedural framework gives flexibility in finding maladministration, in determining that there are 'no grounds for further inquiries' or that a certain recommendation was accepted.[23] Furthermore, in lack of a binding power the EO makes use of several strategies to navigate the complex cosmos of the Union's administration as an influencer, and ultimately to achieve the objectives of the office. In order to gain insight into how these strategies might work in practice, we must also explore issues relating to correlation, causation, and slippery semantics when it comes to the EO's work. In doing so, we must acknowledge not only the difficulty in accessing the 'reality' of the positive change brought by the EO's action but also the multiplicity of factors which may intervene in the ecosystem in which the EO moves.

Our first point of information regarding the influencer work of the EO stems from the office's own strategies that set out how the EO aims to make an impact, as well as the EO's follow-up reports,[24] and especially the *Putting it Right?* reports,[25] that outline how the EU institutions with which the EO was involved responded to the Ombudsman's cases. This fact in itself should prompt us to – again – use caution when discussing the 'impact' of the EO. This is for a number of reasons. For example, the EO might find that there is 'no grounds for further enquiry' when the concerned institution remedied the instance of maladministration in the course of the enquiry. In this case, the 'influencer' role of the EO might have given its fruits, but this might not be visible in the *Putting it Right?* report. Conversely, what the EO classifies as

[19] Regulation 2021/1163, Art 1(4).

[20] Tsadiras (n 1); Krajewski (n 1) 141–42; Hofmann and Ziller (n 2) 4.

[21] Ian Harden, 'The European Ombudsman and Good Administration in the European Union (Book Review)' (2018) 24 *European Public Law* 365, 367; Krajewki (n 1) 143.

[22] European Ombudsman, Ombudsman finds lack of transparency in Commission meetings with tobacco lobbyists' Case OI/6/2021/KR, (2023) available at www.ombudsman.europa.eu/en/news-document/en/168641.

[23] Krajewski (n 1) 157.

[24] The office publishes several follow-up reports where the EO's work is reviewed in detail. These reports tend to be rather detailed and contain information relating to, inter alia, the organisational structure of the office, budget allocation information, as well as case reports. Some of these reports are the *Putting it Right?* Report, the Annual Reports, and the Annual Activity Report.

[25] See for instance, European Ombudsman, 'Putting it Right?- How the EU institutions responded to the Ombudsman in 2019' (2020) available at www.ombudsman.europa.eu/en/doc/follow-up/en/135909.

'satisfactory reply' to a proposal, recommendation or finding of maladministration in the *Putting it Right?* report might be due to external factors (only partially linked to the EO's intervention, such as pressure from the public). The concerned institution might also formally accept a recommendation, while maintaining the old practices in place.[26] There is therefore a risk of both over- and under-estimating the EO's success if we rely on the data available.[27]

In the 2020 strategic document outlining the EO's strategy 'Towards 2024', the office sets out its plan to sustain and improve impact on the EU administration,[28] and achieve a rather ambitious interpretation of the law in order to cover the far-reaching principles of good administration.[29] The plan is centred around four main objectives: (1) to create lasting positive impact on the EU administration by developing more systematic follow-up actions related to the EO's cases and strengthening cooperation with EU institutions; (2) to sustain the relevance of the EO's work by identifying systemic trends in national and EU-level public administration; (3) to increase the visibility of the office by broadening the participation of stakeholders; and (4) to further increase the efficiency of the inner-workings of the office by including flexible and adaptive ways to work, such as design thinking.[30] These mutually reenforcing objectives set out in the office's strategy lay the foundation for the work of the influencer ombudsman. How may that look like in practice? As we elaborated above, the EO's actions take two main lines to achieve the broader goals listed above: reactive and proactive. We discuss these in turn.

The more reactive work of the EO is centred around its mandate, stemming from Article 228 TFEU,[31] to receive and review complaints of maladministration in the activities of Union institutions, bodies, offices and agencies.[32] In these instances, the influencer work of the EO seems to be rather straightforward. The EO receives a complaint concerning maladministration, the office examines the complaint, and then reports its findings along with relevant recommendations, solutions or suggestions to the institution at hand, the complainant and the European Parliament. However, none of these actions bind the institution at hand to comply with or follow the EO's recommendation. In this sense, even in cases where there are formal inquiries following a complaint relating to maladministration, the EO must still work outside the 'boundaries' of the complaint and its potential follow-up actions to eventually achieve positive change. This work can, for instance, take the form of public attention in the media, peer pressure and peer praise mechanisms, shaming, or political

[26] Krajewski (n 1) 163.

[27] See eg Kostadinova (n 14) 1077, who carried out research on the compliance rate with the EO's recommendations based on the EO's own reports.

[28] European Ombudsman, 'European Ombudsman strategy: "Towards 2024" – Sustaining Impact', (2020) available at www.ombudsman.europa.eu/en/strategy/our-strategy/en.

[29] Tanja Ehnert, 'The Role of Comparative Administrative Law in Shaping European Administrative Law – Practitioner's Perspective' (2023) *REALaw.blog* available at https://realaw.blog/2023/05/19/the-role-of-comparative-administrative-law-in-shaping-european-administrative-law-practitioners-perspective-by-tanja-ehnert/.

[30] European Ombudsman, 'European Ombudsman strategy: "Towards 2024" – Sustaining Impact', (2020) available at www.ombudsman.europa.eu/en/strategy/our-strategy/en.

[31] Consolidated Version of the Treaty on the Functioning of the European Union (2008) OJ C 115/47, Art 228.

[32] TFEU, Art 228(1).

pressure. These strategies can both increase the willingness of EU institutions to follow the EO's recommendations, but also have the capacity to reverse initially negative responses.

This particular dynamic is clearly seen in the 2018 EO inquiry on the procedure of appointing the European Commission's Secretary General, Martin Selmayr,[33] which raised significant academic and media attention.[34] On this case, the EO opened an inquiry into the appointment procedure of the Commission's highest civil servant following two complaints to her office on the matter.[35] After an investigation on the basis of failure to respect Articles 4 and 11(a) of the EU Staff Regulations,[36] Articles 8 and 9 of the European Code of Administrative Behaviour[37] and the CCA Rules of Procedure,[38] the EO uncovered four instances of maladministration.[39] On the basis of its investigation, the EO issued a number of recommendations to develop a specific appointment procedure for the Commission's Secretary General that was separate from the procedure relating to other senior posts.[40] While the Juncker-led European Commission 'stood ready' to reassess and improve the procedure,[41] it later rejected the official recommendations of the EO in a written reply where the EO's findings were refuted.[42] More specifically, the then Commissioner for Budget and Human Resources, Günther Oettinger, justified the decision to not follow the EO's recommendations on the basis of a disagreement between the Commission and the Ombudsman on the interpretation of the applicable procedural rules.[43] In their reply to the EO and the subsequent statement, the Commission held that the new Secretary-General was appointed in full compliance with the applicable rules as interpreted by the EU Court and made explicit references to its institutional autonomy in organising its departments and assigning staff members.[44]

[33] Decision of the European Ombudsman on Joint cases 488/2018/KR and 514/2018/KR on the European Commission's appointment of a new Secretary-General.

[34] See for instance the explanation in Päivi Leino-Sandberg, *The Politics of Legal Expertise in EU Policy-Making* (Cambridge, Cambridge University Press, 2021) 190–93.

[35] Recommendation of the European Ombudsman in joint cases 488/2018/KR and 514/2018/KR on the European Commission's appointment of a new Secretary-General.

[36] Regulation No 31 (EEC), 11 (EAEC), laying down the Staff Regulations of Officials and the Conditions of Employment of Other Servants of the European Economic Community and the European Atomic Energy Community, Art 11(a) and Art 4.

[37] European Ombudsman, 'The European Code of Good Administrative Behaviour' (2002) available at www.ombudsman.europa.eu/en/publication/en/3510.

[38] Commission Decision of 07.02.2007 laying down the rules of procedure for the Consultative Committee on Appointments (CCA).

[39] Recommendation of the European Ombudsman in joint cases 488/2018/KR and 514/2018/KR on the European Commission's appointment of a new Secretary-General, para 101.

[40] ibid, Art 9.

[41] European Commission reply to the European Ombudsman Complaints ref. 488/2018 and 514/2018 (2018) C(2018) 3897 final, para 9; Recommendation of the European Ombudsman in joint cases 488/2018/KR and 514/2018/KR on the European Commission's appointment of a new Secretary-General, para 107.

[42] Decision of the European Ombudsman on Joint cases 488/2018/KR and 514/2018/KR on the European Commission's appointment of a new Secretary-General, paras 58–60.

[43] European Commission, 'Statement by Commissioner Günther H. Oettinger on the Decision by the European Ombudsman of 11 February 2019 on the European Commission's appointment of a new Secretary-General' STATEMENT/19/1055 (2019) available at https://ec.europa.eu/commission/presscorner/detail/en/STATEMENT_19_1055.

[44] See European Commission reply to the European Ombudsman Complaints ref. 488/2018 and 514/2018 (2018) C(2018) 3897 final; European Commission, 'Statement by Commissioner Günther H. Oettinger

Upon the rejection of the recommendation by the Commission, is where the 'influencer' role of the EO is most visible. Amidst critical media attention, the office published a scathing press release where the EO held that the Commission did not follow relevant rules in letter or in spirit, thus resulting in maladministration.[45] What followed after the EO's press release was a frenzy stemming from media and academia,[46] as well as EU officials,[47] focusing on issues of corruption and mismanagement within the Commission and even threatening the legacy and integrity of the entire Juncker Commission.[48] The timing of the 'Selmayr scandal' is an important part of the story. The five-month long inquiry and aftermath took place at the end of the Juncker Commission's term and shortly before the European Parliament elections. The scandal, initiated by the EO's inquiry and heightened by the Juncker Commission's rejection of the EO's recommendations, became a hot topic in the elections and especially in the selection of the new President of the European Commission. So much so that the then nominee for the post Ursula von der Leyen made a point to revisit Selmayr's position and appointment upon election.[49] Indeed, in December 2019, a few months after the instatement of the new European Commission under the presidency of von der Leyen, the Commission set up a special procedure for the appointment of the Commission's Secretary General following the EO's recommendations. This action was subsequently endorsed by the European Ombudsman in a press release.[50] Now, we of course must acknowledge that this change in procedure is not solely due to the impact of the EO. Still, having kick-started the investigation and having raised considerable attention to this incident via recommendations, letters and press releases, we must acknowledge that the influence of the EO's work in this case was instrumental – even without the power to issue binding decisions.

on the Decision by the European Ombudsman of 11 February 2019 on the European Commission's appointment of a new Secretary-General' STATEMENT/19/1055 (2019) available at https://ec.europa.eu/commission/presscorner/detail/en/STATEMENT_19_1055.

[45] European Ombudsman, 'Commission should develop new procedure for appointing its Secretary-General PRESS RELEASE NO. 7/2018' (2018) available at www.ombudsman.europa.eu/en/press-release/en/102716.

[46] See for instance, Franklin Dehoursse, 'Selmayr's Appointment: Why this Juncker Crisis is Much More Dangerous for the EU Commission than the Santer Crisis in 1999' (2018) *Verfassungsblog* available at https://verfassungsblog.de/selmayrs-appointment-why-this-juncker-crisis-is-much-more-dangerous-for-the-eu-commission-than-the-santer-crisis-in-1999; Martin Banks and Julie Levy-Abegnoli, 'EU Parliament backs resolution criticising Selmayr appointment – but falls short of demanding his resignation' (2018) The Parliament available at www.theparliamentmagazine.eu/news/article/eu-parliament-backs-resolution-criticising-selmayr-appointment-but-falls-short-of-demanding-his-resignation; David M Herszenhorn, 'Commission slammed over Selmayr promotion' (4 September 2018) Politico available at www.politico.eu/article/martin-selmayr-jean-claude-junker-commission-slammed-over-selmayr-promotion/.

[47] See for instance the reaction of the S&D group in the European Parliament 'S&Ds: the Selmayr scandal was a disgrace for all EU institutions. Commission must adopt new, more transparent, rules by September 2018 and reassess the post' (2018) press release available at www.socialistsanddemocrats.eu/newsroom/sds-selmayr-scandal-was-disgrace-all-eu-institutions-commission-must-adopt-new-more.

[48] Franklin Dehousse, 'Selmayr scandal will tarnish Juncker's legacy' (4 April 2018) Politico available at www.politico.eu/article/martin-selmayr-european-commission-scandal-will-tarnish-jean-claude-juncker-legacy/.

[49] Maïa De La Baume, Florian Eder and David M Herszenhorn, 'Von der Leyen hints at Selmayr exit if she becomes Commission president' (2019) Politico available at www.politico.eu/article/von-der-leyen-hints-at-selmayr-exit-if-she-becomes-commission-president.

[50] European Ombudsman, 'Ombudsman welcomes new procedure for appointing European Commission Secretary-General' (2019) press release available at www.ombudsman.europa.eu/en/case/en/52128.

While the above case received considerable attention and, in that sense, showcases the influencer work of the EO quite clearly, it is also one of the office's most high-profile cases and thus does not do justice to the everyday work of the Ombudsman's office. How does that work look like in the EO's reactive complaint-handling work? Information on the influence of the EO as a positive force for good administration in the EU comes from self-reported data – that is, data that the EO's office itself has compiled and published – presented in the regular *Putting it Right?* reports which are a staple of the EO's work since 2007. The report, the last of which was published in 2020,[51] assesses how the EU institutions involved in EO complaints and inquiries responded to and cooperated with the EO during the inquiry. From the data reported by the EO for 2019, we can see that even though there is no legal obligation for the involved institutions to follow the EO's recommendations,[52] the EO reports that in 79 per cent of the cases closed in 2019 the EU institutions reacted positively and sought to improve their administrative practices. How can we explain this success rate? At present, we do not have sufficient data to answer this question in a satisfactory way. The EO reports provide a few examples of successful cooperation – however, none of negative reactions – and list the 'acceptance rates' of different types of EO recommendations, though without providing explanations as to why (or why not) the cooperation was successful. While this builds a basis for our understanding of the EO's role in promoting norms of good administration in EU institutions – barring the instrumentalisation of public pressure through the possibility to submit Special Reports to the European Parliament in instances of found maladministration[53] – it also raises questions about how this success comes about in respect of the Ombudsman's complaint-handling work.

Of course, things become even more complicated if we were to consider the EO's work outside of reactive formal interventions – that is, inquiries, proposals, recommendations and so on – and instead look at proactive actions. This complication in the work of the EO is recognised by the Ombudsman herself in several reports where the quantitative success, mostly referring to the acceptance rate of the EO's recommendations, and the qualitative success, mostly aimed at creating common norms relating to good administration or actions focused on increasing the visibility of the office, are assessed and accounted for separately. In fact, for the latter, we see the EO really resembling an influencer by establishing initiatives for the recognition of efforts towards good administration, such as through the launching of the Award for Good Administration,[54] as well as by putting emphasis on the visibility of the office online. For instance, Figure 1, originating from the 2022 Annual Management Plan (AMP) of the European Ombudsman's office, sets key performance indicators relating to social media engagement and website visits, as well as improvement targets. The plan also gives a detailed overview of the targets

[51] Reviewing inquiries closed in 2019.

[52] By recommendations we refer to all forms of follow-up taken up by the EO, including recommendations, decisions, suggestions or solutions.

[53] In accordance with Art 4(3) of the Statute.

[54] European Ombudsman, 'Ombudsman launches "Award for Good Administration" Press Release No.12/2016' (2016) available at www.ombudsman.europa.eu/en/press-release/en/72245.

set for social media and web activities that aim to contribute to the third objective of the office – that is, to increase awareness and relevance of the office – which would in turn enable the EO to draw attention to specific issues or debates, raise awareness about good administration, but also exert public pressure. Such work would fall under the umbrella of the EO's proactive actions which are aimed at communication and outreach relating to the EO's work.[55]

Figure 1 Excerpt from: *Annual Management Plan 2022: Measuring and reporting on our performance*

KPI 5	Web activities (composite indicator)		Citizens' awareness
	5a – Visitors to the website	600 000	Real-life relevance
	5b – Advice given through the interactive guide to contact a member of the European Network of Ombudsmen	10 000	
KPI 6	Social media activities (composite indicator)		Citizens' awareness
	6a – Increase of followers on social media		Real-life relevance
	Twitter	+5%	
	Linkedln	+15%	
	Instagram	+25%	
	6b – Number of visits to the website through links posted on our social media channels	3 500	

European Ombudsman, 'Annual Management Plan 2022, (2022) available at www.ombudsman.europa.eu/en/doc/amp/en/152860.

In the relevant reports, the EO categorises this type of work as 'positive influence' in recognition of the softer and more long-term impact that such actions might have.[56] Though, indeed, this type of work is recognised by the EO as part of the office's mandate, there is little information on how this really occurs in practice. From the perspective of the Ombudsman, her influencer role in terms of proactive work is demonstrated in the context of far-reaching and rather (politically) challenging reforms – quite like the Selmayr scandal, own strategic initiatives that aim to share suggestions on existing issues or alert the institutions to matters of public interest, or fact-finding missions that can help the EO to decide whether opening an inquiry is necessary and appropriate. All such actions may already prompt the institution at hand to take action to remedy existing instances of maladministration or prevent (further) maladministration without opening a formal inquiry or investigating a complaint. In these instances, the EO considers these cases settled – as opposed to closed – by the institutions themselves through informal dialogue with the EO during or instead of a complaint. In the 2020 report, the EO gives the example of Case 279/2018/JN on the European Commission's decision to recover funds from a

[55] European Ombudsman, 'Annual Activity Report of the Principal Authorising Officer by Delegation 2022' (2023) available at www.ombudsman.europa.eu/en/doc/aar/en/169272.

[56] See for instance, European Ombudsman, 'Putting it Right?- How the EU institutions responded to the Ombudsman in 2019' (2020) available at www.ombudsman.europa.eu/en/doc/follow-up/en/135909.

company that participated in an EU-funded project in Namibia,[57] which was subsequently settled by the Commission admitting fault during the EO's investigation and repaying the complainant before the EO providing a recommendation.[58]

Lastly, in order to fully grasp how the EO may influence the behaviour of EU institutions in her work to promote good administration, we must also consider the broader context in which the office operates. While the EO itself, as an institution, holds the mandate to identify and investigate maladministration in the EU administration, other institutions and civil society actors are also a part of the puzzle. Working together with the European Parliament, NGOs or civil society, interest groups, concerned citizens, academics, the EO can create common standards of what constitutes good or bad administration that can then be 'enforced' and monitored through multiple angles. According to the EO, this creates an important deterrent effect that can actively prevent instances of maladministration, by creating a high standard for the institutions to act according to the expectations of the public and relevant stakeholders so that there is no need for the official involvement of the EO herself and there is no basis for wider public scrutiny.[59] In this sense, the EO acts as an influencer by co-creating common standards of good administration and setting expectations that are beneficial for the institutions to follow and detrimental for them to ignore. In this way, aside from having the role of a complaint-handling body, the EO becomes an influencer of promoting good administration but also of preventing maladministration.

IV. THE INFLUENCER AND HER FOLLOWERS: CONCEPTUALISING SUCCESS BEYOND COMPLIANCE

What we can see from the above discussion on the role of the European Ombudsman as an influencer of good administration is that the work of the office is complicated and cannot simply be accounted for by the mere compliance rate of the EO's recommendations. This brings us to the next objective of this chapter: to discuss how, as researchers, we can conceptualise the work of the EO as a force for good administration beyond a quantitative account of her complaint-handling work. Yet, throughout the Statute of the EO, there are several mentions to the compliance of the institutions to the EO's recommendations.[60] More specifically, in Article 4 of the Statute, where the reporting obligations of the EO are outlined, Article 4(5) explicitly mentions the compliance rate of the institutions with the EO's recommendations. As stated in the introduction to this chapter, the European Ombudsman's office is not a court and cannot issue binding decisions relating to the quality of the administrative activities

[57] European Ombudsman Decision in case 279/2018/JN on the European Commission's decision to recover funds from a company that participated in an EU-funded project in Namibia.

[58] ibid, para 8.

[59] European Ombudsman, 'Putting it Right? How the EU institutions responded to the Ombudsman in 2019' (2020) available at www.ombudsman.europa.eu/en/doc/follow-up/en/135909.

[60] Regulation 2021/1163.

of EU institutions. Instead, her work relies on issuing formal and informal recommendations which carry normative weight – as it would not be favourable for EU institutions and bodies to be associated with maladministration – but lack legal 'teeth'. However, as we discussed in the previous section of this chapter, whether or not (and to what extent) the relevant institutions follow the formal recommendations of the EO is only a small part of the picture. Can we, then, talk about *compliance* as a sufficient means to understand and assess the success of the EO's work?

Generally speaking, when we talk about compliance in EU law, the notion is situated against means of enforcement that are based on coercion. This would refer to, among others, administrative control, litigation, and sanctions.[61] It is, simply put, usually associated with means of enforcement that are legally binding to their addressees. Departing from this common understanding of the term 'compliance' we can see that there is somewhat of a mismatch between what is ordinarily linked to compliance and the work of the Ombudsman. This is evident already in the first iterations of this report in 2008 under the term of former EO Nikiforos Diamandouros where in addition to compliance, the report also mentions issues or responsiveness and acceptance.[62] Yet, in the history of these follow-up reports, *compliance* remains the primary metric with which the EO measures its success until an abrupt stop in the last report, produced in 2020.[63] All reports produced prior to 2020 make several references to the compliance of EU institutions – including a dedicated section to the overall compliance rate to the EO's recommendations – which drop to zero in 2020. In the latest report, the term compliance is completely replaced by the term *acceptance*, which is significantly more flexible and may include several aspects of the EO's work. In this way, the EO departs from the terminology laid out in the EO Statute and widens the scope of the impact of her work. Does this signal a shift in how the EO envisions her impact as an agent of good administration?

While we do not know the exact motives of the EO in this abrupt change of terminology, one can see the benefits of widening the scope of success of the office's work. Acceptance, when compared to compliance, is a much broader concept that does not carry (comparable) legal weight – it is not commonly linked to bindingness, sanctions, litigation or anything of the like – but also allows for the consideration of wider impact that goes beyond the outcome of a complaint. Though this might or might not have an influence on how the EO understands, monitors, and reports her own work, it does certainly hint towards a larger question about how one can conceptualise the success of the EO's work. Of course, a quantitative account of how far institutions have *complied* with or *accepted* the EO's recommendations can give some insight into how EU administrative procedures and administrative behaviours adapt to principles of good administration, it still leaves several far-reaching questions unanswered.

[61] Edoardo Chiti, 'The Governance of Compliance' in Marise Cremona (ed), *Compliance and the Enforcement of EU Law* (Oxford, Oxford University Press, 2012) 31.

[62] European Ombudsman, 'Follow-up to critical and further remarks – How the EU institutions responded to the Ombudsman's recommendations in 2007' (2008) available at www.ombudsman.europa.eu/en/doc/follow-up/en/3819.

[63] European Ombudsman, 'Putting it Right? How the EU institutions responded to the Ombudsman in 2019' (2020) available at www.ombudsman.europa.eu/en/doc/follow-up/en/135909.

To address such questions, let us first go back to our earlier discussion on the EO as an influencer in the EU administrative space and on how different types of proactive or reactive actions can have different impact. Earlier on, we discussed how, in addition to her work as a complaint-handling body, the EO can – alone or in combination with other actors, such as the Parliament or civil society – have certain norm-setting powers, produce deterrent effects or motivate institutions to respect principles of good administration through several 'soft' mechanisms like peer-pressure or public shaming. All this impact of the EO may easily go unnoticed when we conceptualise success simply on the basis of compliance. Is acceptance a better concept in this regard? Partly, but not completely. While acceptance might indeed broaden the scope of 'compliance' to include interventions outside of complaints – for example own initiatives or settled cases – it still does not completely account for the nuance of the influencer EO. What this warrants, then, is a larger conceptual discussion about how one can grasp the full extent of the EO's work. While this discussion is certainly far beyond the scope of this chapter, we argue that that the focus ought to be put on the establishment of appropriate concepts to understand the influencer role of the Ombudsman not only from the institutional perspective – that is, in terms of compliance, acceptance, responsiveness et cetera – but also from the perspective of the larger environment of EU administration.

Such a discussion will not only enable us, as academics, to study the work of the EO in depth, but can also be of use to the EO herself as an additional consideration when setting up or measuring her work and assess the quality of the EU administration more holistically. How can we then understand this in these broader terms? Generally speaking, the relationship between success and failure of policy-related actions is a very complicated one and, more often than not, is in the eye of the beholder.[64] In the case of the EO, and considering the multiple facets of the office's work, her influencer role can be observed and measured from different perspectives. From an institutional perspective, indeed, measuring success in terms of acceptance and responsiveness seems to be an appropriate metric that can give us a sound foundation to evaluate the work of the EO. From an organisational-culture perspective, and especially referring to the construction and adoption of common norms of good administration, it is much more appropriate to observe how such norms are diffused within EU institutions,[65] how the EO works to raise awareness about them and create a consensus about their importance, and to what extent the institutions are willing to incorporate these norms in their day-to-day operations. Further, if we were to look at the EO in terms of the office's deterrent effect, we must also consider how the institutions react to the (possibility of) public and political pressure attached to instances of maladministration.

The point here is that since the work of the EO is complicated and, to a large extent, relates to the promotion of norms of good administration in a nuanced and

[64] For a more in-depth discussion on the relationship between policy success and policy failure, see chapter 3 of Allan McConnell, *Understanding Policy Success* (London, Macmillan Education UK, 2010).

[65] For an interesting discussion on norm diffusion in the context of international organisations, see Susan Park, 'Theorizing Norm Diffusion Within International Organizations' (2006) 43 *International Politics* 342.

flexible manner, any attempt to *fully* understand the intricate web of influencing the EU administration must also be nuanced and flexible both conceptually and methodologically. An added value of such an approach is that we can operationalise success not only in terms of different sources but also in different directions, involving both the impact and effectiveness of the EO's influencer work and the responsiveness of the EU institutions. Potentially, one might even take this one step further and look beyond the borders of the EU institutions to include the impact of the Ombudsman's work at the level of national administrations through, for example, the European Network of Ombudsmen. Taking such perspective will allow for a much more in-depth exploration of the real work of the EO and understand her success beyond a simple rate of compliance.

V. METHODOLOGICAL CHALLENGES IN STUDYING THE SUCCESS OF THE EO

Let us take this discussion one step further. Having presented the conceptual limitations of the current operationalisation of the EO's success and the benefits of widening the scope of the notion of 'success' as to include the more flexible actions of the office, we now turn our attention to the methodological tools that are necessary to study the EO as an influencer. As briefly discussed in the introduction to this chapter, and as demonstrated in the previous sections, the work of the EO has so far been understood and measured in terms of compliance to or acceptance of recommendations. Widening the conceptual scope of the EO's success, as argued above, at the same time opens a number of methodological questions that require some further consideration. In this final section, we propose a number of methodological avenues that would facilitate an independent and multi-faceted assessment of how the Ombudsman operates as an influencer to shape the conduct of an institution in one way or another, but also why eventually she was or was not able to effectuate the desired change.

There are two particular aspects to this discussion that deserve attention: data and design. We discuss these in turn. At present, data on the work of the EO stems predominantly from the EO's own reports – the data is, in this way, self-reported. Certainly, though helpful at first, self-reported data contain several limitations relating to their validity and generalisability, but also limitations pertaining to their accuracy. This does not mean that the EO's report is not reliable, however one must look a bit further in order to fully capture the dynamics of the interactions between the EU administration and the EO's actions. In short, one must engage in a process of triangulation.[66] Then, depending on the research focus and the conceptual perspective we may take – for instance zooming into the impact of the EO's recommendations, or into the interactions between the EO and the EU institutions – this approach could thus entail choosing a representative sample of Ombudsman's cases, studying

[66] Robert Yin, *Case Study Research: Design and Methods* (London, SAGE, 2009); Todd Jick, 'Mixing Qualitative and Quantitative Methods: Triangulation in Action' (1979) 24 *Administrative Science Quarterly* 602.

the case-files, conducting interviews with the Ombudsman's officials, and with persons working at the concerned institutions and responsible for contacts with the Ombudsman, but also with actors involved in the greater context of the EU administration who are contributing to the EO's work for good administration. In this way, one would be able to take several 'vantage points' and gain a more holistic understanding of the issue by engaging with several sources of data, several methods and several research subjects.

Why is it important to ensure the validity of our data when examining the work of the EO? In relation to the EO's reports, as explained earlier on, one must keep in mind that the acceptance rates listed only capture specific instances of change – that is, an accepted recommendation, a successful inquiry – but do not, and cannot, reflect positive or negative changes that have occurred over time. This would include changes in administrative behaviour and administrative procedures that occurred without opening an official inquiry, initiatives that the institutions took on their own, or changes that were put in place during an ongoing inquiry. This is something the office itself recognises in its reports.[67] This is yet another reason why, when researching the work of the EO through its own reports, we must do so with a grain of salt and should take a much closer look. By deepening our exploration and using the reports as a springboard rather than a catalyst for our evaluation of the EO's work as an influencer, we also do justice to the broader conception of success elaborated earlier on in this chapter.

Of course, in practice this might become somewhat complicated and time-consuming. This is where issues relating to research design come in. First and foremost, when it comes to the overall approach of researching the work of the EO as an influencer, we must acknowledge the key role that interdisciplinarity plays in capturing the multiple facets of this issue.[68] Starting already from the conception of the research problem, for instance on the deterrent effect of the EO or how institutions experience political pressure to adhere to principles of good administration, we can see that in order to appropriately position our research question in the reality of the EU administration we must combine several perspectives. For example, a study that would solely focus on issues of compliance could follow the lines of empirical legal research and base itself on the EO's reports and complementary interviews. On the other hand, if a study were to explore the process of norm diffusion in the EU administration, it would require additional perspectives – perhaps from political science or public administration – in order to empirically capture this process. Similarly, if we were to investigate how the EO uses soft coercion mechanisms to achieve a deterrent

[67] See for instance, European Ombudsman, 'Annual Activity Report of the Principal Authorising Officer by Delegation 2022' (2023) available at www.ombudsman.europa.eu/en/doc/aar/en/169272, 14.

[68] Similar to the above discussion on triangulation, the role of interdisciplinarity here – ie, the process of combining perspectives and insights from different fields of study, such as law, politics and public administration or communications – would allow the researcher(s) to look at the problem from different angles without disciplinary limitations. For a more in depth discussion on the role of interdisciplinarity in research, see: Andrew Barry and Georgina Born, *Interdisciplinarity: Reconfigurations of the Social and Natural Sciences* (Abingdon, Routledge, 2013); Andrew Barry, Georgina Born and Gisa Weszkalnys, 'Logics of Interdisciplinarity' (2010) 37 *Economy and Society* 20; Rolf Hvidtfeldt, *The Structure of Interdisciplinary Science* (Basingstoke, Palgrave Macmillan, 2018).

effect, the primary source of information would be interviews with the 'coercers' and the 'coerced' so that we can grasp how this dynamic plays out. The point here is that the richness of the EO's work must also be represented in our conceptual and methodological choices when exploring and evaluating her influence.

In more practical terms, this approach would indicate a move from a primarily quantitative account of the EO's success towards a primarily qualitative and in-depth exploration of a specific aspects of the EO's work. This move would allow us to get into the 'nitty-gritty' of the EO's work which cannot be captured on a larger and more general scale. Rather, it would allow us to investigate the nuances and particularities of the interactions between the EO and other parties through, for instance, tracing and analysis the constructive dialogue between relevant actors. If one, for example, would want to grasp the dynamics between the EO and the Commission in high profile cases, one would have to closely examine the dialogue between the two institutions during the investigation, conduct interviews with relevant actors, consult documents prepared in the process and identify the strategies used by the Ombudsman. In short, one would have to engage with investigative work in order to be able to gather sufficient information from multiple sources, that can be later synthesised to evaluate the work of the EO's office.

Taking this one step further, several aspects of the EO's work as an influencer which remain unexplored may also require a choice between deductive and inductive qualitative designs. The former referring to inquiries which seek to 'test' the applicability of a theory or a concept[69] – for example the *efficiency* of the EO's inquiries as tools of good administration – while the latter attempt to understand a process that is currently opaque[70] – for example how the EO creates norms of good administration in a specific EU administrative context or what occurs during an EO investigation that motivates the relevant institution to take action. This exercise of specifically identifying the aspect of the EO's work which we wish to explore, designing a research approach that gives the necessary flexibility, and collecting new data through case-files or interviews, among others, will enable us, as researchers, to better grasp how the EO acts as an influencer of good administration in Brussels.

VI. CONCLUSIONS AND PROMISES AHEAD

In the complex world of EU administration, the office of the European Ombudsman plays a key role in providing avenues for citizens to directly challenge or express their concerns about how EU institutions function in practice. Yet, its influence and impact remain rather understudied. As mentioned early on in this chapter, the European Ombudsman is not a court. Her true impact cannot be fully grasped by solely examining case-files. Instead, her influence lays in soft pressure, convincing arguments and persuasion to remedy issues of maladministration and promote principles of good

[69] John Creswell and Vicki Plano Clark, *Designing and Conducting Mixed Methods Research* (London, Sage, 2017) 23; Jonathan Grix, *The Foundations of Research* (London, Bloomsbury, 2019) 98.
[70] Creswell and Plano Clark (n 70) 23; Grix (n 70) 165.

administration in the EU institutions. It is exactly this somewhat 'fluid' nature of the EO's work that makes its impact hard to research and conceptualise. Doing so requires meticulous empirical research, which takes time, patience and resources. Yet, while indeed a difficult endeavour, attempting to capture the EO's influence in Brussels by looking far beyond the factual information contained in case-files has great potential – untapped potential, in fact – to help us understand how the EO acts as a force for good administration.

In this chapter, we have attempted to demonstrate some of the ways in which the European Ombudsman carries out her duties to act as a good administration promotor and a maladministration watchdog. By conceptualising the success of the office beyond the rate of compliance with the EO's recommendations, we propose some conceptual and methodological avenues for the further exploration of the EO's work as an influencer. Given the importance of the EO's role as a forum of accountability in EU administrative governance, further research is needed to assess the actual impact of the EO's work and possibly suggest evidence-based recommendations to increase compliance with good administration principles by EU administrative authorities.

12

Administrification of the Digital Single Market: A New Role for the European Ombudsman in the DSA Framework?

MORITZ SCHRAMM*

I. INTRODUCTION

IN THE 1990S, the EU embarked on the bumpy road of 'agencification' as it established and expanded numerous independent administrative agencies regulating anything from aviation to pharmaceuticals and financial services.[1] Today, the EU embarked on another, arguably even bumpier road. While the emergence of the European 'regulatory state' redistributed regulatory power from Member States to the Union, the new route aims to claw back powers to regulate discourse from private enterprises.[2] Enveloped in a broader political strategy called 'Europe's Digital Decade', the Union passed a significant regulation of online platforms. That regulation is the Digital Services Act (DSA).[3] The DSA's main idea is to co-opt online platforms for Union policies. The DSA aims to overhaul the relationship between

* An earlier version of this chapter was presented at the 'The Evolving Role of the European Ombudsman' Conference at the European University Institute in November 2022. The author would like to thank the organisers and participants for fruitful feedback. All errors in fact or weaknesses in argument remain his. The usual disclaimers apply.

[1] Deirdre Curtin, 'Satellite Executive Power' in Deirdre Curtin, *Executive Power of the European Union* 1st edn (Oxford, Oxford University Press, 2009); Merijn Chamon, *EU Agencies: Legal and Political Limits to the Transformation of the EU Administration* (Oxford, Oxford University Press, 2016).

[2] European integration is often understood in predominantly constitutional terms. However, it also features a crucial administrative dimension: Peter L Lindseth, *Power and Legitimacy: Reconciling Europe and the Nation-State* (Oxford, Oxford University Press, 2010).

[3] The Digital Services Act was published in the EU's official journal on 27 October 2022 at L 277 p 1–102 under the full title Regulation (EU) 2022/2065 of the European Parliament and of the Council of 19 October 2022 on a Single Market For Digital Services and amending Directive 2000/31/EC (Digital Services Act).

For an overview see: Martin Husovec, *Principles of the Digital Services Act* (Oxford, Oxford University Press); Martin Eifert and others, 'Taming the Giants: The DMA/DSA Package' (2021) 58 *Common Market Law Review* 987.

platforms and EU citizens. Both aspects – co-opting platforms for public policy and restructuring how platforms treat EU citizens – crucially rely on one mechanism. That mechanism applies public law ideas, methods, and institutions to private governance. According to the DSA, platforms shall act more like administrators.[4] Platforms shall work 'with due regard for fundamental rights', 'proportionate' and 'fair'.[5] In short: the EU aims to *administrificate* online platforms.

This chapter argues that the European Ombudsman (hereinafter Ombudsman) is uniquely positioned to make an important – but possibly overlooked – contribution to that endeavour. No institution but the Ombudsman could draw from such deep pockets of experience to infuse concepts and practices of good administration into the burgeoning administrification of online platforms in Europe.

The chapter outlines how the 'Ombudsman' – who is currently an Ombudswoman – could consult EU institutions and platforms to navigate the ever-growing, increasingly fundamental rights-sensitive and regulatory co-opted administrification of online platforms in Europe. Very large online platforms (hereafter VLOPs) create a digital space and regulate and police that space. In doing so, platforms are partly co-opted by the European Union and Member States. Platforms exercise these governance elements – creating, regulating, policing – in private form. Platforms are private companies. Analogising them to public administrators, therefore, necessarily highlights some similarities while omitting differences. However, that governance operations' sheer size, their normative and socio-political implications and their thickening entanglement with public policy, function and mandate begs the question of how well those 'private bureaucracies' (Jack Balkin) fare if vetted against the principles of good administration.[6] Since we put vast chunks of digital governance into the (increasingly regulated) hands of private organisations, these organisations' administrative practices should reflect the grander socio-political significance at stake. The Ombudsman is uniquely positioned to help aligning platforms' ultimately profit-oriented organisational structure and, potentially, their internal culture with emerging administrative and bureaucratic demands.

If the Ombudsman would get involved, it would likely choose the form of an 'inquiry' according to Article 3 Ombudsman Statute. Such an inquiry would differ from most Ombudsman initiatives on two accounts. First, platforms' private bureaucracies are formally no EU institutions (there are, however, EU institutions involved). Second, the initiative's focus would be proactive rather than reactive. The Ombudsman would consult the European Board of Digital Services, Digital Services Coordinators

[4] *En passant*, Giovanni De Gregorio touched upon this phenomenon as he rightly argued that the DSA leads to an 'administrativisation' of content moderation. However, De Gregorio does not further explore the ramifications of that administrative dimension and instead focuses on a constitutionalist lens, see further Giovanni De Gregorio, *Digital Constitutionalism in Europe: Reframing Rights and Powers in the Algorithmic Society* 1st edn (Cambridge, Cambridge University Press, 2022) 213. In the US, others also analogized platforms to administrative actors, sometimes highlighting how platforms' growing size and increasing concern to stomp out hate speech incentivised platforms to develop administrative-like content moderation structures. See especially Kate Klonick, 'The New Governors: The People, Rules, and Processes Governing Online Speech' (2018) 131 *Harvard Law Review* 1598. Others highlighted how the regulatory environment in the US incrementally requires platforms to adapt mechanisms, norms, and procedures known from administrative law, see especially Hannah Bloch-Wehba, 'Global Platform Governance: Private Power in the Shadow of the State' (2019) 72 *SMU Law Review* 27.

[5] See eg Art 14(4) DSA.

[6] Jack M Balkin, 'Free Speech Is a Triangle' (2018) 118 *Columbia Law Review* 2011, 2021–32.

(Member State institutions) and platforms on how to imbue a private bureaucratic system with 'public' values, principles and procedures. Thereby the Ombudsman would help prevent maladministration in the burgeoning administrification of private platform governance in Europe.

The chapter progresses in five steps. It briefly contextualises platform administrification (section II) and problematises the missing link between administrative mandate and private structures within platform companies (III). Based on this problem analysis, the chapter draws from organisational sociology (IV) and law (V) to theorise why and how involving the Ombudsman would be advantageous. Last, the chapter argues that such an inquiry would be covered by the Ombudsman's mandate (VI).

II. THE PHENOMENON: ADMINISTRIFICATION OF THE DIGITAL SINGLE MARKET

The private governance structures of massive online platforms like Meta or X – so-called VLOPs in DSA legalese – can be portrayed as growing systems of administration.[7] That is for two complementary developments. On the one hand, regulatory schemes like the Digital Services Act impose administrative law-inspired reforms upon platforms. On the other hand, platform administrification comes from within. Maintaining the infrastructures to process vast amounts of data and police the communication of hundreds of millions of users requires a certain degree of formalisation, hierarchy and principled decision-making.[8]

This section briefly conceptualises platforms as administration (A) and then portrays several key regulatory dicta effectively administrificate VLOPs' private governance (B).

A. Platforms as Administration

Very large online platforms – any that has more than 45 million users in the EU (Article 25 DSA) – may be conceptualised as functional administrators.[9] Of course,

[7] The section builds on Moritz Schramm 'Platform Administrative Law: A Research Agenda' (July 1, 2024) SSRN via: https://dx.doi.org/10.2139/ssrn.4898542.

[8] Whether the whole 'architecture' of platforms changes to a more decentralised model remains to be seen. Although current content moderation regimes are certainly no Weberian bureaucracy but a complicated and intricate *assemblage* of quick-fixes, workarounds and competing interests, most were, at the end of the day, quite hierarchical. When launching the Twitter competitor Threads, Meta promised to make it interoperable, that is functionally connecting its communicatory flow to other social media networks, such as Mastodon. If that would entail a departure from Meta's current centralised content moderation regime remains to be seen.

[9] Different authors described platforms and especially their 'content moderation' practices as akin to administration or bureaucracy. See eg speaking of 'private bureaucracy' Balkin (n 6) 2028 et seq; Bloch-Wehba (n 4); describing the emerging bureaucratic elements without labelling them as such Klonick, 'The New Governors: The People, Rules, and Processes Governing Online Speech' (n 4) 1630 et seq; Evelyn Douek, 'Content Moderation as Systems Thinking' (2022) 136 *Harvard Law Review* 526; in general De Gregorio (n 4) 80 et seq; advocating for a more administrative law-informed perspective Moritz Schramm, 'Where Is Olive? Or: Lessons from Democratic Theory for Legitimate Platform Governance' (*The Digital Constitutionalist*, 26 January 2022) https://digi-con.org/where-is-olive-or-lessons-from-democratic-theory-for-legitimate-platform-governance/.

online platforms are not *public* administration or EU institutions in the formal sense of the word. VLOPs are private, profit-seeking organisations rationalised by obligations towards their shareholder(s) instead of the public interest. However, VLOPs' ability to (unilaterally) make and enforce rules vis-à-vis millions of individuals transformed VLOPs from mere technology providers into social controllers.[10] Further, as shown below, the EU's advancing co-optation of platforms incentivises platforms to establish such administrative structures. Ultimately, this creeping administrification refutes labelling VLOPs as solely 'private' actors.[11] VLOPs are already auxiliary agents for public power. This was the case on the Member State level, for example, via the German *Netzwerkdurchsetzungsgesetz*, but also on the EU level, for example, since the ECJ decision *Glawischnig-Piesczek* and especially since the Digital Services Act.[12]

Understood functionally, concepts and practices like administration, bureaucracy and even administrative law are not necessarily limited to public institutions, especially in global and transnational governance.[13] From a functional perspective, administrative organisations make and enforce rules in individualised decisions vis-à-vis individuals on matters traditionally considered relevant from a public law perspective, like free expression and commerce. Typically, administrative organisations are embedded in a broader, higher-ranking normative system, operate on a somewhat clearly defined mandate, are subject to external control and accountability, and are staffed with highly skilled experts.[14] Even though we must be careful not to adorn private governance operations with possibly legitimising labels of public/administrative law or constitutionalism, analysing and reforming private governance from a public law perspective may prove fruitful.[15] As Evelyn Douek noted:

[10] These lines are, of course, always blurry since the design of technologies, especially in the sector of communication, necessarily reflects normative preconceptions and sentiments. In other words, already technology itself is not 'neutral' but a mechanism of social control. See famously Lawrence Lessig, *Code and Other Laws of Cyberspace* (New York, Basic Books, 1999). For recent debates regarding large language models see eg Paul Friedl, 'Dis/Similarities in the Design and Development of Legal and Algorithmic Normative Systems: The Case of Perspective API' (2023) 15 Law, Innovation and Technology 25.

[11] For illuminating background from political philosophy see Linnet Taylor, 'Public Actors Without Public Values: Legitimacy, Domination and the Regulation of the Technology Sector' (2021) 34 Philosophy & Technology 897.

[12] See eg C-18/18 *(Glawischnig-Piesczek)* [2019] European Court of Justice ECLI:EU:C:2019:821; Clara Rauchegger and Aleksandra Kuczerawy, 'Injunctions to Remove Illegal Online Content under the eCommerce Directive: Glawischnig-Piesczek' (2020) 57 Common Market Law Review 1495; Martin Eifert, 'Das Netzwerkdurchsetzungsgesetz und Plattformregulierung' in Martin Eifert and Tobias Gostomzyk (eds), *Netzwerkrecht* (Baden-Baden, Nomos, 2018).

[13] For administrative law see recently Rodrigo Vallejo, 'The Private Administrative Law of Technical Standardization' (2022) 40 *Yearbook of European Law* 172; Rodrigo Vallejo, 'After Governance?: The Idea of a Private Administrative Law' in Poul F Kjaer (ed), *The Law of Political Economy* (Cambridge, Cambridge University Press, 2020); Rodrigo Vallejo Garreton, *The Idea of Private Administrative Law (Thesis)* (Florence, European University Institute, 2021); see already Benedict Kingsbury, Nico Krisch and Richard B Stewart, 'The Emergence of Global Administrative Law' (2005) 68 *Law and Contemporary Problems* 15; and recently again Sabino Cassese, *Advanced Introduction to Global Administrative Law* (Cheltenham, Edward Elgar Publishing, 2021).

[14] Regarding public (executive) administrative power: Deirdre Curtin, 'Administrative Executive Power' in Deirdre Curtin, *Executive Power of the European Union* (Oxford, Oxford University Press, 2009).

[15] For the prevalence and danger of constitutional metaphors as legitimising descriptors of private governance see Josh Cowls and others, 'Constitutional Metaphors: Facebook's "Supreme Court" and the Legitimation of Platform Governance' [2022] *New Media & Society* 1, 16 et seq. See further Thomas Kadri, 'Juridical Discourse for Platforms' (2022) 136 *Harvard Law Review (Forum)* 163.

'Like administrative agencies, platforms play multiple roles all at the same time – businesses, rule-writers, and rule-enforcers – but while administrative law requires separations of functions to mitigate concerns about bias, no such measures exist within platforms.'[16]

Two complementary thrusts drive this development. On the one hand, platforms respond to societal demands for more transparency, procedural fairness and accountability. In other words, to remain operational, platforms must moderate.[17] On the other hand, platforms' administrification also owes to increasing co-optation by States or the EU to enforce the rule of law online. Regulatory endeavours like the *Netzwerkdurchsetzungsgesetz*, copyright law, acts against terrorism online, or the DSA impose mounting procedural and organisational requirements on platforms.[18] Platforms must deal with notices, state reasons and take down content that might be illegal.[19]

B. Regulatory Administrification of Platforms

To better understand the Ombudsman's potential role in making platforms better administrators, we must first outline the different regulatory approaches existing in Europe, especially the Digital Services Act.

The administrification of online platforms began with domestic approaches like the German *Netzwerkdurchsetzungsgesetz*, intensified in specific areas like the prevention of terrorist content online, and culminated, for the time being, in the Digital Services Act (DSA).[20] The DSA administrificates online platforms' structures, procedures and rules at different levels.

First, on a *structural* level, the DSA is likely to inject steroids into the already accelerating process of administrification. Platforms shall, for example, according to Article 16(1) DSA:

> put mechanisms in place to allow any individual or entity to notify them of the presence on their service of specific items of information that the individual or entity considers to be illegal content. Those mechanisms shall be easy to access and user-friendly, and shall allow for the submission of notices exclusively by electronic means.

Further, they shall 'state reasons' when removing content (Article 17 DSA) which must be 'clear and easily comprehensible and as precise and specific as reasonably

[16] Douek (n 9).

[17] See especially Tarleton Gillespie, *Custodians of the Internet: Platforms, Content Moderation, and the Hidden Decisions That Shape Social Media* (New Haven, Yale University Press, 2019).

[18] See eg Balkin (n 6) 2015 et seq.

[19] C-18/18 *(Glawischnig-Piesczek)* (n 12) ss 33–47; Rauchegger and Kuczerawy (n 12); Daniel Holznagel, *Notice and Take-Down-Verfahren als Teil der Providerhaftung: Untersuchung des rechtlichen Rahmens von Verfahren zur Beanstandung und Verteidigung von Inhalten im Internet, insbesondere auf 'User Generated Content'-Plattformen* (Tubingen, Mohr Siebeck, 2013).

[20] Gesetz zur Verbesserung der Rechtsdurchsetzung in sozialen Netzwerken (Netzwerkdurchsetzungsgesetz – NetzDG) vom 1. September 2017 (BGBl. I S. 3352), das zuletzt durch Artikel 3 des Gesetzes vom 21. Juli 2022 (BGBl. I S. 1182); Regulation (EU) 2022/2065 of the European Parliament and of the Council of 19 October 2022 on a Single Market For Digital Services and amending Directive 2000/31/EC (Digital Services Act).

possible' (Article 17(4) DSA) and give information on redress mechanisms (Article 17(4) and Article 17(3)(f) DSA). Then, whenever users disagree with the 'clear and comprehensibly reasoned' decision made by the platform, users may access internal complaint-handling systems (Article 20 DSA). These shall be electronic, free of charge, easy to access and user-friendly. Wherever platforms realise they erred in deleting content the platform 'shall reverse its decision … without undue delay' (Article 20(4) DSA). Further, platforms shall 'take the necessary technical and organizational measures' to empower a network of users that notice content that is illegal or violates a platform's terms of service. In other words, platforms shall arrange and rely on groups of users patrolling the speech of other users. These so-called 'trusted flaggers' shall have 'particular expertise and competence for the purposes of detecting, identifying and notifying illegal content' (Article 2(2)(a) DSA). Even though said trusted flaggers will be certified by the national competent authorities (called 'Digital Services Coordinator' in the DSA context), they effectively patrol the platforms as freelance 'sheriffs'. Reflecting their expertise and alleviated organisational status, platforms grant trusted flaggers a special kind of 'administrative' procedure, speeding up policing of flagged content (Article 22 DSA). In turn, platforms are under broad and possibly far-reaching due diligence responsibilities whenever they become 'aware of any information giving rise to a suspicion that a serious criminal offence … is taking place or is likely to take place' (Article 18 DSA). Lastly, an entirely new class of certified private adjudicators shall subject content moderation to external, independent scrutiny (Article 21 DSA). These adjudicators imperfectly emulate the logic of judicial review of administrative action. However, their decisions are non-binding, and their potential to effectively protect fundamental rights vis-à-vis platforms remains questionable.[21]

Hopefully, all these obligations entail major organisational overhauls at platforms. The primary role model, unambiguously, is public and mainly administrative law. Internal and external control procedures, formalised complaint mechanisms and control procedures, a duty to pass and perhaps even investigate possible criminal behaviour: many core DSA rules emulate principles of administrative law.

Second, on the *procedural* level, administrative law's imprint on the norms of contemporary platform governance becomes even more visible. The DSA outlines broad procedural yardsticks for how platforms interact with users.[22] Also, these procedural yardsticks mostly originate from administrative law. For example, when enforcing their rules – that is, policing their users – platforms shall respect public law principles like proportionality and the fundamental rights of their users. Most importantly, Article 14(4) DSA states that platforms

> shall act in a diligent, objective and proportionate manner in applying and enforcing … restrictions …, with due regard to the rights and legitimate interests of all parties involved, including the fundamental rights of the recipients of the service, such as the freedom of expression, freedom and pluralism of the media, and other fundamental rights and freedoms as enshrined in the Charter.

[21] See in detail Moritz Schramm, *The Emulation of Courts in the Digital World: Platforms, the Digital Services Act, and the Oversight Board* (Cambridge, Cambridge University Press *forthcoming*).

[22] Cf Gerhard Wagner and others, 'Taming the Giants: The DMA/DSA Package' (2021) 58 *Common Market Law Review* 987, 1009 et seq.

As argued above, terms of service are platforms' main normative instruments to regulate the spaces they create. Applying and enforcing these rules in an 'objective and proportionate manner' with 'due respect' for fundamental rights essentially transforms the formally private relationship between user and company into a public-law style relationship governed by (ill-defined) powers, partially effective but sometimes arbitrary enforcement, and fundamental rights.[23] As it is 'axiomatic' for any administrative law style system, the DSA also provides for ex-post review of platform decisions.[24] This ex-post review is internal – the above-mentioned internal complaint-handling systems (Article 20 DSA) – and external – the so-called out-of-court dispute settlement bodies (Article 21 DSA).[25]

However, the DSA's attempts to make platforms more like public administrators remain fragmented. Especially on the normative level, meaning the norms platforms eventually enforce, the DSA remains largely silent. Especially the extent to which the DSA 'binds' platforms to EU fundamental rights is unclear.[26] As we saw above, platforms must act in a 'proportionate' way and pay 'due regard' to EU fundamental rights. However, they must only when 'applying and enforcing' their terms of services vis-à-vis users – not when *making* those norms. *E contrario*, fundamental rights and proportionality are immaterial to the terms of service's creation and substance. Admittedly such formalist differences may not be decisive in practice. Enforcing a rule that is 'proportionate' and 'with due respect for fundamental rights' might generally safeguard that nothing disproportionate or in violation of fundamental rights reaches users. However, given the lack of regulatory incentives, we may assume that platform rulemaking will remain as ad hoc in the future as it is today.

That being said, one cannot help but wonder what level of regard is indeed 'due' for platforms. Since platforms remain private enterprises, their 'due regard' might very well be different from that of public enterprises. Especially the argument that extensive fundamental rights protection is costly could shield platforms from demanding claims. While public actors might not easily claim that protecting fundamental rights is just too expensive, a business whose profit mainly depends on scalability might. Therefore, Article 14 DSA could remain a somewhat ceremonial provision: platforms may now publicly claim to pay 'due regard' to users' fundamental rights, but for a list of circumstances, due regard does not equal complete protection.

III. THE PROBLEM: ADMINISTRIFICATION AS MYTH AND CEREMONY?

Based on the outlined context, the administrification of platform governance, this section highlights the problem with that endeavour. Drawing from organisational

[23] Balkin speaks in this context of 'co-optation' of platforms by states for public policy, cf Balkin (n 6) 2019 et seq.

[24] PP Craig, *EU Administrative Law* 3rd edn (Oxford, Oxford University Press, 2018) 250.

[25] See Daniel Holznagel, 'The Digital Services Act Wants You to "Sue" Facebook over Content Decisions in Private de Facto Courts' [2021] Verfassungsblog: On Matters Constitutional https://intr2dok.vifa-recht.de/receive/mir_mods_00010865.

[26] Arguing that Art 14 DSA 'establish[es] indirect horizontal effect' of EU fundamental rights for platforms:João Pedro Quintais, Naomi Appelman and Ronan Ó Fathaigh, 'Using Terms and Conditions to Apply Fundamental Rights to Content Moderation' (2023) 24 German Law Journal 881.

sociology, it appears that such administrification, at least in parts, risks remaining mere ceremonial sugar-coating, detached from platforms' internal practices.[27] The argument is simple. We know from organisational sociology that changing habitualised governance practices within large organisations is challenging. Organisations are quick to erect formal, ceremonial structures that conform to the organisation's institutional environment and accommodate public demands.[28] However, simultaneously, organisations are equally quick to decouple internal practices from these external, institutionalised reforms.[29] John Meyer and Brian Rowan told us that organisations in post-industrial society 'dramatically reflect the myths of their institutional environments instead of the demands of their work activities'.[30] Simply put, large and publicly visible organisations – like online platforms – often flaunt certain ceremonial structures, advancing their perceived legitimacy without remodelling their internal structures and practices.

The DSA seeks to infuse public and administrative law procedures into private governance. Achieving that goal requires a fundamental overhaul of platform structures, procedures, normative underpinnings and personnel. Platforms are structured to generate profit, not to protect fundamental rights or maintain procedural safeguards. As an EU regulation with considerable potential fines (Article 74 DSA), the DSA might incentivise such structural and procedural changes as far as those structures and procedures are *clearly defined* and align, more or less, with platforms' business interests.[31]

However, whenever the DSA's administrification attempts lack clear definitions and are at odds with the platforms' business interests, platform reform will remain ceremonial rather than substantive. Many of the DSA's procedural impositions are vague, qualified and adjective-laden. For example, platforms shall 'handle complaints submitted through their internal complaint-handling system in a timely, non-discriminatory, diligent and objective manner' (Article 20(4) DSA). The DSA does not detail what exactly 'diligent' and 'objective' procedures would entail. We still know too little about platforms' internal operations, the habitualised practices of their personnel, and the norms and values underpinning their choices. Much of what we know – buzzword Facebook leaks – points toward a corporate culture that favours growth, user engagement (the euphemism for the time users spend

[27] For the largely canonised sociological bases see prominently John W Meyer and Brian Rowan, 'Institutionalized Organizations: Formal Structure as Myth and Ceremony' (1977) 83 *American Journal of Sociology* 340; Paul J DiMaggio and Walter W Powell, 'The Iron Cage Revisited: Institutional Isomorphism and Collective Rationality in Organizational Fields' (1983) 48 *American Sociological Review* 147; Walter W Powell and Paul DiMaggio (eds), *The New Institutionalism in Organizational Analysis* (Chicago, University of Chicago Press, 1991); Swaran Sandhu, 'Grundlagen und Kernbegriffe des Neo-Institutionalismus' in Swaran Sandhu, *Public Relations und Legitimität* (Weisbaden, Verlag für Sozialwissenschaften, 2012); critically assessing the scholarly reception of one of DiMaggio and Powell's concepts Mark S Mizruchi and Lisa C Fein, 'The Social Construction of Organizational Knowledge: A Study of the Uses of Coercive, Mimetic, and Normative Isomorphism' (1999) 44 *Administrative Science Quarterly* 653.

[28] Foundationally: Meyer and Rowan (n 27).

[29] ibid.

[30] ibid 341.

[31] This aspect is explained in much greater detail in Schramm (n 21).

on a programme) and profit over sound, balanced practices regarding rulemaking and rule-enforcement – not even to speak of the company's data mining.[32] So, even though the sheer size and functional logic of platforms partially mirrors administrative functionality, we must assume that online platforms' normative underpinning and cultural embedding reflect their profit-oriented nature.

Since, for example, implementing individualized, in-depth assessments of complaints in the context of Article 20 DSA would inflict potentially staggering costs on platforms, it appears possible that platforms will instead adopt 'ceremonial' procedures that invoke the perception of legitimacy without deeper-running modifications to governance. In turn, phrased in sociological parlance: platforms may design 'a formal structure that adheres to the prescriptions of myths in the institutional environment' and thereby demonstrate that they 'act[…] on collectively valued purposes in a proper and adequate manner'.[33] Yet, these formal structures often remain 'decoupled' from organisations' actual work activities.[34] Hence, the DSA's goal to administrificate platforms may further ceremonies but not necessarily trigger the fundamental mood-swing towards more 'responsible and diligent behavior' by platforms that the EU rightly considers '[e]ssential for a safe, predictable and trusted online environment and for allowing Union citizens and other persons to exercise their fundamental rights'.[35]

IV. THE SOLUTION: THE OMBUDSMAN'S POTENTIAL ROLE

The previous section argued that although platforms functionally resemble aspects of administrative entities, their underlying structure, normative underpinning and personnel quite naturally reflect their private, profit-oriented nature. As organisational sociology indicates, this makes the DSA's goal to administratificate the platforms' procedures, structures and rules even more difficult. If faced with public demands requiring painful internal restructuring, organisations conform only ceremonially to needs while veiling essentially unchanged practices behind a series of novel institutions, practices and publicly declared doctrines.

This brings us to the crucial role of the European Ombudsman in all this. The Ombudsman's core expertise lies in overseeing large-scale and complex administrative

[32] Cf Julie Cohen, *Between Truth and Power: The Legal Constructions of Informational Capitalism* (Oxford, Oxford University Press, 2019); Adrian Daub, *What Tech Calls Thinking: An Inquiry into the Intellectual Bedrock of Silicon Valley* (New York, Farrar, Straus and Giroux, 2020); Jillian York, *Silicon Values: The Future of Free Speech under Surveillance Capitalism* (New York, Verso, 2021); Shoshana Zuboff, *The Age of Surveillance Capitalism: The Fight for a Human Future at the New Frontier of Power* (New York, PublicAffairs 2019); and especially for Facebook (although similar things presumably apply to all tech giants): Jeremy B Merril and Will Oremus, 'Five Points for Anger, One for a "Like": How Facebook's Formula Fostered Rage and Misinformation' *The Washington Post* (26 October 2021) www.washingtonpost.com/technology/2021/10/26/facebook-angry-emoji-algorithm/; Sheera Frenkel and Cecilia Kang, *An Ugly Truth: Inside Facebook's Battle for Domination* (New York, Harper, 2021).

[33] Meyer and Rowan (n 27) 349.

[34] ibid 357 et seq.

[35] DSA recital 3.

organisations, structures and practices. As Krajewski noted, its 'jurisdictional remit, accessible proceedings and the creative development of normative standards' are the Ombudsman's greatest strength.[36] Due to her unique standing, independence, experience and autonomy, the Ombudsman may nudge large-scale administrators into compliance. In the case of online platforms, the Ombudsman could play a crucial role in guiding, assisting and monitoring the administrification of platforms' private governance in Europe.

Such guidance, assistance and monitoring by the Ombudsman would have three goals, one is more sociological regarding the platform's personnel and practice, whereas the other two focus directly on the platform's administrative procedures.

A. Coupling

From a sociological perspective, the Ombudsman's involvement in the administrification of online platforms in Europe would have to *couple* the formal structures and procedures demanded by the DSA with the companies' personnel, its habitualised practices and the organisation's actual structural patterns. Sociologists posit that '[o]rganizational control efforts, especially in highly institutionalized contexts, are devoted to ritual conformity, both internally and externally'.[37] To maintain this 'ritual conformity' as cost-efficient and quickly as possible, profit-driven organisations '*decouple* structure from activity and structures from each other'.[38] Translated to the administrification of platforms' private governance, this decoupling might lead to a duality of, on the one hand, publicly visible, DSA-conforming rituals and, on the other hand, publicly invisible activities untouched by and uncoupled of administrative ideals.

The EU published the DSA in its official bulletin on 27 October 2022. Implementing it takes time. Therefore, any Cassandra-like prophecies regarding a possible decoupling of administrative rituals at platforms are premature. Yet, given the tremendous task imposed, the Union – including the Ombudsman – might proactively engage with platforms to put the DSA's ambitious goals to work. Concretely, the Ombudsman's role in coupling the DSA's structural and procedural targets with platforms' practice could entail reviewing plans by the platforms, sharing best practice examples, providing guidelines for personnel development and recruiting and guiding platforms to unravel their rulemaking and policing functions from entirely profit-oriented functions.[39]

[36] Michał Krajewski, *Relative Authority of Judicial and Extra-Judicial Review: EU Courts, Boards of Appeal, Ombudsman* (Oxford, Hart Publishing, 2021) 139.

[37] Meyer and Rowan (n 27) 361.

[38] ibid 361 (emphasis added).

[39] From a critical perspective one might question whether it is ultimately possible to disentangle an infrastructure's technical construction and the normative preconceptions underpinning choices, patterns and practices considered merely 'technical'. From that perspective Douek's proposal to disentangle different functions on the platforms appears perhaps hard to implement if not to fully de-commercialise platforms.

For the discussion see Langdon Winner, 'Do Artifacts Have Politics?' (1980) Daedalus 109, 121; Bruno Latour, 'Morality and Technology' (2002) 19 *Theory, Culture & Society* 247; concretely for large language models: Friedl (n 10).

In other words, the Ombudsman could help establish a more administration-spirited culture and practice at the platforms. Aiming for elusive notions like culture and practice may sound negligible. But they are not. As Emily O'Reilly repeatedly showed, 'maladministration' can manifest in various forms. Improper internal and informal practices certainly are among them.[40] Given the level of discretion the DSA grants to platforms in designing their 'diligent', 'objective' and 'proportionate' internal procedures, the social norms and preconceptions permeating the internal discussions and reform efforts at those platforms will be decisive.

Further, neither the DSA nor the platforms arguably have any other option but to define more or less loose targets and then adapt procedures to the specific structures of each platform. Since platform infrastructures vary significantly among companies and public regulators arguably should not superimpose their likely simplistic understanding of how platforms work onto the former.[41] Regulating platforms is necessary. Crafting such regulations is not so easy.[42] For some experts, individualised and ex-post-focused reforms like the DSA do not suffice. For example, Evelyn Douek recently called for the introduction of a 'separation of functions' within platforms, which would disentangle some of the platform functions (rulemaking, policing) from the profit-driven, overall functionality.[43] Interestingly, the final version of the DSA even adopted that proposal. However, it did so in a superficial form. In Article 41, the DSA demands that platforms establish a 'compliance function'. The precise distinction between this 'compliance function' and the roles of already existing compliance officers, legal departments and auditors has yet to be clarified. In fact, the provision seems quintessentially ceremonial as platforms may comply with it when designating a single person (!) to constitute their compliance function, cf Article 41(1)(1) DSA. Given the scale of the operations, that is an impracticable solution. Therefore, whether the DSA ultimately institutionalises public law elements like a separation of functions or effective fundamental rights protection crucially depends on the platforms' practical and cultural receptivity to that idea but not the DSA itself.

The Ombudsman's strategic inquiry and initiative tools could be crucial in advancing such receptivity. Currently, the 'burden' to build novel institutions, structure new procedures and proceduralise formerly arbitrary structures squarely rests with platforms. As Kate Klonick's work on the genesis of Meta's Oversight Board

[40] Just recently, for example, the Ombudsman opened strategic inquiries into how the ECB deals with 'revolving door' cases, ie whether former ECB agents take up employment in the private sector too quickly, Case OI/1/2022/KR. In that case, the Ombudsman directly scrutinised the ECB staff's informal practices – even after leaving the ECB. Among other things the Ombudsman suggested that 'where the ECB considers that a request from a staff member to take up an occupational activity while on unpaid leave poses risks that cannot be adequately mitigated by restrictions or when restrictions cannot be effectively monitored or enforced, it should not authorise such a request'.

[41] Douek, for example, staunchly criticised what she perceived as oversimplifying standard picture of content moderation and advocated for a more 'systemic' approach, cf Douek (n 9).

[42] Francisco De Abreu Duarte, 'From Platforms to Musk to … Protocols?' (*The Digital Constitutionalist*, 31 October 2022) https://digi-con.org/from-platforms-to-musk-to-protocols/.

[43] Douek (n 9) 586 et seq.

showed, platforms' internal institution-building might yield innovative results.[44] Yet, several caveats seem warranted. On the one hand, Meta, then Facebook, had an intrinsic and inner-organisationally legitimated interest in creating the Oversight Board as CEO Mark Zuckerberg pushed the project.[45] This would not be the case for most reforms incentivised by the DSA, as platforms presumably perceive the DSA's administrification primarily as cost-inflicting, burdensome, and 'eurocratic'. Therefore, the 'enthusiasm' displayed by some Meta executives during the Oversight Board's genesis is unlikely to re-emerge in other companies or Meta itself when implementing the DSA. Quite the contrary. In 2023, Meta referenced the EU's regulatory policies for temporarily halting the introduction of its newest social media app 'Threads' in Europe.[46]

Further, we should not forget that Meta's autonomous creation of the Oversight Board undeniably led to a novel and innovative institution with promising facets but, ultimately, falls way short of any meaningful 'judicial' or even 'supreme court-like' control as which it was announced in 2018.[47] Therefore, building new institutions that would effectively administratificate the platform's private governance arguably requires external guidance from an administrative law perspective. In contrast, without such external advice, emergent institutions will likely be imbued with US American preconceptions of due process and free speech, lacking real control capacities and 'teeth', and aim to respond to what companies consider global concerns that not necessarily align with those of the European Union (here, again, the buzzword is data protection).

B. Rulemaking

Apart from the abstract point of coupling the DSA's structural and procedural regime to the platforms' actual practice, the Ombudsman is uniquely positioned to consult platforms and EU regulators with their rulemaking. As mentioned above, the DSA does not regulate platform rulemaking. Albeit demands to 'democratise' platform-rulemaking have become more prominent in recent years, concrete policy-proposals on how to do it are scarce.[48]

So far, platform's US legal departments and governance teams are responsible for platform rulemaking. This has two consequences. First, the normative underpinning

[44] Kate Klonick, 'The Facebook Oversight Board: Creating an Independent Institution to Adjudicate Online Free Expression' (2020) 129 *Yale Law Journal* 2232.

[45] ibid 2425 et seq, 2449–51. See also Kate Klonick, 'Inside the Making of Facebook's Supreme Court' *New Yorker* (12 February 2021) www.newyorker.com/tech/annals-of-technology/inside-the-making-of-facebooks-supreme-court.

[46] This policy might be subject to change. As of July 2023, Meta appears to be in a power struggle with European authorities over privacy, its business model, and the potential monopoly emerging if Threads surpasses Twitter in Europe.

[47] See Douek (n 9); Klonick, 'The Facebook Oversight Board: Creating an Independent Institution to Adjudicate Online Free Expression' (n 44); Cowls and others (n 15).

[48] See eg Giovanni De Gregorio, 'Democratising Online Content Moderation: A Constitutional Framework' (2020) 36 *Computer Law & Security Review* 105374; from a theoretical perspective Schramm (n 9); proposing a 'legislative body' for Facebook Klonick, 'The Facebook Oversight Board: Creating an Independent Institution to Adjudicate Online Free Expression' (n 44).

of the people who draft these rules does not necessarily reflect the norms and values enshrined in the DSA or the Charter. Even though most companies now feature some form of 'civic engagement' in the rulemaking process, these steps usually touch only the top layer of rules, even though many of the most consequential rules are hidden on lower levels of specific guidelines.[49] Squaring these cautious proceduralisations with the normative acquis of EU (and global and US) administrative law could be widely inspirational for platforms. That is especially the case for administrative rulemaking. Dipping into administrative law would offer a finetuned baseline fit into complementary systems of EU administration (eg, in the context of data protection).[50] Since platforms will work closely with Member States and EU institutions, aligning them with basic tenets of administrative law appears imperative to normatively develop platforms' internal dealings. Hence, even if the Ombudsman refrains from directly engaging with platforms, it may guide their administrification via consulting with the Digital Services Coordinators.

Based on previous inquiries and initiatives, the Ombudsman could, for example: Help platforms build structures for accountable and inclusive rulemaking, especially for rules concerning or affecting marginalised groups and issues; Support platforms in developing inclusive and comprehensive participatory mechanisms and increase stakeholder participation; Aid platforms identify hiring criteria for staffers working on rulemaking that balance normative diversity, procedural accountability and technical feasibility; Assist formulating guidelines for rulemaking that the Digital Services Coordinators could disseminate; Coordinate with the Digital Services Coordinators and make unified recommendations on what types of rules, norms, practices, hiring criteria and procedural aspects improving rulemaking would be ideal from an administrative perspective.

Such input would be especially important as the Commission fills out the blanks of the DSA. So far, many concepts in the DSA remain vague and untested. Interpretative guidelines, recommendations and, eventually, litigation by the Commission will specify the DSA down the road. Here, the Ombudsman could offer considerable administrative expertise to craft these specifications.

C. Rule-Enforcement

Further, the Ombudsman could help platforms on the level of platform rule enforcement. Today, platforms enforce different types of rules in various procedures.

[49] This is also explained in detail in Schramm (n 21).

[50] On EU administrative rulemaking see eg Joana Mendes, *Participation in EU Rulemaking: A Rights-Based Approach* (Oxford, Oxford University Press, 2011); Deirdre Curtin, Herwig Hofmann and Joana Mendes, *ReNEUAL Model Rules on EU Administrative Procedure Book II – Administrative Rulemaking*, vol II (Herwig Hofmann and others eds, 2014); Carl Fredrik Bergström and Dominique Ritleng (eds), *Rulemaking by the European Commission: The New System for Delegation of Powers* 1st edn (Oxford, Oxford University Press, 2016). For normative input from a more global perspective see Kingsbury, Krisch and Stewart (n 13); Richard B Stewart, 'The Normative Dimensions and Performance of Global Administrative Law' (2015) 13 *International Journal of Constitutional Law* 499. For a critical account on participatory elements in administrative rulemaking see famously Richard B Stewart, 'The Reformation of American Administrative Law' (1975) 88 *Harvard Law Review* 1667.

On the one hand, platforms enforce public rules (eg, criminal law, copyright, etc) vis-à-vis their users. On the other hand, platforms enforce their own rules (terms of service and cascading layers of more specialised rules). This rule enforcement rests on two pillars: human enforcement by so-called 'moderators' and algorithmic enforcement.[51] Both mechanisms have their difficulties. Human moderators are typically underpaid individuals who review thousands, sometimes tens of thousands, of pieces of content per day.[52] Most human moderators are not embedded in the local norms, which might be necessary to balance freedom of expression properly against other interests.[53] Further, the quality of human moderation varies. Balancing free speech with other fundamental rights cannot be fed into a factory-like process.[54] Content moderation is something other than assembling a Ford model T. While large workforces can upscale repetitive, streamlined tasks, content moderation is only redundant on its surface level. Upon closer inspection, many cases are complex and diverse.

Algorithmic moderation, in turn, skyrocketed during the Covid-19 pandemic (because human moderators could not come to the office). Algorithmic moderation is easier scalable than human moderation and, once implemented, much cheaper for platforms. However, even though the industry propagates 'artificial intelligence' as the solution to many of its administrification problems, the automated tools' capabilities are limited, sometimes biased and error-prone.[55]

The Ombudsman could – ideally in coordination with the Digital Services Coordinators – help platforms safeguard what Paul Friedl calls 'normative tutelage'.[56] The DSA translates European norms and values into a regulatory program. As shown above, the gist of this regulatory program relates only mediately to platforms' practice. Platforms enjoy broad discretion when implementing many parts of the DSA. Platforms shall implement certain procedural values and specific steps (eg, provide reasons). Yet, the detailed procedural design lies pragmatically in the platform's hands. This might disrupt transferring the DSA's normative tutelage to the platforms' rule-enforcement – especially if the latter relies on automation. Given the Ombudsman's experience with in-depth analyses of complex regulatory and highly technical administrative operations, strategic insights into *how* exactly

[51] For a good overview see MacKenzie F Common, 'Fear the Reaper: How Content Moderation Rules Are Enforced on Social Media' (2020) 34 *International Review of Law, Computers & Technology* 126; for an in-depth discussion see Klonick, 'The New Governors: The People, Rules, and Processes Governing Online Speech' (n 4); Douek (n 16); Kate Klonick, 'Of Systems Thninking and Straw Men' (2023) 136 *Harvard Law Review Forum* 339.

[52] *The Moderators* (Directed by Adrian Chen and Cieran Cassidy, Field of Vision 2017) https://fieldofvision.org/the-moderators.

[53] Klonick (n 4) 1635 et seq; see also from a more ethongraphic perspective Sarah T Roberts, *Behind the Screen: Content Moderation in the Shadows of Social Media* (New Haven, Yale University Press, 2019).

[54] Douek forcefully makes this point in Douek (n 16).

[55] Robert Gorwa, Reuben Binns and Christian Katzenbach, 'Algorithmic Content Moderation: Technical and Political Challenges in the Automation of Platform Governance' (2020) 7 *Big Data & Society* 205395171989794; Caroline Sinders, 'Toxicity and Tone Are Not The Same Thing: Analyzing the New Google API on Toxicity, PerspectiveAPI.' (*Medium.com*, 24 February 2017) https://medium.com/@carolinesinders/toxicity-and-tone-are-not-the-same-thing-analyzing-the-new-google-api-on-toxicity-perspectiveapi-14abe4e728b3.

[56] Friedl (n 10) 14 et seq.

private rule enforcement might be effectively administrificated would be of tremendous value.

Therefore, regarding rule enforcement, the Ombudsman could: Analyse and assess the practices currently in place regarding human and algorithmic moderation from an administrative perspective; Help platforms structure their rule enforcement in line with the DSA's normative tutelage; make recommendations regarding 'good enforcement' practices from other highly technical fields; Coordinate with the Digital Services Coordinators and make unified recommendations on what types of rules, norms, practices, hiring criteria and procedural aspects improving rule enforcement would be ideal from an administrative perspective.

V. THE OMBUDSMAN'S MANDATE: WHAT IS ADMINISTRATION?

The previous section explored three substantive areas – coupling, rulemaking and rule enforcement – in the private governance of online platforms, in which the Ombudsman might take up an own-initiative inquiry. This section briefly outlines why such an initiative would be within the Ombudsman's mandate even though platforms are private entities and, therefore, no EU administration in the formal sense.

A. A Simple Argument

The argument is simple. On the one hand, EU institutions like the Commission or the newly established European Board for Digital Services, which consults the Commission and coordinates the Member States' Digital Services Coordinators, are undeniably within the remit of the Ombudsman. These institutions will play a crucial role in supervising platforms' administrification.[57] Article 1(3) of the Ombudsman Statue states that the Ombudsman 'shall help to uncover maladministration in the activities of the Union institutions, bodies, offices and agencies'. Although this mandate is expansive, it also clarifies that '[n]o action by any other authority or person may be the subject of a complaint to the Ombudsman'. However, the Ombudsman may act upon complaints or upon its own initiative. According to Article 3(3) of the Ombudsman Statute states:

> The Ombudsman may conduct own-initiative inquiries whenever he or she finds grounds, and in particular in repeated, systemic or particularly serious instances of maladministration, in order to address those instances as an issue of public interest. In the context of such inquiries, he or she may also make proposals and initiatives to promote administrative best practices within Union institutions, bodies, offices, and agencies.

Platforms themselves are, clearly, not Union bodies. Directly reviewing their co-optation as the Union's administrative agents appears, therefore, outside of

[57] See further Suzanne Vergnolle, 'Putting Collective Intelligence to the Enforcement of the Digital Services Act: Report on Possible Collaborations between the European Commission and Civil Society' Conservatoire National des Arts et Métiers (CNAM) Paper Series, 2023.

the traditional contours of the Ombudsman's mandate. Yet, as shown above, the EU approaches platforms through several actors (courts, regulators), by various means (legislation, recommendations, codes of conduct, etc) and under continuous supervision. It would be wrong to dissect platforms' administrative power entirely and artificially from the Union's regulatory framework. That framework makes platforms more and more into administrators. It is characteristic for the digital transformation that old distinctions between public and private, Union power and non-Union power appear increasingly dated.[58] It is, in turn, characteristic for EU law to have practical effect (*effet utile*). Overcoming conceptual constrictions by erecting a 'new order' is the very essence of the European project.[59] Clearly, the public/private distinction still carries weight and EU institutions rightly seek to respect the boundaries of their mandate. Yet, the writing is on the wall. Private enforcement of EU law will increase. The EU will have to find ways to deal with that. Committing private administrators to good administration as early as possible appears, therefore, prudent.

Therefore, my proposal builds on this power of the Ombudsman to launch own-initiative inquiries into EU administrative actors. As described in the sections above, platform administrification happens – to a degree – under the auspices of EU actors such as the Commission or the European Board of Digital Services Coordinators. The Ombudsman's anchor points are the Commission and the European Board of Digital Services.

B. The Commission

But even if the Ombudsman would, for now, leave private actors that act on behalf of the EU aside, it may investigate traditional EU institutions. The Commission assumes a crucial role in enforcing the Digital Services Act vis-à-vis very large online platforms, centralizing enforcement power comparable to competition law. Berlaymont shall 'develop Union expertise and capabilities, including, where appropriate, through the secondment of Member States' personnel' (Article 64(1) DSA). Further, it has the power to launch inquiries, inspections and enforce obligations vis-à-vis VLOPs (Articles 65–73 DSA). It may issue fines (Article 74 DSA) and, crucially, may establish regimes of 'enhanced supervision' for VLOPs if they fail to mitigate risks adequately (Article 75). Although extensively described in the DSA, the Commission's powers are not clearly defined and delineated. Ultimately, they remain subject to the normative assessment of the Commission. Since improving the administrification of platforms may mitigate risks, involving the Ombudsman in said administrification would be beneficial. Including the Ombudsman as early as possible in that process offers considerable benefits to both institutions. The Commission can rely on the Ombudsman external expertise in administrative governance.

[58] For a rich description of the ongoing rearrangement of powers in the digital era see De Gregorio (n 4); see also already Deirdre Curtin and Linda Senden, 'Public Accountability of Transnational Private Regulation: Chimera or Reality?' (2011) 38 *Journal of Law and Society* 163.

[59] Famously: *van Gend & Loos* [1963] ECLI:EU:C:1963:1 (European Court of Justice).

Apart from competition law, the Commission largely has only limited experience with enforcing the regulation it churns out. If said enforcement requires organisational reform within the regulated entities, inexperienced regulators may fall for ceremonial would-be-reforms. In turn, including the Ombudsman in enforcing the DSA – even if only as a consulting body – might improve the emerging 'administrative' situation hundreds of millions of platform users in Europe. Even the tiniest of improvements would be scaled up significantly.

C. The European Board of Digital Services

Apart from centralized enforcement efforts by the Commission, the DSA sets up its very own regulatory actor. That is the European Board of Digital Services. Apart from VLOPS, which are arguably the heart of the matter, enforcing the DSA relies heavily on national competent authorities, the 'Digital Services Coordinators'. The European Board of Digital Coordinators will coordinate those national authorities. It shall 'contribut[e] to the consistent application' of the DSA and 'assist[...] the Digital Services Coordinators with the supervision of the very large online platforms' (Article 47(2)(a) and (c) DSA). In other words, the European Board of Digital Services is an EU institution that shall help Member State institutions to supervise the administrification of private platform governance. The Ombudsman could lend her expertise to that Board.

A possible counterargument could be that since the DSA creates the European Board of Digital Services, supervising platform administrification is a task exclusive to that board, the Commission and the national competent authorities. However, the Ombudsman would not replace EU institutions in fulfilling their mandate but only complement their expertise and, thereby, avert maladministration by EU supervisors (and, by extension, platforms acting on behalf of the EU). Clearly, so far, the Ombudsman's approach remains typically reactive to existing maladministration.[60] Yet, *preventing* maladministration to manifest in the Union's huge and somewhat unprecedented co-opting of private power seems much more efficient than waiting for problems to entrench. Further, the Ombudsman inevitably works in fields principally entrusted to other institutions. Whether asylum law, competition or human resources – maladministration may occur in virtually any situation where a Union actor acts vis-à-vis individuals or the Member States. Like a shadow, the Ombudsman shall follow the Union's growing executive and shall seek to improve its workings. If principal competence of more specialised institutions would hinder the Ombudsman to infuse her expertise, the Ombudsman would be largely out of work, given that specialised agencies exert most executive functions in the EU's own administration. The Ombudsman's job is not only to hold the sprawling EU executive accountable but also to foster good administration more generally. This includes offering advice

[60] For example, the Ombudsman investigated conspicuous 'revolving door' policies at EU institutions, most recently at the European Investment Bank, see Case 611/2022/KR, Decision of 31 October 2023. Another perennial area of concern is the fundamental rights record of EU agencies handling border controls and asylum procedures, eg Case SI/4/2022/MHZ, Decision of 23 February 2023.

to specialised bodies like agencies, boards or, potentially, private actors that administer Union law. Review, remedies and recommendations by the Ombudsman do not equate to usurping the functional role of the actor that is primarily responsible.

The European Ombudsman's potential role becomes even clearer when looking at the strengths and limitations of the European Board of Digital Services, the national Digital Services Coordinators and the Commission. All these bodies focus on the 'digital' and 'commercial' aspects of the DSA. The experts deployed by these institutions to supervise how platforms implement basic administrative law principles like hierarchy and deference, proportionality, due process and fundamental rights will, in all likelihood, overwhelmingly *not* have an administrative law background. Although administrification is pervasive, it is often cloaked in the terminology and thinking of private law, private governance and managerial rather than administrative language. Of course, all these private and economic elements are vital for platforms. They will not – and should not – be entirely displaced by public administrative jargon. Yet seriously protecting fundamental rights in private, profit-oriented spaces requires strong public law input. In that sense, the Ombudsman does bring a unique perspective to establish an ethos, form a canon of norms, and hire a college of people that are at least aware of the public and administrative law dimension the whole operation carries. As this whole endeavour constitutes a humongous challenge, including the Ombudsman to offer external guidance would prove beneficial – even if the Commission might be already aware of all these aspects.

How the Ombudsman would eventually disseminate her perspective in the process depends much on the receptivity of the relevant bodies. But drafting frameworks, codes of conducts, and offering recommendations what 'good administration' would entail in a novel context like the content moderation machinery of a social network or the de-listing efforts of a search engine would be an easily attainable yet potentially lasting form of influence.

D. Attribution

Lastly, one could indeed question whether a formalist, entity-focused understanding of the Ombudsman's mandate still matches the reality of Union power. The Ombudsman's mandate is to control maladministration in the 'activities' of EU institutions, as per Article 1(3) of the Ombudsman Statue. But what are activities 'by' EU institutions? All these institutions are large organisations and not natural persons. Hence, defining what constitutes an act by EU institutions and what does not is a matter of *attribution* – and thereby is open to interpretation. Establishing attribution of acts to legal entities must consider the relevant context and object and purpose of the attribution regime. The object and purpose of the Ombudsman's mandate is to advance good administration in the EU. If the form of that EU administration evolves, the Ombudsman should follow suit.

If the Commission or an agency takes an action, it is within the remit of the Ombudsman. If the Commission or an agency outsources that action, which then gets messed up, it would be outside of the Ombudsman's remit. For example, border controls conducted by Frontex are within the Ombudsman's limit. Border controls conducted by private contractors or other actors – even if acting on behalf of the agency –, according to a narrow understanding of attribution, would be outside the Ombudsman's mandate.[61]

The problems of that reasoning are palpable. Privatising governmental tasks may be considered more efficient or effective – nonetheless privatisation remains an act of public power.[62] Platforms moderate – that is, delete, restrict visibility or otherwise impact – online communication of hundreds of millions of EU citizens. In the DSA framework, platforms may, for example, delete 'illegal content', which is, according to Article 3 lit. h DSA content that 'is not in compliance with Union law or the law of any Member State which is in compliance with Union law, irrespective of the precise subject matter or nature of that law'. Therefore, when platforms enforce legal provisions of the EU or the Member States they act on behalf of the Union. Even though regulation evidently may not level the difference between a private corporation and EU institutions, escaping principles of good administration by outsourcing administrative power to corporations would erode the effective application of EU law. Ultimately, we face a classic question of attribution and responsibility. The EU expands its administrative capabilities not only through agencies or increasingly complex constructions weaving together Member States and Union actors. With the DSA, these constructions expand into another dimension. As explained above, crucial administrative powers are bestowed upon large online platforms. According to Article 16, 20 DSA, platforms enforce, for example, domestic criminal law vis-à-vis EU citizens, regulate their speech and structure their economic, political and cultural communication. Especially here, the principle of good administration is under threat. Not because administrators misbehave but because a whole class of actors must learn how to administrate in the first place.

VI. CONCLUSION

This chapter argued that the Ombudsman could contribute fundamentally to accelerating the administrification of private platform governance in Europe. Based on organisational-sociological scholarship, the chapter hypothesised that platforms might struggle to adapt to the administrative law-inspired structures, procedures and rules imposed on them by the DSA. To avoid that the DSA yields mainly empty

[61] For the complexities of linking legal responsibility with practical ability at the EU border see Melanie Fink, *Frontex and Human Rights: Responsibility in 'Multi-Actor Situations' under the ECHR and EU Public Liability Law* 1st edn (Oxford, Oxford University Press, 2018); in the US, even war is (partially) privatised: Laura Dickinson, *Outsourcing War and Peace: Preserving Public Values in a World of Privatized Foreign Affairs* (New Haven, Yale University Press, 2011). See further, Joyce De Coninck, *The EU's Human Rights Responsibility Gap: Deconstructing Human Rights Impunity for International Organizations* (Oxford, Hart 2024).

[62] The US discourse here is particularly relevant as many critical executive tasks (eg, warfare, prisons) have been partially privatised there: Laura Dickinson, 'Organizational Structure and Culture in an Era of Privatization: The Case of United States Military and Security Contractors' in Susan Rose-Ackerman, Blake Emerson and Peter L Lindseth (eds), *Comparative Administrative Law* 2nd edn (Cheltenham, Edward Elgar Publishing, 2017).

ceremonies at the platforms, the Ombudsman could take on a strategic initiative to help the Commission, Digital Services Coordinators, that is, the national competent authorities, and platforms to achieve structural, far-reaching reform. To this end, the chapter outlined three core areas in which the Ombudsman could contribute: First, the Ombudsman could safeguard sociological coupling of DSA demands with platform activities (informal practices, hiring criteria, etc). Second, the Ombudsman could consult the national Digital Services Coordinators and platforms to help platforms implement principles of good administration in rulemaking and, third, in rule enforcement.

To conclude, a few words on the likelihood that the Ombudsman indeed makes such a bold move. Evidently, it would be a huge leap and may test the limits of the Ombudsman's mandate. Yet, as argued above, pushing limits, shredding conceptual constraints and acting pragmatically rather than formalistically is deeply embedded in the European Union's DNA. Digital corporations will only become more powerful. Most likely, the European Union will seek to further co-opt these companies. Eventually, platforms will become an undeniable, administrative reality. The Ombudsman should help shaping that reality.

13

Transparency that is Fit for Purpose: The European Food Safety Authority's Experience with the European Ombudsman and Proactive Transparency

DIRK DETKEN AND LAURA WEEMERING

TRANSPARENCY IS A guiding value for the European Food Safety Authority (EFSA). EFSA is a decentralised agency of the European Union (EU) tasked with the assessment and communication of food and feed associated risks. Since its foundation in 2002, EFSA implemented several policies and tools to embed transparency in its daily operation and execution of its tasks. With the entry into force of Regulation (EU) 2019/1381, the so-called 'Transparency Regulation',[1] EFSA is subject to a new ambitious law embedding 'proactive' transparency into its work. The European Ombudsman (EO) has in the past years played a significant role in the development of EFSA's transparency approach. This chapter further explores EFSA's experience with the EO and sets out how the EO can help to shape proactive transparency to ensure that transparency in the EU remains fit for purpose.

I. THE IMPORTANCE OF TRANSPARENCY

Transparency is essential to deliver effectively on EFSA's mission,[2] vision[3] and tasks. EFSA was set up in 2002, in response to a series of food scares in the EU, to restore

[1] Regulation (EU) 2019/1381 on the transparency and sustainability of the EU risk assessment in the food chain and amending Regulations (EC) No 178/2002, (EC) No 1829/2003, (EC) No 1831/2003, (EC) No 2065/2003, (EC) No 1935/2004, (EC) No 1331/2008, (EC) No 1107/2009, (EU) 2015/2283 and Directive 2001/18/EC [2019] OJ L231/1, ('the Transparency Regulation').

[2] EFSA's mission is: 'Safety in the food chain from farm to fork is at EFSA's core. EFSA contributes to protecting human life and health, taking account of animal health and welfare, plant health and the environment. EFSA will deliver independent and transparent scientific advice to policy makers, through cooperation with our partners, and in an open dialogue with society.' See EFSA, *EFSA Strategy 2027 – Science, safe food, sustainability* (Publications Office of the European Union 2021), available at www.efsa.europa.eu/sites/default/files/2021-07/efsa-strategy-2027.pdf, 5.

[3] EFSA's vision is 'Safe food and sustainable food systems through transparent, independent and trustworthy scientific advice.' See ibid.

consumers' confidence in the risk regulation of food and feed related matters.[4] With Regulation (EC) 178/2002, known as the 'General Food Law' or the 'GFL',[5] EFSA was established as an impartial source of scientific advice to ensure a high-level protection of public health, taking account of animal health and welfare, plant health and the environment. Within its mandate, EFSA carries out risk assessments to support the European Commission, the European Parliament and Member States' risk management decisions. In addition, EFSA communicates the risk assessment findings to raise public awareness and understanding of food and feed related risks. Transparency is thus not only fundamental to enable scientists and risk regulators to make well founded risk-assessments and decisions, but also instrumental to enhancing public trust in the output of science-based institutions such as EFSA. Specifically, as EFSA was set up to assure trust and confidence in the sensitive matter of EU food safety, transparency is crucial for the functioning of the agency.

EFSA's institutional commitment to transparency is prominently embedded in its founding Regulation, the GFL and its recent amendment by the Transparency Regulation.[6] Where the EU Treaties enshrine transparency by linking it to open decision-making,[7] Article 6(2) of the GFL specifically states that '[r]isk assessment shall be based on the available scientific evidence and undertaken in an independent, objective and transparent manner'. More importantly, Article 38 sets out that '[t]he Authority shall carry out its activities with a high level of transparency',[8] which commits EFSA in the subsequent (sub)paragraph and articles to proactive transparency. Following these commitments, EFSA systematically publishes a wide range of documents on EFSA's website.

II. STRENGTHENING REACTIVE TRANSPARENCY

Over the past two decades, an overarching legislative approach to transparency in EU governance is based on 'reactive' transparency, in the form of public access to documents (PAD).[9] PAD is a firmly established fundamental right of citizens and natural or legal persons residing or having its registered office in a Member State

[4] Commission of the European Communities 'White Paper on Food Safety', COM(1999) 719.

[5] Regulation (EC) No 178/2002 laying down the general principles and requirements of food law, establishing the European Food Safety Authority and laying down procedures in matters of food safety [2002] OJ L31/1, ('the GFL').

[6] Transparency Regulation (n 1).

[7] See, eg: Consolidated Version of the Treaty on the Functioning European Union [2008] OJ C115/13, ('TFEU'). Art 15(1) and (2) state that: '1. In order to promote good governance and ensure the participation of civil society, the Union institutions, bodies, offices and agencies shall conduct their work as openly as possible. 2. The European Parliament shall meet in public, as shall the Council when considering and voting on a draft legislative act.'

[8] Art 38 of the GFL (n 5) as amended by the Transparency Regulation (n 1).

[9] See especially: Regulation (EC) 1049/2001 regarding public access to European Parliament, Council and Commission documents [2001], OJ L145/43 (the 'PAD Regulation') and Regulation (EC) No 1367/2006 on the application of the provisions of the Aarhus Convention on Access to Information, Public Participation in Decision-making and Access to Justice in Environmental Matters to Community institutions and bodies [2006] OJ L264/13 ('the 'Aarhus Regulation').

of the EU,[10] inter alia enshrined in Article 15 of the Treaty of the Functioning of the European Union (TFEU).[11] As foreseen in Article 15(3) of the TFEU, Regulation (EC) 1049/2001 on public access to EU institution documents (the 'PAD Regulation')[12] governs this right. Under the PAD Regulation, citizens can request access to documents held by institutions that are 'drawn up or received by it and in its possession, in all areas of activity of the European Union'.[13] As citizens must exercise their right for PAD and access is provided only following a request for access to specified documents, this instrument is called 'passive' or 'reactive' transparency. The PAD Regulation has since its founding been applicable to EFSA through Article 41 of the GFL. With the amendments of the GFL by the Transparency Regulation, both the applicability of the PAD Regulation and the so called 'Aarhus Regulation' (EC) No 1367/2006[14] regarding inter alia access to environmental information, have been more explicitly emphasised, further embedding reactive transparency into EFSA's operation.

Although the PAD Regulation itself is a robust framework, originating from 2001 and has never been amended since, the practicalities of access to documents are constantly evolving. In the past 20 years, technological, legislative and societal developments such as advances in digital communication and changing public expectations towards institutional information have had a strong impact on PAD requests and their handling. While the digital transformation of the past two decades undoubtedly eased the exercising of the right to PAD for citizens and the processing of requests for institutions, this and other developments including the entry into force of the Aarhus Regulation also contributed to an increased complexity of the handling of requests compared to when the Regulation entered into force. A growing body of EU Court judgments interpreting the PAD Regulation helps EU institutions understand how to process PAD requests accordingly to the applicable legal framework. To further guide EU institutions keeping up with innovations, challenges and other changes in this ever-evolving field of transparency, the EO also provides relevant guidance on the processing of PAD requests. The EO for example issued recommendations on implementing appropriate administrative, organisational and technical measures that allow for a smooth identification of documents in the scope of a PAD request[15] and that make the redaction of sensitive information more efficient.[16] Similarly, the EO provided recommendations that focus on ensuring the seamless technical

[10] For readability, hereinafter 'Any citizen of the Union, and any natural or legal person residing or having its registered office in a Member State' will be abbreviated to 'citizens'.

[11] TFEU (n 7), art 15(3) first para: 'Any citizen of the Union, and any natural or legal person residing or having its registered office in a Member State, shall have a right of access to documents of the Union institutions, bodies, offices and agencies, whatever their medium, subject to the principles and the conditions to be defined in accordance with this paragraph.'

[12] PAD Regulation (n 9).

[13] PAD Regulation, ibid, art 2(3).

[14] Aarhus Regulation (n 9).

[15] See, eg, Decision in Case 1616/2016/MDC on the alleged failure by Frontex to make public Serious Incident Reports concerning Frontex or joint operations in Bulgaria, 17 November 2017, paras 18 and 19.

[16] See Decision in Cases 1808/2018/FP and 1817/2018/FP on how Frontex handled a request for access to its operational plans and interpreted Article 10(1) of Regulation 1049/2001, 7 May 2019, suggestion for improvement.

communication with PAD applicants, the accessibility of requested documents[17] and the timely processing of PAD requests.[18]

EFSA greatly values this work of the EO: As the Ombudsman has been established to increase EU citizens' confidence in the workings of EU institutions, EFSA carefully considers the EO's recommendations, knowing that these are to the benefit of the citizens the EO is assisting as well as the institutions it aims to strengthen. EFSA therefore not only considers recommendations that are directly addressed to its administration, but also keeps a close eye on all EO inquiries that delve deeper into transparency related topics, to implement best practices and anticipate its administration where needed. An example is EFSA's use of the Connect.EFSA platform for communicating with PAD applicants and providing access to the requested documents.[19] EFSA uses the platform to engage with the public and other stakeholders on a variety of topics, among which requests for information (RFI), access to documents (PAD) and public consultations.[20] By combining these engagements in one tool, several queries can be accessed from one entry point. Furthermore, the tool provides an overview of the status of all submitted PAD applications and long-term access to the documents requested. The EFSA connect tool thus enhances the interaction with the PAD applicants before, during and after the processing of the PAD requests, enabling the easiest possible exercise of the right of PAD. Nevertheless, and as recommended by the EO,[21] PAD applications can still be processed by e-mail where this is the preference of the PAD applicant. To further guide applicants in their PAD requests, EFSA launched in 2023 a webinar explaining how PAD applications are handled, including tips for making a PAD application[22] and explaining the guidance for PAD applicants. To further increase the transparent communication with the public, EFSA intends to operationalise in the processing of PAD applications the use of an IT tool that will support the calculation of the time needed to process a specific access request based on statistical analysis of data collected throughout the recent years taking into account inter alia the number of documents requested, the typology of documents concerned and the number of third-party authors to be consulted. Such a tool should provide applicants with additional insights in what EFSA is able to process within the timeframes of the PAD Regulation. This and other technical measures ensure that EFSA's processing of PAD requests is better fit for the modern context.

[17] See, European Ombudsman, Decision in Joined Cases 1261/2020/PB and 1361/2020/PB on issues related to how the European Border and Coast Guard Agency (Frontex) communicates with citizens in relation to its access to documents portal, 15 December 2022, para 21 and recommendation.

[18] See, eg, Decision on how the European Food Safety Authority (EFSA) dealt with a request for public access to documents related to a proposal to restrict lead in ammunition (Case 2124/2021/OAM), 14 November 2022, recommendations; Recommendation on the time the European Commission takes to deal with requests for public access to documents (strategic inquiry OI/2/2022/OAM), 28 March 2023.

[19] Available at connect.efsa.europa.eu/RM/s/new-ask-efsa-request.

[20] See, for more information, EFSA's toolkit: www.efsa.europa.eu/en/applications/toolkit.

[21] See, eg, Decision in Case 104/2020/EWM on the European Border and Coast Guard Agency's refusal to deal with a request for public access to documents based on procedural grounds, 20 February 2020, para 8 and recommendation; and Joined Cases 1261/2020/PB and 1361/2020/PB (n 16), paras 7 and 23.

[22] See, EFSAchannel, 'Webinar on EFSA Guidance for public access to documents applicants', 15 May 2023 [Youtube-video], www.youtube.com/watch?v=zHpzCuICdkg.

The work of the EO has also helped EFSA to re-evaluate its transparency approach and practices. As EFSA is committed to the highest level of transparency, it aims to ensure the *widest access to documents it holds*, both in the number of documents as in the information contained therein. Depending on the number of documents and pages requested, the nature and origin of those documents and the width and depth of the specific assessments of the documents, providing access can in practice be a time-consuming exercise. In EFSA's case, many documents in its possession originate from third parties, and can contain information which can be considered commercially sensitive. The careful assessment of such information to ensure that EFSA provides the widest access to documents except for the duly justified confidential information, within the timeframes provided by the PAD Regulation, proves to be a challenging activity. The EO has further supported EFSA in the processing of complex PAD cases. Taking into account the guidance of the EO, EFSA is increasingly communicating with PAD applicants to process their request(s), for example by providing lists of documents that fall in the scope of a request and engaging with document owners as soon as possible, ensuring that EFSA's reactive transparency approach is fit for purpose.

III. TOWARDS 'PROACTIVE' TRANSPARENCY

Now, EFSA is entering a new chapter of transparency, which allows citizens more actively to exercise their right to public access to documents. Following amendments of the GFL by the Transparency Regulation, EFSA is empowered to increase the level of transparency. In addition to proactively publishing output[23] and process[24] related documents, now also systematically documents and data supporting the scientific outputs are published. After the publication of the non-confidential versions of authorisation or approval dossiers on the OpenEFSA Portal,[25] the public is consulted on the submitted data and studies at an early stage of the risk assessment,[26] in order to guarantee that EFSA has access to all relevant information available. These proactive and systematic publications together with the public consultation, and the transparency in the risk assessment process, allows interested parties to

[23] All the scientific outputs of EFSA are publicly available in the EFSA journal; an open access online scientific journal which is updated continuously. The EFSA journal contains all outputs from Scientific Committees and Panels, as well as outputs of EFSA, which are not prepared by such Scientific Committees and Panels, see EFSA, 'EFSA Journal' [webpage], efsa.onlinelibrary.wiley.com/journal/18314732.

[24] EFSA publishes a multitude of corporate and procedural documents such as practical arrangement and decisions on transparency and independence, rules of procedure, working procedures as well as minutes, participants list, agenda, the opinions of the Scientific Committee and Panels, including minority opinions and the web-stream and audio- and video recording of the management board meetings. See, for example, EFSA, 'Corporate documents and Publications' available at www.efsa.europa.eu/en/about/corporatedocs; EFSA 'Calender', www.efsa.europa.eu/en/events/advanced-search and; 'Calendar Management Board Meetings', www.efsa.europa.eu/en/events/advanced-search?f%5B1%5D=event_participant%3A121&sort=computed_sort_date&order=desc.

[25] The OpenEFSA Portal is available at: open.efsa.europa.eu.

[26] See: EFSA, 'Public consultations' www.efsa.europa.eu/en/calls/consultations.

scrutinise EFSA's work. These 'transparency amendments' are therefore expected to increase the accountability of – and trust in – the agency[27] and ultimately strengthen the role of EFSA in the EU food safety system.[28]

EFSA is fully committed to the mandate to making documents and data on this scale accessible and is about to implement these new transparency obligations while delivering efficiently and effectively on EFSA's tasks of risk communication and risk assessment. Having proactive transparency at the heart of the risk assessment process and providing transparency at this number of documents, is however a new endeavour in EU administration. Where EFSA can draw for its reactive transparency on a 20-year experience with the PAD legal framework, best practices from other EU bodies and guidance from the EO, now under the Transparency Regulation ongoing administrative and legislative interpretive choices need to be made for the proportionate implementation of these new obligations into EFSA's administration. A challenge of making publicly available huge amounts of technical information, is potentially ensuring its meaningfulness for the public. For EFSA's risk communication responsibilities and overall mission, it is relevant to consider the comprehensibility of the information made available. Whilst for the traditional engagement activities, great efforts are put to contextualise information, it is time-wise too early into the implementation of this new legislation to assess how the public perceives this level of transparency.

IV. FUTURE OUTLOOK: THE EO'S ROLE IN SHAPING 'PROACTIVE' TRANSPARENCY

For risk assessment and risk communication to be effective, efficient and coherent, the EO can help to further shape what meaningful proactive transparency is. In the past years the EO has already been guiding EU bodies how to make transparency serve the citizen with recommendations on proactive transparency. This occurred specifically in the field of decision-making processes, interactions and topics that generate public interest: the EO for example gave practical advice to keep records of meetings between EU institutions and interest representatives, and to render such records public.[29] Moreover, the EO continues to recommend to proactively provide documents in relation to policy areas and topics that generate public interest and

[27] See, eg, Transparency Regulation (n 1), rec 12: 'Transparency of the risk assessment process contributes to greater legitimacy of the Authority being acquired in the eyes of the consumers and general public in the pursuit of its mission, increases their confidence in its work and ensures that the Authority is more accountable to the Union citizens in a democratic system. It is therefore essential to strengthen the confidence of the general public and other interested parties in the risk analysis underpinning the relevant Union law, and in particular in the risk assessment, including the transparency thereof as well as the organisation, functioning and independence of the Authority.'

[28] See: EFSA, *Programming document 2022–2024* (Publications Office of the European Union, 2022).

[29] European Ombudsman, 'Practical recommendations for public officials' interaction with interest representatives', SI/7/2016, 24 May 2016.

documents that are necessary for public participation.[30] The scope of the proactive transparency obligations that EFSA is subject to is however more ambitious showing the novelty of the Transparency Regulation EFSA is exposed to.

To live up to the transparency commitments on the scale of the Transparency Regulation, improvements and adaptations of EFSA's transparency approach are continuously needed. Since the entry into force of the Transparency Regulation, EFSA has taken substantive administrative, organisational and technical measures to deliver on this new mandate. Now the transparency infrastructure is crystallised out, a transparency approach needs to be found that delivers effectively and efficiently on EFSA's task to fully serve the citizen for whom it was founded.

[30] See Decision on how the European Commission dealt with a request for public access to documents concerning the negotiations for the procurement of COIVD-19 vaccines (Case 2206/2021/MIG), 18 July 2022; Decision in Joint Cases 85/2021/MIG and 86/2021/MIG on the European Commission's refusal to give public access to documents concerning the purchase of vaccines against COVID-19, 12 May 2021.

14

The European Ombudsman as an Influencer: An Insider's Perspective

AIDAN O'SULLIVAN

THIS CHAPTER WILL outline how the strategy of the third European Ombudsman (EO), Emily O'Reilly, has been devised and implemented over the past decade and the challenges of the EU context in which it was implemented. The chapter concludes with some of the tactics used by the Ombudsman's team to implement the strategy in practice.

I. A BROAD MANDATE AND A CHALLENGING CONTEXT

When first elected by the European Parliament in 2013, Emily O'Reilly took a broad view of her mandate to assist as many European citizens and residents as possible. She viewed the evolution of the Office in its historical and legal context, rooted in the Maastricht Treaty (1992) which crucially established 'citizenship of the Union'[1] and created the EO as the EU body to which those new EU citizens could seek help when dealing with EU administration.[2]

In the strategy for her first term, 'Towards 2019', Emily O'Reilly defined the mission of the Office as firstly to 'serve European democracy'.[3] Given the success of the first strategy, and following her re-election in 2019, the follow-up adopted five-year strategy 'Towards 2024' refined the mission of the Office further as 'to help to support European citizenship'.[4] This broader view of the mandate, as compared to both previous Ombudsmen, has guided the work of the Ombudsman and the Office over the past decade.

While handling complaints from citizens and residents of the EU is the core business of the Office, given this wider view of the mandate, the Office does a lot more.

[1] Treaty on European Union [1992] OJ C 191, Art 8(1).
[2] ibid, Art 138e.
[3] European Ombudsman, 'Towards 2019', Strategy, 17 November 2014, www.ombudsman.europa.eu/en/publication/en/58332.
[4] European Ombudsman, 'Towards 2024 – Sustaining Impact', Strategy, 7 December 2020, www.ombudsman.europa.eu/en/strategy/our-strategy/en.

'Towards 2024' elaborates on how the EO delivers on the mission: 'We do this by listening to citizens, to our stakeholders, and by working with the institutions of the EU to help to create a more accountable, transparent, ethical and effective administration.'[5] In short, the EO aims to advocate for a more democratic EU.

Any successful strategy must take account of the context within which it is to be executed. As a democratically elected office holder, the EO must always be aware of the political, economic and social context in which European citizens and residents experience their lives. Over the past decade, the EU and its administration have faced many difficult challenges.

First, EU scepticism, allied to the rise of extreme nationalist sentiment and autocratic political regimes, is a strong feature of contemporary Europe. Other forces, in our neighbourhood and globally also threaten the European vision of multilateralism.

In this more 'geopolitical EU', the EU administration is becoming increasingly involved 'on the ground' on issues such as migration, security and even health. This is challenging for an EU administration traditionally focused on a technical and regulatory role. EU agencies, for example, have a more extended 'hands on' role in relation to the protection of migrants in the Mediterranean while the European Commission, for the first time ever, has created an EU stockpile of medical supplies.[6]

At the same time, the EU has faced several policy challenges: the climate emergency, the rule of law within the EU, the migration crisis, the banking and financial crisis, Brexit, global trade disputes and digital challenges including surveillance and artificial intelligence.

While the global regulatory influence of the EU is now widely recognised via the 'Brussels effect',[7] this makes the EU the target of intense lobbying, which makes the issues of lobbying transparency and ethics even more relevant to protect the public interest.

The years of 2020–23 were dominated by the Covid-19 pandemic with an obvious impact on the work of the entire EU administration. The subsequent Covid-19 economic recovery plan – which includes common EU borrowing – represents a new chapter in the evolution of EU integration. Citizens will need to know the where, how and why of the distribution of the recovery funds and hold the EU institutions accountable for this spending.

Finally, many Europeans have increasingly higher expectations of public administrations and often expect instant responses to their concerns and requests. Given contemporary technology and social media tools, citizens have understandably less tolerance for delays when dealing with the public administration.

II. STRENGTHENING EUROPEAN ADMINISTRATIVE STANDARDS: STRATEGY AND TACTICS

Against this background, the EO identified two major implications for the work of the Office. First, the EO recognises that the EU has, in general, high standards of

[5] ibid.

[6] European Commission, 'COVID-19: Commission creates first ever rescEU stockpile of medical equipment', Press Release, 19 March 2020, ec.europa.eu/commission/presscorner/detail/en/IP_20_476.

[7] Anu Bradford, *The Brussels Effect: How the European Union Rules the World* (Oxford, Oxford University Press, 2020).

administration, ethics and transparency – when compared to other global actors and even many Member States.[8] The EU institutions – acting as role models – should set global administrative standards. Pluralist democracy is part of what sets Europe apart from many other parts of the world, and a well-functioning public administration is a vital support to Europe's democratic structures. Second, the EU has set itself the goal of transforming Europe in a green, digital and fair way. The first Strategic Foresight Report[9] of the Commission from 2020, which provided a longer-term perspective on EU policymaking, viewed this goal through the prism of resilience. In its report, the Commission defines resilience as 'the ability not only to withstand and cope with challenges but also to undergo transitions in a sustainable, fair and democratic manner'. The EO believes the quality of the EU administration is a strength. However, it sees vulnerabilities such as a lack of citizen participation and the potential for undue lobbying influence. Transparency and participation boost legitimacy; their absence erodes it. If the EU is to become more resilient, its administration must strengthen transparency, ethics and democratic accountability.

The EO strategy[10] combines four mutually re-enforcing objectives: to achieve lasting positive impact on the EU administration, to be of real-life relevance to citizens, to increase citizens' awareness of its work and to become internally efficient, given the limited resources of a small office.

Over the past decade, the EO has used various tactics to implement this strategy. The Office has provided leadership as an acknowledged, trusted and independent authority on issues of good administration, has used the full scope of its formal and soft powers, and has strengthened cooperation and dialogue with the EU institutions to ensure the continued improvement of administrative practices.

The Office has proactively selected areas of key importance to citizens for systemic inquiries and EO initiatives. Example are EU-US trade talks,[11] Commission expert groups[12] or Frontex.[13] The EO and her team strive to remain aware of the changing dynamics of the EU and the political, social, economic and legal context. They engage in, and contribute to, relevant debates and developments on European democracy and administration.[14] The Office has engaged with and learnt from its stakeholders, including EU researchers and legal experts. The Office has boosted its cooperation with the European Network of Ombudsmen,[15] and other Member

[8] European Ombudsman, 'Towards 2024 – Sustaining Impact', Strategy, 7 December 2020, www.ombudsman.europa.eu/en/strategy/our-strategy/en.

[9] European Commission, '2020 Strategic Foresight Report', 9 September 2020, commission.europa.eu/strategy-and-policy/strategic-planning/strategic-foresight/2020-strategic-foresight-report_en.

[10] European Ombudsman, 'Towards 2024 – Sustaining Impact', Strategy, 7 December 2020, www.ombudsman.europa.eu/en/strategy/our-strategy/en.

[11] European Ombudsman, 'Further steps to increase TTIP transparency necessary', Press Release, 7 January 2015, www.ombudsman.europa.eu/it/press-release/en/58669.

[12] European Ombudsman, 'Citizens need to know more about expert groups' advice to Commission', Press Release, 2 February 2016, www.ombudsman.europa.eu/de/press-release/en/63520.

[13] European Ombudsman, 'How Frontex can ensure respect for migrants' fundamental rights during "forced returns"', Press Release, 6 May 2015, www.ombudsman.europa.eu/en/press-release/en/59744.

[14] European Ombudsman, 'Ombudsman calls on Member States to back EU Transparency Register', Press Release 11/2014, 16 April 2014,www.ombudsman.europa.eu/en/press-release/en/54096.

[15] European Ombudsman, 'About the European Network of Ombudsmen', www.ombudsman.europa.eu/en/european-network-of-ombudsmen/about/en.

States' bodies, international networks and organisations to identify and promote the higher standards and good practice, for example in relation to fundamental rights and governance issues.

Given Emily O'Reilly's background as a journalist, she has always placed an emphasis on ensuring that the Office communicates its work online and offline in a clear manner, using language that is both accessible and compelling to a wide audience. The Office has, at every step of executing the strategy, engaged deeply with the European Parliament and its committees on the broad range of issues of mutual concern, while always maintaining independence. The Office has also tried to develop a participatory approach with its stakeholders and multipliers, such as civil society organisations, media, businesses and other organisations for them to be part of an ecosystem that can positively influence the EU administration.

III. ASSESSING AND INCREASING IMPACT

With this clear strategy, executed with the above-mentioned tactics, how does the EO make an impact? Assessing how this impact is achieved requires an understanding of that wider role of the EO, as detailed above, and not a narrow view of the Office as simply a complaint-handling body. This wider role of EO 'influence' has not yet been very well examined academically; as such, academic scrutiny normally comes from largely a classic EU administrative law perspective.

When the EO launches a major inquiry, based on a complaint or on her own-initiative, different elements have combined to convert that inquiry and its findings into real impact. It is a combination of legal arguments, arguments about good administrative practice, targeted inter-institutional outreach, stakeholder outreach, smart media communications, political contextual awareness and the networking conducted by senior EO staff, which make the difference in terms of influencing the EU administration. These efforts also need to be ongoing and not just during the formal inquiry. In a classic complaint handling body, the work would often be considered completed at the closing of an inquiry. However, under the strategy of the EO, each of the formal inquiry steps actually provide pillars around which all the other work of media communications, outreach and networking are built upon, and the work continues long after the end of an inquiry.

The EO aims to build up an ecosystem of stakeholders, which can be allies on various issues of concern and can vary from topic to topic. Academics have an important role to play, being proactive on various issues, to critique the impact on the EU institutions but also the performance of the EO. Civil society has a dual role as both an agent for change and as a source of potential complainants. Journalists also increasingly turn to the EO, who see her as an agent of change, including on many high-profile cases over the past decade. The EO has also carefully chosen to launch own-initiative inquiries in a strategic manner, into topics that were often not subject to many complaints but needed systemic attention, for example, into the lack of Council legislative transparency.[16]

[16] Recommendation of the European Ombudsman in case OI/2/2017/TE on the Transparency of the Council legislative process, 15 May 2018.

Such influence includes not only the direct formal responses and follow up to EO inquiries, but also the ripple effect over time across the wider 'Brussels bubble' on specific issues – highlighted at the right time – and of the resulting cultural change and expectations change over time. In October 2022, the EO published a major Impact Report, which detailed the key inquiries and issues where the Office has had a positive impact over the past decade.[17]

One good example of the EO achieving impact over time, as listed in the Impact Report, was the inquiry into corporate sponsorship of presidencies of the Council of the EU. In response to the EO's findings, the Council did eventually agree to issue guidelines[18] on corporate sponsorship for Member States holding the six-month EU presidencies. The inquiry led to improved transparency around this issue, with most Member States holding the presidency starting to list their corporate sponsorship on their official presidency websites, allowing Parliament, civil society and the media to monitor the issue. This inquiry was opened following a complaint from a non-governmental organisation in 2019, following the corporate sponsorship of an American multinational of the Romanian presidency that year. The EO office already conducted such an inquiry in 2005/06, but the EO's proposed solution was rejected by the Council at the time. This new inquiry was different, as the EO used a variety of tactics and tools to influence, not just the Council, but also the wider range of actors in the EU milieu that were concerned by the issue.

Each of the pillars of the inquiry, the opening letter, the reply of the Council, the EO recommendation and the closing decision, were all published by the EO and then distributed to a wide variety of interested civil society, academic and media stakeholders, which acted as further multipliers. All relevant European and national parliament committees were contacted, along with several interested MEPs and national MPs, who exerted further pressure on the Council via parliamentary questions[19] and/or media work.

The inquiry, culminating in the recommendation,[20] was concluded swiftly, in comparison to the previous related inquiry. The 2019 recommendation assessment was short and drafted in accessible language, ensuring it would be accessible to a wider audience, and thus influence a lot more key stakeholders. The EO also took a pragmatic approach and recommended only that new Council guidelines be adopted, rather than calling for a ban of sponsorship as such. The EO's team contacted directly certain Member States' permanent representations in Brussels, who would be discussing the issue within the Council, to highlight with them directly the importance of the issue. Most of the stakeholders the EO's team reached out to over this period, whether in the Parliament, Council or in civil society, were already well-known as good relations had been built up over several years. Such an approach to an inquiry,

[17] European Ombudsman, 'Impact of the European Ombudsman', 10 October 2022, www.ombudsman.europa.eu/en/document/en/161700.

[18] Council of the European Union, 'Sponsorship of the Presidency of the Council of the European Union: guidance on best practice', Brussels, 30 June 2021, 10325/21.

[19] European Parliament, 'Council sponsorships', Parliamentary Question E-003909/2019, 20 November 2019, www.europarl.europa.eu/doceo/document/E-9-2019-003909_EN.html.

[20] Recommendation of the European Ombudsman in case 1069/2019/MIG on sponsorship of the Presidency of the Council of the European Union, 6 January 2020.

and such networking and influencing was deployed on all major EO inquiries and initiatives over the past decade, building upon the high-quality inquiry work, thus underpinning much of the Office's impact.

Any assessment of the impact of the EO cannot exclude the issue of resources available. The EO Office has a staff of 75, which is expected to deal with administrative issues in the whole EU administration, covering all major EU institutions and bodies, over 50 EU agencies around Europe and also the European External Action Service (EEAS)'s delegations around the world. In the academic literature, this aspect is often not mentioned in assessments of the work of the EO. One 2020 academic paper,[21] which compared the oversight roles of the EO and the European Court of Auditors (ECA), gave a positive assessment of the work of the EO. It should be noted that the ECA has over 1,000 staff in comparison to the very limited resources of the EO. Indeed, several EU oversight bodies – the EO, European Data Protection Supervisor (EDPS), European Public Prosecutor Office (EPPO) and the European Anti-Fraud Office (OLAF) – regularly inform the budgetary authorities of being under resourced, which is a topic worthy of further attention.

Finally, another priority of the current EO since 2013 has been to boost the relevance and impact of the European Network of Ombudsmen[22] (ENO), which is an informal network of nearly one hundred ombudsman bodies across Europe. The EO has introduced parallel inquiries and initiatives, whereby a regional or national ombudsman would undertake a relevant inquiry at that level, and at the same time the EO would undertake an inquiry at EU level on the same issue, and both would coordinate. As many issues today, such as migration or AI in public administration, affect European, national and regional levels, such multi-level cooperation between ombudsmen can only be of benefit. The EO also organises regular webinars with staff of the ENO offices, to share good practice on issues of common concern. In the past, the annual ENO conferences took place in various cities around Europe but the current ombudsman has hosted them in Brussels (or Strasbourg) in order to introduce the ENO members and their staff more into the EU machinery and also invite senior representatives of the EU institutions. This approach helps 'Europeanise' those ENO members and staff interested, and also helps introduce real experience from the national and regional levels to the EU representatives based in Brussels.

IV. CONCLUSION

This chapter has sought to explain in detail how the EO strategy has been devised and implemented over the past decade. Emily O'Reilly was the first European Ombudsman office holder to draft such a multi-year strategy. It is yet to be seen whether the next

[21] A Wille and M Bovens, 'Watching EU Watchdogs Assessing the Accountability Powers of the European Court of Auditors and the European Ombudsman' (2020) 44 *Journal of European Integration* 183.

[22] European Ombudsman, 'About the European Network of Ombudsmen', www.ombudsman.europa.eu/en/european-network-of-ombudsmen/about/en.

Ombudsman continues this practice of drafting such a strategy document, collaboratively with staff and stakeholders, to provide a cohesive and transparent framework to underpin a strategic approach to improving standards in EU administration.

This chapter has outlined the strategy, its effectiveness, looked at the real-life context in which the Ombudsman strategy was executed and assessed its impact with cited examples. It is the view of the author that, given the limited resources of the EO and the absence of binding powers, the EO has had considerable influence in driving improvements in the EU administration over the past decade.

Index

www.ingramcontent.com/pod-product-compliance
Lightning Source LLC
LaVergne TN
LVHW020159140225
803739LV00003B/75
9781509975600